EUROPE BETWEEN THE SUPERPOWERS

A Council on Foreign Relations Book

COUNCIL ON FOREIGN RELATIONS BOOKS

EUROPE BETWEEN THE SUPERPOWERS

The Enduring Balance

A. W. DePorte

New Haven and London   Yale University Press

1979

Published with assistance from the foundation established in memory of Philip Hamilton McMillan of the Class of 1894, Yale College.

Designed by John O. C. McCrillis and set in Baskerville type. Printed in the United States of America by LithoCrafters, Inc., Chelsea, Michigan.

Published in Great Britain, Europe, Africa, and Asia (except Japan) by Yale University Press, Ltd., London. Distributed in Australia and New Zealand by Book & Film Services, Artarmon, N.S.W., Australia; and in Japan by Harper & Row, Publishers, Tokyo Office.

Library of Congress Cataloging in Publication Data

DePorte, Anton W
    Europe between the superpowers.

    Bibliography: p.
    Includes index.
    1. World politics—1945–   2. Europe—Politics and government.   3. United States—Foreign relations—Europe.
4. Europe—Foreign relations—United States.
5. Russia—Foreign relations—Europe.   6. Europe—Foreign relations—Russia.   7. Balance of power.
I.   Title.
D843.D374   327'.11'09   78-8123
ISBN 0-300-02229-8

Contents

Preface

Tesman: "But, good heavens, we know
nothing of the future."

Lovborg: "No, but there is a thing or two to be
said about it all the same."

Ibsen, *Hedda Gabler*

This book deals mostly with the past but is addressed mainly to the future. It is not a history of European-American relations since the beginning, nor even since 1945. It is an essay on a set of closely interrelated matters:

—The decline and death of the classical European state system.

—The emergence as a consequence of this demise, and as a byproduct of the cold war it gave rise to between the United States and the Soviet Union, of a bipolar system dominated by the two superpowers which includes the states of Europe but is no longer centered on Europe.

—The consolidation of this new system to the point that it now stands quite independently of its cold war origins and could well survive indefinitely because it serves the interests of so many states, and particularly of those with power to change things.

Any study of the postwar European state system that comes to this conclusion cannot avoid considering why so much analysis of European-American relations has tended, as we can see now, to overemphasize the successive challenges to the new system and underemphasize the factors making for strength and durability. If the structural stability of Europe since the 1950s and the power stability that underlies it have been overlooked by many observers, a principal cause, I think, has been an insufficient appreciation of the historical roots of current events. What has often been missing is the conviction, as Robert M. Grant has put it, that "History is not just one thing after another."[1] We cannot understand how events of 1945, 1949, and 1954 provided solutions to problems created in 1870, for example, if we do not consciously and coherently bring 1870 and the years after into the picture. Such historical perspective should be a principal contribution of scholarship to the understanding of the events of our times.

Europeans have reasonably well understood if not always relished the implications of their past for the power constellation in which they have

1. Robert M. Grant, *Augustus to Constantine* (New York: Harper & Row, 1970), p. xiii.

found themselves since 1945. This chastening but sober knowledge has in itself provided one of the elements of strength of the new system. Though 1945 was undoubtedly a watershed year in European and world history, it was not the Year One of the world we live in. What has happened in Europe since 1945 cannot be understood without considering what happened before, and quite long before. This is most certainly not a call to invoke Munich or the fall of the Roman Empire to explain current events. Such practices do not use history to reinforce understanding but debauch both. Rather, we need to find some coherent framework of understanding that links the European past and present beneath the rush of events that have bewildered public, official, and scholarly thinking about the life of the last three decades. With due regard for the difficulty of the task and the tentativeness of the outcome, it is my purpose in this book to do that.

The thesis of this essay is that the new state system of Europe is what it is because of why and how the old system declined and fell and because of the way the United States and the Soviet Union then slowly worked out their relations with each other in the circumstances they confronted—partly inherited, partly of their making—at the end of World War II. The argument of the book runs in this way:

—The European state system that emerged at the end of the Middle Ages was characterized, for over four centuries, by ceaseless diplomatic maneuvering and frequent wars among the member states but also by the continued existence of almost all of them. This phenomenon, by no means universal in state systems, was the outcome of the successful working of a constantly shifting but generally maintained balance of power among the principal states.

—The system which contained Spanish, Austrian, and French bids for hegemony was not able to contain the power of the German state that emerged after 1870. Leaving aside all questions of motivation and responsibility, the power of Germany was organized on such a scale by 1914 compared to its neighbors' that it would have been able to win World War I and establish its hegemony in Europe but for the intervention of the United States. The seeming restoration of the old European system after 1918—the touchstone of normalcy for much American thinking about Europe—was artificial, unnatural, and transitory and was swept aside by German power even before war broke out again in 1939. But the brief German hegemony established in 1940 was undone by two countries whose power was organized on a yet higher scale, the United States and the Soviet Union. It was then clear that the old European state system, which had failed in its most essential task of maintaining internal balance and the independence of its member states, was gone beyond recall.

—World War II had profound, precise, and lasting consequences for the international scale of power and therefore for the state system of Europe. Germany was not only defeated in 1945 but destroyed as a power and a state. The resolution of the German problem in this way left the United States and the Soviet Union dominant over two halves of a divided Europe. The new superpowers then might have defined their relations to each other in any of several ways. The cold war, for example, might possibly have been avoided. If so, the division of Europe it consolidated might have been confirmed many years before it was. Conceivably, though less likely, that division might even have been averted or at least attenuated. But it was not surprising, in light of both history and power relations, that the new superpowers found themselves on the road of competition rather than cooperation after 1945. A series of specific disagreements between them, beginning in Eastern Europe, reignited preexisting ideological differences into a total confrontation. But this then led to a process by which each institutionalized its presence in Europe and thereby gave structural stability to the military division of the continent produced by German defeat in 1945. As a by-product of their cold war conflict, and without quite realizing what was happening, the superpowers thus produced a dynamic amplification and institutionalization of the status quo, establishing a bipolar European state system utterly unlike the old one and far more firmly rooted in power realities than that had been in its final half-century.

—In this new system the European states found themselves dependent in varying degrees on one or the other superpower. Even so, the system has fulfilled for them the primal function of a state system: maintenance of their national independence, however severely (but not necessarily unchangeably) circumscribed in practice, particularly in Eastern Europe. It has even preserved peace. And, not by chance, the problem of German power, which had destroyed the old system, has been resolved by the cold war more securely and lastingly than it was likely to have been in any other way, including even an agreement by the superpowers soon after 1945 either to divide or reunite Germany. The cold war had the effect of cementing the two parts of divided Germany into the two blocs in such a manner as not only to remove the issue of unification from the realm of practical politics but to do so with the consent of the larger part of Germany. The arming of the Federal Republic of Germany in 1955, by completing this resolution of the German problem, reduced still further whatever chance there might still have been to devise some other kind of European settlement and system.

—The new bipolar system has now endured since 1955 and given rise to Euratlantic and Eurasian subsystems, symmetrical in their structural roles but asymmetrical in that the former rests largely on consent, the latter on coercion. The Atlantic alliance itself has developed as the outward and visible form of an inward and immanent community, which, because of the multiplicity and intimacy of relationships among the member states, has proved itself to be much more than an epiphenomenon of the cold war: more structured, more stable, and continuously useful to the members with respect to providing solutions to their security, political, and economic problems, new as well as old.

—Much has happened in Europe since 1955, and there have been many challenges to the new system—"subjective" challenges aimed to change it and "objective" challenges that, whatever the motives behind them, seemed likely to do so. Many of these challenges made a great stir at the time; none made any significant change in the system. This fact, once it is recognized, leads us to consider why the system has been so surprisingly stable. There seem to be two reasons: because it so well serves most of the interests of most of the participants most of the time—particularly those with power to affect it—and, even more profoundly, because it accurately reflects the facts of power as between the United States and the Soviet Union on the one hand, and between them and the states of Europe on the other. The qualitative power primacy of the two superpowers over all others and the stabilizing implications for their relations of weapons so powerful as to be almost unusable have been central to this situation. The very stability of Europe, conversely, is a sign of how unchanged in its fundamentals the European power balance between and within the blocs has been for the last quarter century. The cold war—seen as one phase of American-Soviet relations—may be over, but the relations of the superpowers remain, as they have been since 1945, the key to the stability (or not) of any international system, regional or global, and to the peace and independence (or the reverse) of most other states, and certainly those of Europe.

An explanation is in order with respect to my use of certain words. I find the notion of a "system" of states is useful to an enterprise that tries to find patterns beneath events, but I make no claim to use the word in an original or even a rigorous way. I use it to describe a group of states the major part of whose important foreign interactions are with each other over a considerable period of time.

I should emphasize also that I use the words "stability" and "challenge" with entire objectivity. Stability is not necessarily good, nor are efforts to change it bad. On the contrary, stability can keep injustice intact. I am quite aware, for example, that describing the postwar European system as stable leaves aside the involuntary participation of the countries of Eastern Europe in that stability; the circumscribed character of their independence; the effects of the division of Germany on German sensibilities; the effects of Europe's loss of autonomy and status on the feelings of many Europeans. Not only does the word "stability" neglect the human aspects of these problems but it risks leading us to overlook the fact that challenges to unwelcome forms of stability from these and other sources can obviously invite destabilizing developments and even, if they are strong enough, the breakup of the system. But neither ethical judgment nor empirical analysis is precluded or prejudiced by using the words themselves to describe situations of fact. Whether we like or do not like things that are, the first task of analysis is to be clear about *what* they are and, as far as possible, *why*.

In this connection, however, I must admit that, having arrived as objectively as possible at an analysis of events affecting Europe since 1945, I find considerable virtue in the particular stability that they have brought about *as compared to feasible alternatives*. If we did not have the system we have, what other would we be likely to have and what would *its* "virtue" be? We must proceed very carefully here. I have found in doing the research on this book that much of the discussion of modern European history and the cold war concludes that some course of events other than the one that took place would have been better and also, in many cases, not so difficult to bring about if only particular decisions had been different from what they were. I have therefore given considerable attention to the many disputed might-have-beens of prewar, wartime, and postwar history. The inherent difficulty of reaching persuasive judgments on such "iffy" questions—particularly of keeping wishfulness at bay—is increased because of the state of evidence available to us: too sparse on the Soviet side, almost too plentiful on the American. In many cases I prefer to avoid dogmatism by admitting that no definite judgment is possible rather than to pretend to a certainty that cannot be sustained. Within these limits, I have reached the conclusion, rather to my surprise, that while there were many occasions when different decisions might have given events a different direction, it is not clear, considering the course of World War II, or even World War I, that it would have been possible to bring about a state of affairs in Europe that would have been better than the one we have known since 1945—better for peace, which was preserved despite tensions threatening war; better for the states of Europe as such, whose independence could no longer be maintained in the old European state system but has been preserved, in however limited a way, in the new; better, even, for the "greatest good of the greatest number" of the peoples of Europe in terms of the liberal democratic values which I hold.

In most of the debated cases, I am not convinced that the more attractive alternative futures were really available to decision-makers at the time—not just in retrospective fantasies—and that the more plausible alternative decisions were likely to have produced better outcomes. For that reason I think the postwar system, built over a decade and more of acute tensions sometimes threatening war, can yet be given high marks for providing stability, even if in a sense inadvertently, and at least fair marks for the kind of stability. In any case this system, like all that prove viable, has been well rooted in power realities. If not an inevitable outcome of history, it was at least a natural one.

I do not want to seem to be presenting a panegyric of the cold war. What has happened since 1945 has had high costs and many victims, in particular the countries and peoples of Eastern Europe. For the United States, the costs have included not only the losses incurred in two wars and the resources devoted to defense but the attitude of wartime exceptionalism that cold war tensions allowed to be dangerously perpetuated in peacetime, with all the consequences that has had for the blance of American institutions and for the intellectual and moral climate of the country.

Facing all the costs and victims of the cold war squarely, and even grimly, we nevertheless cannot assume that some other course of events would have had fewer. War between the superpowers seemed possible on more than one occasion. Some form of Soviet control over Western as well as Eastern Europe was no inconceivable thing in light of the local European power balance after 1945. A German drive for unification by force or unsettling diplomacy sounds fantastic only because the cold war and the new European system have succeeded so well in making this impossible that we now overlook the achievement. These, which are among the more likely alternatives to what did happen, are not attractive prospects. Others that seem more attractive turn out on examination to be implausible.

If, as I believe, the present state of Europe is utterly unlike its past yet linked by iron bands of causation to the past, what if anything that is sensible can we say about the future? We must not be dogmatic about what may happen in time to come, for the most important events are often the most unforeseeable. We must, in particular, avoid projecting the present. But, though we cannot predict the future, we can try, with Eilert Lovborg, to think about it intelligently. The most careful way to do this is to look at present institutions, practices, forces, and trends—the subjects of this book—as things the future will have to contend with. The stronger they are, and the power weights behind them, the more powerful will have to be any impetus that might work to change them in the future. This study has emphasized where we are and how we got there with respect to European-American relations because the legacy of these things will be part of the future with which governments and peoples will have to live. *That* is what we can know about the future by properly understanding the present as the outcome of the past.

In the case under discussion, we have had enough experience to know that the new system in Europe has effectively performed its basic tasks for the member states—survival and maintenance of peace—for three decades. This gives some reason to believe that its essential structures and functions, if tended and kept responsive to changing conditions, will remain much as they are in the absence of some truly significant shift in the power relationships of the member states which underlie the system. For all the economic recovery of both Western and Eastern Europe since 1945 and other marked changes, there has been no such power shift since the system took its present form in the mid-1950s. Those who think they foresee power changes on that scale may fairly claim to foresee also major shifts in the European system; others should not. As one who does not, I suggest that the system which has lasted from 1955 until today— 1978—may well last as long again, that is, until 2001. Beyond that sonorous date even those who are most impressed with the stability of the results of World War II should fall silent. The future, as General de Gaulle said, lasts a long time.

Analysis stops here, but the conclusions reached have implications for public policy that are worth pursuing. Notwithstanding all the international problems that press on our attention from around the world, it is useful for Americans to think carefully about their relations with Europe, not because the relationship is in crisis but because it is in as exemplary a state of stability as anything can be in a revolutionary world. But stability is a special case of change, not the natural order of things. There will continue to be challenges to European stability, not least from the fact that the superpowers, though they have stabilized their relations in Europe, are far from having done so elsewhere in the world. Problems from outside as well as from inside Europe can reverberate against its stability. We must be clear how that stability was achieved if we are to do what is necessary to maintain or improve on it if, as I believe, it continues to be in the interest of the United States to do so.

Informed support for a continuing American role in Europe can be strengthened if policymakers and the public understand that that role is as natural as deep historical roots can make anything and as likely to be longlived as anything useful can be in the face of what Tennessee Williams calls the world's passion for declivity. Insofar as that happens, Europeans will continue to place confidence in the system of which, since 1945, they have found themselves part. Insofar as both Europeans and

Americans do so, the system will be seen to be strong, useful, normal, and enduring, not a transition back to an irrecoverable past or a way station to an imagined future, whether dream or nightmare. Challenges to the system after so many years and so many other challenges can then be seen in a more time-balanced perspective, as not likely to be mortal. Policy problems can be approached in a more serene spirit, as adjustable.

A study which has emphasized structural stability and, by implication, points to preservation of that stability as a policy goal, runs the risk of seeming to argue for endlessly pursuing the same policies that have brought us to the (relatively) tolerable present it describes. Nothing could be farther from my purpose. Mindless pursuit of established policies can sometimes be the worst way to maintain a desirable stability. The point was pungently made a century ago by Lord Salisbury:

> The commonest error in politics is sticking to the carcasses of dead policies. When a mast falls overboard you do not try to save a rope here and a spar there in memory of their former utility; you cut away the hamper altogether. And it should be the same with a policy. But it is not so. We cling to the shred of an old policy after it has been torn to pieces; and to the shadow of the shred after the rag itself has been thrown away.[2]

May this *not* be the case with American policy toward Europe. Let us, however, balance the most open-minded approach to policy with a true sense of the historic context in which policy must be made.

2. Lady Gwendolen Cecil, *Life of Robert Marquis of Salisbury* (London: Hodder and Stoughton Limited, 1921), vol. 2, p. 145.

Acknowledgments

The formal sources of this book are the research and commentaries of many other writers. The published literature on this subject is vast. Some of it has stood up well to the passage of time. Much has not. I am indebted to the authors of both kinds: to the former for the sound insights they have provided, to the latter for leading me to search for the abiding factors in the postwar situation which they overlooked or undervalued in their preoccupation, understandable but limiting, with the current policy problems of their time. The selected bibliography therefore includes the more important titles for understanding the historiography as well as the history of the period. I should like to acknowledge a particular debt to the three books which contributed most to my own systematic thinking about modern Europe: Hajo Holborn's *The Political Collapse of Europe*, to which the present work is in some sense a sequel, Harold van B. Cleveland's *The Atlantic Idea and Its European Rivals*, and Paul Seabury's *The Rise and Decline of the Cold War.*[1]

I completed the book while a fellow at the Council on Foreign Relations during 1976-77. There cannot be a more hospitable setting for research, writing, and the exchange of ideas. To my friends at the Council and in the Department of State and elsewhere I extend my thanks for their help in many forms. None of them, of course, nor the Council nor the Department, is in any way responsible for what I have written.

A. W. DePorte

East Providence, Pennsylvania
November 1, 1978

1. Hajo Holborn, *The Political Collapse of Europe* (New York: Knopf, 1951), Harold van B. Cleveland, *The Atlantic Idea and Its European Rivals* (New York: McGraw-Hill, 1966); Paul Seabury, *The Rise and Decline of the Cold War* (New York: Basic Books, 1967).

CHAPTER 1

The European State System

The first order of business for any state is to ensure its own survival. Even the most powerful and the most isolated states have not been free of the risk of extinction. In ages when physical contact among peoples was tenuous and rulers were least able to organize the resources of their states to coerce either their subjects or their neighbors, they nevertheless did try to influence the affairs of other states and, in many cases, to absorb or annihilate them. Whole systems of states have disappeared from history in this way. But in other systems the contact and conflict among the member states—their international relations—led not to the disappearance but to the survival of most of them over long periods.

The modern European state system was (for it no longer exists) of this type. Far from living in a state of nature the countries of Europe were until recently members of a system one characteristic of which was their survival as independent political entities. The similarities between the gross outlines of the map of Western and Central Europe of 1500 and that of today are striking. The most conspicuous difference arises from a single particular cause: the many small states inhabited at the earlier date by people who already belonged to the Italian and German linguistic-cultural communities were absorbed into the unified Italian and German states in the nineteenth century when the power of the national idea cut across (though by no means displaced) more conventional concepts of state relations and thus undermined the legitimacy of most of the Italian and German states—that is, international sanction of their right to exist. But apart from this, most of the European states that existed in the late Middle Ages still exist.

The European state system worked as well as it did because of its flexibility. It did not rest on a once-and-for-all distribution of power and status among its members but underwent a constant process of change. Boundaries and patterns of power and influence were altered ceaselessly, populations and economic, social, and intellectual systems changed out of recognition—more so perhaps than in any other time or place in the history of the world. Some states did disappear from the map, for shorter or longer periods, occasionally forever. But the conspicuous characteristic of this system was that most of the member states survived all fluctuations of power, rank, and frontiers for 500 years or more. As all things changed, the states themselves persisted, along with the fundamental structure of the relations among them that made their survival possible.

We take for granted, because it is so familiar to us, this truly extraordinary phenomenon—so much so that the final breakdown of the European state system in World War II is still often thought to be no more than a temporary departure from a millennial normalcy (much as conservative Chinese may have thought for decades that all that happened in their country after 1912 was only one more "time of troubles" between dynasties). In fact, the radically new situation of postwar Europe can be seen as it is only if the brute fact of the death of the prewar state system is analytically—and emotionally—grasped. It is therefore worth considering why the fundamental stability of the defunct European state system ensured the survival of the member states over so long a period and why, after so many vicissitudes, it finally collapsed in our time. Such a review would provide essential perspective on how these same states have tried to ensure their survival (and other interests) in a radically different international environment. Postwar Europe emerged from the prewar state system; the long success and the circumstances of the recent death of the old system strongly color what has happened since 1945.

European nationalism and most of the nation states long antedate the French Revolution, and it is somewhat arbitrary where to begin a discussion of the modern state system. Much can be said for using the year 1494 to mark the beginning of that continuous and intense political interaction among all or most of the states of Western Europe which characterizes the modern period. When Charles VIII of France invaded Italy in that year, Spain and the Empire also quickly became involved. There then began among them, and eventually others, a constant series of wars, alliances, and political maneuvers—in short, the system which continued until 1940.

The general outline of European international history from this point of view is familiar. During most of the sixteenth century the two Habsburg monarchies, led by Spain, seemed on the way to dominating Western Europe, but their power was inadequate to overcome the resistance of France, England, and others. Led by Austria, they tried again after 1618, and failed again. France, after building a successful coalition to check the Habsburgs, then took their place in a drive for European hegemony. By 1714 this effort had been blunted too.

During the eighteenth century the Western European state system gradually merged with the partially autonomous system of Eastern Europe—which had followed a quite different path, marked by the progressive disappearance of most states into the polyglot Turkish,

Austrian, and Russian empires. At the end of the century France tried to establish control over the entire European system, and almost succeeded for a time, only to fail by 1815. Most of the nineteenth century passed before one state seemed to be pushing again toward regional hegemony—and perhaps Germany's actual effort dated only from World War I itself. In any case, the Germans failed, in what seemed like yet another success of the old European state system in preserving the independent nations against the strongest among them but was, in fact, something quite different.

The supreme characteristic of the European system up to 1914—the survival of most of its member states despite almost constant competition and rivalry—arose from the fact that their interplay in war and peace worked in such a way that no one state, or even a group of states, could gain lasting ascendancy over the rest or blot out a neighboring state without others intervening to prevent it. Louis XIV won all of his earlier wars—but then went on from stalemate to defeat and left France weaker, in proportion to its neighbors, than he had found it. Napoleonic France established hegemony over Europe for a time but could not maintain it. In one conspicuous case a substantial state *was* wiped from the map: Poland, in the partitions of 1772, 1793, and 1795. But the uniqueness of this case may be said to demonstrate the validity of the general proposition. It also points to Poland's spectacular geographic vulnerability vis-à-vis stronger powers—a fact to which I will return in discussing the origins of the Soviet-American conflict in Europe in 1945, which first took visible form, not by chance, with respect to Poland.

The balance of power system worked to maintain the independence of the member states over many centuries and in the face of challenges in part because of almost mechanical forces. If any state seemed to be getting overly powerful and ambitious in proportion to the others, the others sooner or later leagued together to set limits to the threat (though often creating a new one, which then set the process in motion again). The more important states in any given generation were fairly well matched in totaling the material resources they were able to bring to bear in international politics—the scale of their power—including in the calculation the quality of their organization and leadership; and lesser states were usually protected as buffers or auxiliaries of the greater.

In part, however, the system also worked because, after a time, the participating states came to believe that it would, so that their ambitions and calculations were adjusted accordingly. Going further, a kind of international ethic of self-restraint eventually grew up in the eighteenth and nineteenth centuries which condemned any drive to European hegemony, or any threat to the very existence of an established state, as an improper challenge to a satisfactory system. In the eighteenth century itself, the partition of Poland was widely considered a scandal and a crime (even by Maria Theresa, one of its perpetrators). Self-restraint was reinforced in the nineteenth century by the horrid example set by the French Revolution and Napoleon and by the fear on the part of conservative governments that excessive international turmoil created risks of unleashing France or reviving the "revolution" which outweighed any possible gain to their state interests.

There was, as noted previously, a partial suspension of all these considerations in the mid-nineteenth century, when the disappearance of large numbers of Italian and German states was condoned by many who otherwise took the balance of power most seriously. To them, the national idea had claims of its own and, besides, these changes did not seriously disrupt the basic balance in any case, since the vanished states were mostly very weak. But apart from this, the balance of power remained the keystone of the European state system up to World War I, mechanically effective, accepted as such, and buttressed by psychological and even ethical acceptance of its legitimacy.

The main characteristics of the old European system are worth noting as points of contrast with the system which succeeded it in the mid-twentieth century. First, the system was very fluid. The states did not oppose and ally themselves in rigid patterns. The growth and decline of the power and ambitions of each constantly affected the system, regrouping its elements. Of course, some traditional alignments and enmities lasted for considerable periods, frequently for geographical reasons. England versus France, France versus the House of Austria, Austria versus Prussia: these long-term antagonisms sometimes bred popular sentiments which could impede the readjustments called for by changing power calculations. But the large states formed and reformed their groupings; the smaller ones changed protectors. The Triple Alliance and Triple Entente of pre-1914 days were the exception to the general rule (and were a good deal less firm, in any case, than is remembered). The balance of power system was only occasionally more or less bipolar; usually it had many poles, or none.

Second, the system was much more colored by ideological considerations than is often thought. They, too, along with conflicts arising out of dynastic, geographic, and economic factors, were among its components. We tend to think that our era is more or less exceptional in its use of ideological definitions, or cloaks, or rationalizations, for state antagonisms. In fact, the presence of ideology as a component in foreign policy—not necessarily a dominant one—is the rule rather than the exception. The calculus of power has rarely been pure.

The political rivalries and alignments of the sixteenth and seventeenth centuries were strongly colored by religious controversy, though obviously this went hand-in-hand with other considerations. The rather brief period between 1714 and 1789, often held up as the norm for a kind of pure "national interest" international politics to which the world might return, was in fact the only era of post-Reformation history relatively free of ideological issues. The nineteenth century was full of ideology, and not only during the revolutionary and Napoleonic wars. Affairs in Eastern Europe were particularly colored by it. Imperial Russia, for example, set great store during much of the century on defending conservatism in the belief that change risked revolution and that revolution—liberal or national—was a threat to both itself and its neighbors. Was it truly in Russia's power interest to restore Habsburg rule in Hungary in 1849 and thus save the rival monarchy? One can doubt it. Something of these considerations (among others) entered also into the "Three Emperors' Leagues" in the 1870s and 1880s. The role of France in Europe, at least up to 1870, was similarly colored, in the opposite sense.

This is not to exaggerate the importance of ideologies in the modern European system but only to point out that the interweaving of ideological considerations with others has been more common than exceptional in European international politics.

Third, though the member states of the European system almost all maintained their existence over the centuries, the distribution of power among them—and therefore of rank—frequently shifted in response to changes in population, economic strength, and the quality of political leadership and military organization. The great powers could wish that the system would preserve their rank as well as their existence, but this was not always the case. During the sixteenth century Spain, France, Austria, and England were the leading powers. In the seventeenth Holland and Sweden joined the list, although both fell out in the eighteenth along with Spain, while Prussia and Russia were then added. By the time the Seven Years' War began in 1756—that is, before the Industrial Revolution—the European system, characterized by five great powers amidst a crowd of lesser states, was firmly fixed in the pattern it would hold (except for the formal but questionable addition of Italy after 1861) until 1918.

The emergence of the Concert of Europe in the nineteenth century confirmed the wide gap between the great powers and the others, and it is remarkable that this structure held together despite revolutionary economic and social changes for over a century. As a result, however, the great powers by 1914 had come to take their status so much for granted that those which then felt it threatened were ready to run great risks in its defense. The very stability of this aspect of the system had reduced its ability to adapt to changing conditions of power.

Fourth, the *absolute* amount of power (however defined) at the command of practically all governments in 1900 for use in foreign policy was greater than those of 1700 enjoyed, and they, in turn, possessed resources beyond what their predecessors controlled in 1500, but at any given time the power positions of the great powers of the day relative to each other tended to be, or to become, stable. None of the great powers was strong enough to overwhelm the others.

This resulted, in part, from the slow and rather uniform pace (by modern standards) of economic and demographic growth in all the European states up to the nineteenth century. But this alone does not account for the special success of the European system over so many centuries, for in other systems of the past one state sometimes decisively vaulted ahead of the others in power even though its population or economic resources did not conspicuously outclass its rivals. Something about the way in which the successful state organized its resources and pursued its goals compared with the others gave it a clear-cut advantage over them. The causes of the rise of empires may be even more multiple and disputed than those of their fall, but it is clear that the power at the disposal of a government has more complex roots than the number of people and the economic resources of the territory under its authority. These factors by themselves, therefore, cannot account for the stable or transitory character of a given multimember international political system.

Two cases come to mind of systems which may be compared to the European state system. In the first, the states that occupied the territory of Alexander's empire in the last three centuries before Christ, after a period of balance of power relations among themselves, were confronted and then overwhelmed by Rome, a state whose power was organized so effectively in comparison to theirs as to be on an entirely grander scale. Somehow it made better use of what it had.

In the second case, the rather self-contained system among the states of fifteenth-century Italy experienced a similar fate. Venice, Milan, Florence, the Papal States, and Naples, among others, maintained their independence for many decades in a classic balance of power pattern. But once France and Spain entered Italian affairs, the scale on which their power was organized overwhelmed the system of the smaller states.

It is piquant—and perhaps relevant to European problems of our own time—to note that there were, then, Italians such as Machiavelli who urged their countrymen to unite to resist the foreign barbarians who threatened the independence of them all. Italy no doubt had the material and human resources to constitute a power on the same scale as its conquerors—provided, of course, that the country was suitably organized. The Italians were conscious of a common nationhood and certainly of their cultural superiority to the invaders. The resources were there and the need for unity was felt and articulated, but the effort was not made in the first generation of foreign occupation, nor for more than three centuries afterward. The population, wealth, and sophistication of sixteenth-century Italy did not suffice to prevent its falling into dependence on neighbors that used their resources more effectively for state purposes.

It remains mysterious why one state or people organizes itself more effectively than another, but the life-span of a state system may depend as much on such factors as on decisive disparities that may develop in the physical resources of the principal members. In either case, the uniform scale of power among the principal members on which any balance of power must rest can be disrupted, and the disruption of the system itself may then follow.

There were, of course, times when one European state did seem to have changed the scale of power then prevalent. The geographical sweep of the empire of Charles V, the skillful utilization (for the period) of the resources of France under Louis XIV, the even more dramatic use of French resources by the Revolution and Napoleon—all these threatened to permanently upset the European balance. None did so, however, because the change of scale was either illusory or ephemeral or was eventually matched by comparable developments (including effective use of coalition resources by individually weaker states) among the other members of the system.

When the European state system emerged in 1815 from the greatest and last of the challenges to its existence which it was to survive, two possible threats to the scale of power in the existing state system were then seen by many. Some, impressed by the eruption of French power between 1789 and 1815, feared a renewal of aggression from that quarter. Others began to think that the French danger had been exorcised only to be replaced by the awesome power of Russia. Neither fear was, for that time, realistic, for industrialization—which would go far, before the century was out, to transform the scale of power in Europe—had scarcely begun to have an impact on international affairs. But while fear of France was anachronistic, those who saw Russia as a menace to the state system were premature but prophetic.

When Russia entered the European system in the mid-eighteenth century, it of course struck people's imagination by reason of its vastness.

But whatever potential for power its size represented was more than compensated for at the time by its small population and economic backwardness and administrative weakness. Thus, Russia did not at first have any real impact on the *scale* of European politics; it entered the system, at about the same time as tiny but well-organized Prussia, as one great power among others.

But as such Russia played a role in Europe from the start which is sometimes overlooked by those who contrast the Soviet Union's sudden appearance in Central Europe and elsewhere as a superpower after 1945 only with its weakness and semi-isolation during the interwar period. It is essential to remember that Russian troops occupied Berlin as early as 1760 and fought in northern Italy in the 1790s. When Averell Harriman at Potsdam congratulated Stalin on the Red Army's capture of Berlin, the latter recalled, with a sound sense of the continuity of his country's foreign policy, that in 1814 the Russians had been in Paris.

As one power among others, Russia was an increasingly important participant after 1740 in European politics. After 1815, generations of British statesmen were obsessed to an exaggerated degree with the Russian threat to the Middle East, India, and the Far East. Much of British diplomacy in the nineteenth century was taken up with checking Russian power. And a number of people began to see Russia as something more than one great power among others. The most familiar of these prophets was Alexis de Tocqueville, who wrote, in the 1830s:

> There are now two great nations in the world which, starting from different points, seem to be advancing toward the same goal: the Russians and the Anglo-Americans.
>
> Both have grown in obscurity, and while the world's attention was occupied elsewhere, they have suddenly taken their place among the leading nations, making the world take note of their birth and of their greatness almost at the same instant.
>
> All other peoples seem to have nearly reached their natural limits and to need nothing but to preserve them; but these two are growing. All the others have halted or advanced only through great exertions; they alone march easily and quickly forward along a path whose end no eye can yet see.
>
> The American fights against natural obstacles; the Russian is at grips with men. The former combats the wilderness and barbarism; the latter, civilization with all its arms. America's conquests are made with the plowshare, Russia's with the sword.
>
> To attain their aims, the former relies on personal interest and gives free scope to the unguided strength and common sense of individuals.

The latter in a sense concentrates the whole power of society in one man.

One has freedom as the principal means of action; the other has servitude.

Their point of departure is different and their paths diverse; nevertheless, each seems called by some secret design of Providence one day to hold in its hands the destinies of half the world.[1]

Tocqueville was right in foreseeing both a new scale of power for twentieth-century international politics and the states that would benefit from that change. What he could not see was the way in which the bipolar world was to come into being. Neither Russia nor the United States initiated the change of power scale in Europe, but Germany. It was not Germany, however, which was to benefit from that change, but Russia and the United States. Telescoped in those two sentences are the decline and fall of the European system I have described and the emergence, since 1945, of a wholly different kind of system which is no mere transition to a restoration of the old order, now irrevocably gone, but a firmly established and probably longlived successor to it.

1. Alexis de Tocqueville, *Democracy in America*, trans. George Lawrence (New York: Harper & Row, 1966), pp. 378–79.

CHAPTER 2

Dissolution of the System

The period 1895–1905 marked the beginning of a transformation of the international power system. Soon after 1900, for example, Great Britain abandoned its "splendid isolation" to enter into an alliance with one non-European power, Japan, and to begin to forge a "special relationship" with another, the United States. The emergence at that time of these two non-European countries as important factors in international affairs was itself a signal of the transformation underway. The convergence of power rivalries on the Far East in the 1890s pointed to the development of a truly *world* power structure, still centered on Europe but no longer confined to it. This situation was very different from the colonial rivalries of the seventeenth and eighteenth centuries, the competition in the Middle East opened by Napoleon's invasion of Egypt, the partition of Africa, and the international ramifications of Britain's position in India. For the first time most of the European powers had continuing major security concerns—and opportunities—in areas far from Europe and met there, not only each other, but new non-European powers.

This expansion of the geographic dimensions of international rivalry was closely related to the transformation of the scale of power then underway in Europe. The pacesetter after 1870 was the newly unified German Empire. After the success of the Prussian military system in the wars of 1866 and 1870, all the European states except Great Britain shifted over from small professional armies to the principle of universal service. The costs of this system, and of new developments in weaponry, mounted rapidly. In some countries the growth of industry and wealth made it possible to pay these costs with relative ease; others found it more difficult to keep up. As a result of the convergence of all these developments, the absolute international power of all major states increased markedly as compared with the recent past, but disparities among them also increased. Mass armies put new importance on population; modern weapons—especially navies—on industry; both on economic power and each country's ability to pay for these things. Some, in short, advanced rapidly toward a wholly new scale of power; others lagged farther and farther behind.

Table 2.1 shows not only the upward spiral of the arms race but also

Table 2.1   Defense Expenditures of European Powers
(in millions of dollars)

Army

	Austria-Hungary	France	Germany	Great Britain	Italy	Russia
1870	37	75	48	67	32	98
1880	62	114	91	75	41	130
1890	58	142	121	88	56	123
1900	60	139	168	107	54	162
1910	73	188	204	138	81	266
1914	143	197	442	147	92	324

Navy

	Austria-Hungary	France	Germany	Great Britain	Italy	Russia
1870	4	35	6	49	7	12
1880	4	43	11	51	9	19
1890	6	44	23	69	23	22
1900	9	73	37	146	24	42
1910	14	74	103	202	41	47
1914	38	90	112	237	49	118

Total

	Austria-Hungary	France	Germany	Great Britain	Italy	Russia
1870	41	110	54	116	39	110
1880	66	157	102	126	50	148
1890	64	186	144	157	79	145
1900	68	212	205	253	78	204
1910	87	262	307	340	122	312
1914	182	287	554	384	141	441

Source: Quincy Wright, *A Study of War* (Chicago: University of Chicago Press, 1942), vol. 1, pp. 670–71.

the sharp differences in the perceived (and self-perceived) standings of the six great powers.

As these decades passed Austria-Hungary and Italy competed for the lowest position among the significant military powers. France lost much ground, not only to Germany but to Russia on land and not only to Britain but to Germany and Russia at sea. The Russian army, still the most costly in Europe in 1910, lost ground rapidly to the German in the last few years of peace, but that was balanced by a late spurt in navy-building. The British fell behind in relative army expenditures but in 1914 managed to spend more on their navy than the next two greatest naval powers together and to enjoy a better relative position over their most likely enemy, Germany, than they had enjoyed over France in

1870. The most conspicuous factor overall was the rise of German military power, which, particularly on land, set new standards of cost.

Relative expenditures on armaments reflected, as noted, not only the policies of each government and its priorities for using its resources but also more underlying factors: population and industrial strength. Tables 2.2, 2.3, and 2.4 provide the data on which those contemporary statesmen who paid attention to such things could base their predictions of the future distribution of power and rank in Europe—calculations which could not but color current policy actions.

The stagnation of the French population stands out conspicuously against the growth of the rest. By 1910 Germany had very clearly outstripped all its European neighbors except one, Russia, whose population put it in a class of its own in Europe. But population figures, though much thought about by contemporaries, are a less reliable index of present national power—whatever they might indicate as to the future—than industrial strength. The production of iron and steel are important yardsticks. French expenditures on armaments were overshadowed by Germany's, but how much wider the discrepancy in iron and steel production! By 1914 Great Britain was no longer the industrial leader of Europe. How startling it is to see that backward Russia, on the eve of World War I, was already producing almost two-thirds as much steel as advanced Britain. In modern industry, as in defense expenditures, Germany was setting a new standard for power in Europe. But it was as overshadowed in industry by the United States (which in 1913 produced 32 million tons of steel) as in population by Russia.

Neither the course nor the outcome of World War I is implicit in these tables. France, for example, made a better military showing than such numbers would suggest, Russia made a worse, and American participa-

Table 2.2   Population of European Powers
(Home territory, in millions)

	Austria-Hungary	France	Germany	Great Britain	Italy	Russia
1870	36	36	40	31	27	82
1880	37	37	43	35	28	93
1890	41	38	49	38	30	110
1900	45	39	56	41	32	133
1910	49	39	64	45	35	163
1914	52	39	65	45	37	171

Source: Quincy Wright, A Study of War (Chicago: University of Chicago Press, 1942), vol. 1, pp. 670–71.

Table 2.3   Production of Pig Iron and Ferro Alloys in Europe
(in millions of tons)

	Austria-Hungary	France	Germany	Great Britain	Italy	Russia
1880	0.46	1.73	2.47	7.87	0.02	0.47
1890	0.97	1.96	4.10	8.03	0.01	1.0
1900	1.46	2.71	7.55	9.10	0.02	3.2
1910	2.01	4.04	13.11	10.17	0.36	3.4
1913	2.38	5.21	16.76	10.42	0.43	5.1

Sources: For Russia, Peter I. Lyashchenko, *History of the National Economy of Russia,* trans, L. M. Herman (New York: Macmillan, 1949), pp. 529, 688; for the others, Ingvar Svennilson, *Growth and Stagnation in the European Economy* (Geneva: United Nations Economic Commission for Europe, 1954), p. 257.

tion lay beyond prediction in 1914. Organization of resources, morale, and leadership, then as always, counted for much, and so did the play of circumstances. Nevertheless, the broader the sweep of time considered, the more likely that such "underlying" factors as population and industry will proportionately influence the relations among nations. Thus, someone who in 1914, for example, tried to conjure up the contours of the entire political landscape for the half century before and after could not but notice—whatever his explanations for the phenomena—the decline of Austria-Hungary and France, the growing eclipse not only of them but of Great Britain by Germany, and the prospect that Russia, if it could organize its growing power more efficiently, and the United States, if it should choose to amplify the participation in major international affairs that it began in 1898, would both, in a·more or less

Table 2.4   Production of Steel Ingots and Castings in Europe
(in millions of tons)

	Austria-Hungary	France	Germany	Great Britain	Italy	Russia
1880	0.12	0.39	0.73	1.32	—	—
1890	0.52	0.68	2.14	3.64	—	0.4
1900	1.17	1.57	6.46	4.98	0.14	1.5
1910	2.17	3.41	13.10	6.48	0.73	3.48
1913	2.61	4.69	17.60	7.79	0.93	4.83

Sources: For Russia, 1890 and 1900 in A. J. P. Taylor, *The Struggle for Mastery in Europe 1848–1918* (London: Oxford University Press, 1954), p. xxx; 1910 and 1913 in N. Peacock, ed. *The Russian Yearbook for 1915* (London: Eyre & Spottiswoode Ltd., 1915), p. 209; for the others, Ingvar Svennilson, *Growth and Stagnation in the European Economy* (Geneva: United Nations Economic Commission for Europe, 1954), p. 260.

foreseeable future, overshadow even German power. The future pattern of relations among all these states was, of course, uncertain, but their relative weights on the scale were discernible.

If 1945 could not be seen precisely from 1914, neither could 1914 be made out in 1871, the first year of the next-to-last phase of the European state system. The defeat of France by Prussia ended forever the prospect—already outdated by then—of French hegemony in Europe. But while the German Empire emerged as the strongest military power after its victories over Austria and France, its success was seen at the time as modifying but not upsetting the traditional balance of power system. This view was due in part, of course, to the fact that the national "unification" of Germany (as of Italy earlier) was sanctioned by opinion and exempted to some extent from the normal power calculus. More important, however, was the circumspect policy of Germany under the rule of Bismarck. The period up to 1890 was filled with diplomatic crises, but the main thrust of German policy was to keep Europe quiet, the status quo intact, frontiers unchanged. Far from feeling moved to counter or check increased German power, Great Britain—the supposed traditional "holder of the balance" in Europe—often worked with Bismarck to restrain those restless states that were suspected of threatening the existing settlement: France, unwilling to accept the territorial and power political results of 1870, or Russia and Austria-Hungary, trying to exploit the continual decline of Turkish power in the Balkans or to prevent each other from doing so. In this period German power and policy were respected but not unsettling.

Bismarck, however, created a state whose industrial power soon began to outrun that of its neighbors and provided means of action to those who, succeeding him in office after 1890, found his foreign policies too narrow for the resources at their command. Defense expenditures, industrial production, and even population began to rise at a rate which outclassed France and Austria-Hungary and threatened to rival Great Britain. Germany's belated efforts to take part in the game of colonial partition in Africa and Asia and to make its weight felt in Europe, not only effectively but conspicuously, were no more reprehensible than any other state's. But they came at a time when xenophobic popular nationalism was moving toward its disastrous climax as a factor in international affairs and, above all, when German power was visibly threatening to overshadow that of its European rivals. The disturbance created by Germany in the international atmosphere was thus intense.

Bismarck had been in alliance or entente with every major state except France. His successors dramatically altered this situation by dropping the tie to Russia, which then formed an alliance with France, and by

launching a colonial and naval policy which increasingly frightened
Great Britain. While remaining estranged from France in Africa and
from Russia in the Middle East and Asia, Great Britain in the 1890s
began to consider the implications of the new course in German policy.
The Boer War brought home that, from supposed balancer, Britain was
moving into dangerous isolation. Attempts to reach agreement with
Germany—aimed in large part to restrain Russia's expansion in the Far
East—failed. The Germans apparently thought that Britain could never
settle its quarrels with France and Russia and would therefore have to
come wooing Berlin again, at better terms.

The Germans, however, miscalculated. First, Britain formed an alliance with Japan in the Far East and an entente with the United States.
It next settled its colonial quarrels with France, in 1904, and those two
powers then passed from détente to *Entente Cordiale* (though never, it
might be noted, to alliance). Russia's defeat at the hands of Japan in
1904–1905 made it easier for France's ally and Britain to come to terms
in Asia, in 1907, and for the three of them to establish what became
known as the Triple Entente.

The Anglo-Russian tie was never as strong as the Franco-Russian or
even the Anglo-French, and the Triple Entente was in no way to be
compared, in mutual political commitment, to the Austro-German alliance of 1879. But public opinion in Europe thought it saw two armed
blocs confronting each other. Defense expenditures shot up and a period of almost permanent tension set in about 1905 during which a
succession of crises threatening war accustomed many to think that a
final test of arms between the two camps was inevitable.

Germany had the resources to maintain the most powerful army in
Europe and at the same time to build up, particularly after 1906, a
powerful fleet. But German diplomacy put these assets to poor use. The
fleet led neither to a bargain with Britain nor to the logical opposite, a
continental bloc against it. Indeed, one can wonder if Germany's leaders
coherently thought of the navy as having any precise use other than
serving, as Chancellor Bethmann-Hollweg said in 1912, "the general
purposes of her greatness."[1] Certainly Admiral von Tirpitz's "risk
theory" (so like General de Gaulle's "tear off an arm" nuclear strategy
sixty years later) did not deter the British from going to war with
Germany in 1914 for fear of sustaining unacceptable (though not fatal)
damage, nor did Germany's fleet save its colonies or protect the homeland from the ravages of blockade when war came. The naval buildup

1. A. J. P. Taylor, *The Struggle for Mastery in Europe, 1848–1919* (London: Oxford
University Press, 1954), p. 478.

simply squandered resources that might have been used more effectively by the German army, and, even more seriously, deepened at both the public and official levels the estrangement of Britain and Germany.

German attempts to break up the Entente Cordiale and the Triple Entente in a series of crises ended by strengthening both. For all their power, the German leaders secured little from these crises (Morocco in 1905–1906 and 1911, Bosnia in 1908–1909). They found themselves too late for substantial expansion in Africa and Asia and surrounded in Europe, as they came to feel, by a ring of hostile powers. Meanwhile, Germany's one reliable ally, Austria-Hungary, was visibly sliding down the power scale. The practical destruction of Turkey-in-Europe during the Balkan wars of 1912–1913 at the hands of Russian protégés immediately raised the question whether the polyglot Habsburg monarchy might not soon fall victim to external and internal Slav irredentism backed by Russia.

Faced by this prospect, the Austrian government decided in July 1914 that offense was the best defense and resolved to crush Serbia, once the murder of Archduke Franz Ferdinand supplied the pretext. Austria-Hungary received the firm and consistent backing of Germany in this policy—indeed, the reluctant Hungarian prime minister would probably not have permitted Austro-Hungarian action against Serbia without having been convinced that Germany favored it. Germany was strong enough, perhaps, to have risked restraining the Austrians. But it had successfully backed them in diplomatic clashes with Russia in 1908–1909 and again in 1913, and these precedents, which emboldened the Austrians in 1914, did not discourage the Germans from pursuing the same policy, firmly and clearly. They saw no reason to abandon their one ally, with whose survival they had gratuitously and imprudently entangled themselves. Besides, the Germans—studying the population and production statistics cited above and appraising the still incomplete program of Russia's rearmament—may have thought themselves at the peak of their power advantage vis-à-vis Russia. Neither Germany nor Austria-Hungary sought war with Russia, Serbia's Slavic patron, or a general European war, but both were conscious of the risk and willing to take it.

Russia, though not yet fully recovered from its 1905 defeat, concluded that its international prestige and Balkan interests would not permit it to be humiliated again by Germany and Austria-Hungary as it had been in a comparable crisis in 1908–1909. Some Russians may also have judged—unlike the case in the nineteenth century—that a patriotic war in these circumstances was likely to ward off social upheaval at home and consolidate the shaken monarchy. Finally, many Russian leaders probably agreed with Foreign Minister Sazanov's view that "to feel the stronger and yet to give way to an opponent whose superiority consists solely in his organization and discipline" was "humiliating."[2]

France, for its part, was certainly in no position to abandon its best ally to defeat by Germany—which would result, of course, in the overturn of the European balance of power to France's most serious detriment. The French, indeed, hardly dared jeopardize their alliance by trying even to exercise diplomatic restraint on Russia. They too could read the statistics, from their own point of view, and could judge that a severe diplomatic defeat for themselves and their ally might be more dangerous for their future than war (as they envisaged it). In any case, it scarcely mattered what France did—or Great Britain either—once the events of July 1914 were launched by Austria-Hungary's desperation, Germany's consent, and Russia's decision not to permit the crushing of Serbia. Military technology interlocked with the play of the alliance system to create a kind of inevitability.

Until the early 1890s German strategists, facing the prospect of a two-front war, had planned to stand on the defensive in the West and concentrate against Russia. After 1894 the plan was reversed; it was decided that France, unlike vast Russia, could be knocked out of the war at once by a strong blow and that, thereafter, Germany could turn east at leisure and with the best chance of final and total success. Between 1897 and 1905 the German strategic plan was refined to provide that the attack on France would not proceed frontally against the strong French position in the Vosges mountains but through Belgium. In 1900 the German Foreign Office was told of this plan to violate Belgium's neutrality, which Germany along with the other powers was committed to uphold, and it raised no objection.[3] This fundamental political decision appears never to have been debated in the German government.

This being the German strategy, it is doubtful that either France or Great Britain (only ambiguously committed to France but traditionally sensitive to the fate of Belgium) could have remained out of a German-Russian conflict even if one or both had decided at the last minute to accept Russian defeat and German ascendancy in Europe as preferable to war. British indecision in the crisis has been much criticized, but they could not have stopped the implementation of the German war plan whatever they did. Indeed, the German government itself could not

2. Quoted in C. L. Mowat, ed., *The New Cambridge Modern History*, vol. 12, *The Shifting Balance of World Forces, 1898–1945*, p. 152.

3. Hajo Holborn, *A History of Modern Germany 1840–1945* (New York: Knopf, 1969, p. 346.

have stopped the execution of the Schlieffen plan, for there was no other.[4]

> Henceforth from the moment the Russians mobilized their army, Germany had to declare war on Russia in order to be able to break off relations with the latter's ally, France, and thereby gain the excuse for presenting an ultimatum to Brussels demanding the unopposed passage of the German army. In other words, since the strategic planning was exclusively concentrated on a general war, the German government was forced at a certain point of a crisis to assume the responsibility for opening a general European war, irrespective of whether or not all the diplomatic means for settling, or at least localizing, the conflict had been exhausted.[5]

That is, the Germans acted in such a way, once war with Russia was certain, as to make sure that France also entered the conflict. In moving against France through Belgium, they were not blind to the prospect that Britain also might go to war but they were quite indifferent to it, taking for granted that Britain could play no significant military role in the short war they—like everyone else—foresaw.

The course and consequences of World War I are more important for this discussion than its immediate causes. But the events of July 1914 are significant here because, behind the specific details, most of the participants seem to have been aware of the wider crisis which their international system was undergoing. It has been argued that the rigidities of the two alliances escalated a Balkan quarrel into a world war. But, while it is true that both groupings tightened their bonds after 1911, it is also true that there remained distinct possibilities of change. Anglo-German, Russo-German and even Franco-German détente had their advocates in the respective countries. These very possibilities, whatever their prospects if war had not come in the summer of 1914, led to fear on all sides that allies, if abandoned in the crisis, might move toward the enemy camp. The crisis, which in effect lasted only one week, suddenly revealed in circumstances of utmost tension how high the stakes were. The Austrians believed that their survival as a state was at stake; the French thought that their own survival as a great power obliged them to support Russia even in a remote quarrel; Russia felt too weak—at home as well as abroad—to accept a diplomatic defeat of the magnitude implied by

---

4. Hajo Holborn, "Moltke and Schlieffen," in *Makers of Modern Strategy*, ed. Edward M. Earle (Princeton, N.J.: Princeton University Press, 1943), pp. 172–205. On William II's last-minute and futile notion of standing on the defensive in the West and moving first against Russia, see Holborn, *Modern Germany*, pp. 423–24.

5. Holborn, *Modern Germany*, p. 348.

Austria's demands on Serbia; and the Germans were conscious at the same time of their present power, of the isolation their diplomacy had done so much to create, and of the longer term threat posed by Russia's population and resources to their own position.

The British found the unity to enter the war in neither desperation, hope, nor fear, but in moral indignation—concern for a "scrap of paper." Their shortsightedness is more to be wondered at than the concerns, however narrow and muddled, of the continental powers. For, in fact, the war itself confirmed what most of the participants more or less grasped at the outset: that the balance of power on which the European state system was based had already been upset and could no longer fulfill its most fundamental purpose, to guarantee the survival and the status as great powers of the principal member states.

In this sense, World War I, which revealed and precipitated a long-growing transformation, was by far the fundamental international event of the twentieth century. Europe has been adapting to its consequences ever since.

The first shock to the nations that went to war in August 1914 came when their expectations of a short conflict were disappointed. Guided by the examples of the Franco-Prussian conflict of 1870 and the recent Balkan wars, every government had expected that the war would be decided by a few battles. Every military machine was organized (as best it could be, and with very different levels of efficiency) to that end. Instead, the French offensive against Germany in the Vosges failed at once; the German advance through Belgium into France was halted in the epic battle of the Marne, in early September; and the Russian advance into East Prussia, though it helped to relieve the German pressure on France, met a catastrophic defeat at the end of August. The participants thus surprisingly found themselves deadlocked, at least in the West, and years of bloody attacks and counterattacks across northern France made little appreciable difference in the situation, nor did the subsequent entrance into the war of smaller countries, nor sideshow campaigns like Salonika, Gallipoli, and Mesopotamia.

In these unexpected circumstances more underlying power factors in each country came to the surface, for better or worse. France focused its resources with extraordinary persistence on holding the line established in September 1914. Great Britain, which found itself much more involved in continental land warfare than it had ever expected, slowly found the industrial and human resources needed for that effort as well as for maintaining its naval superiority. Russia, on the other hand, forced on the defensive by the end of 1914 and practically cut off from its Western allies, began to undergo social disintegration. Germany was able to organize its population and industry to a point which allowed it practically to absorb Austria-Hungary into its war effort, to hold the line if not to advance on the Western front, and gradually to wear Russia down to surrender.

The decisive year of the European war was 1917. Two revolutions in Russia produced a new regime which, to maintain itself in power at whatever cost, signed first an armistice and then a peace with the Central Powers (at Brest-Litovsk, in March 1918) that pushed the new Soviet state back to the Russian frontiers of the mid-seventeenth century. Victorious in the East, Germany was now in a position to shift its full power to the Western front. With no better allies than Austria-Hungary, Bulgaria, and Turkey, Germany had succeeded in organizing its power for war on such a scale, despite an increasingly effective Allied blockade, as to defeat Russia and to be on the edge of defeating France and Great Britain as well. The war by early 1918 made clear what some had feared before: that German power could not be contained by any combination of European states. And the Germans were ready with a program of war aims which would convert their victory into a permanent postwar hegemony of Europe, strategic and economic.

1917 was, however, a decisive year for Europe in an even more fundamental sense. With Russia at least temporarily removed from the game by defeat, dismemberment, and the nature of its new government, and with Germany apparently on the brink of establishing its hegemony over the continent, the entrance of the United States into the war suddenly transformed a European war into a world war and reversed the results about to be achieved on the continent. American power reached the Western front in time to prevent French and British defeat by the last German offensive (March-July 1918) and then in sufficient volume to force Germany, in its turn, to surrender.

Great Britain, France, and (ironically) Russia were thus saved from subordination to Germany. But the old self-contained European state system was not saved, for its member states had been unable to defend themselves against the power of one of them. German unity, so long delayed, proved to be more than the old European system could live with. The national fact had triumphed, but at the expense of the long-standing international structure. Unlike the case of Napoleonic France, it was not a coalition of European states that finally defeated the exceptional member of the system, but, rather, the entrance onto the scene of a new and outside power—one which the victorious Allies, in their enthusiasm, might well have seen as a *deus ex machina*. The independence of the European states was maintained only because, as Canning had said in 1826, the New World had been called into existence to redress the balance of the Old.

CHAPTER 3

Indian Summer of Europe

The combatants had gone to war in 1914 with largely negative objectives. They wanted to avoid diplomatic defeat, loss of allies and status, or upset of the European balance of power. As the fighting went on, however, territorial objectives were advanced on all sides. France, of course, wanted the restoration of Alsace-Lorraine; Russia wanted the straits and portions of Turkey-in-Asia; Britain and France together made plans to partition the Arab-speaking part of the Turkish Empire; Italy and Rumania were brought into the war on the side of the Entente (now called the Allies) with promises of Austro-Hungarian and Turkish territory. The scope of German ambitions was shown in the treaty of Brest-Litovsk, signed with the new Bolshevik government of Russia in March 1918. The Ukraine, Poland, the Baltic littoral, and Finland were detached from Russia and set up as dependent states, bound to Germany by close economic ties. Germany had equally ambitious plans for Western Europe.[1]

Most of these plans were not made public in wartime, however, and all the participants came to realize that annexationist aims were not sufficient to mobilize domestic morale for the drawn-out and bloody struggle in which peoples as well as armies were increasingly involved. The length and intensity of the war had the effect of escalating war aims on all sides. Each government tried to justify the war to its own people not only by claiming to be defending a beleaguered fatherland against

---

1. A plan drawn up by Chancellor Bethmann-Hollweg in September 1914 called for the annexation of the iron mines of Lorraine and possibly of the French coast from Dunkirk to Boulogne; French reparations of such a size as to prevent rearming for fifteen or twenty years; a trade treaty with France that would make it a German economic satellite; the annexation of Liege and perhaps of Antwerp in Belgium and the reduction of the rest of the country to economic and strategic vassalization to Germany; and the establishment of an economic federation around Germany including the Netherlands, Denmark, Austria-Hungary, and Poland, and possibly other countries as well as France and Belgium. The German colonial empire in Africa was to take in Portuguese, Belgian, and French colonies. Fritz Fischer, *Germany's Aims in the First World War* (New York: Norton, 1967), pp. 103–06. This, the program of the supposedly moderate civilian chancellor, would have put an end to the prewar European system and the independence of the member states, except perhaps, for a time, of Great Britain. And Bethmann-Hollweg's aims were by no means the most ambitious set forth in high circles in wartime Germany.

wanton aggression but also by holding out the hope that victory would produce a better international system than had existed before 1914.

This was easiest for the Germans because it was clear that victory would establish their hegemony in Europe and thus, from their point of view, a more satisfactory system than the alleged "encirclement" of the uneasy prewar balance of power. The Allies, who also realized what German victory would mean, had as their negative objective the preventing of such an outcome. But they found it difficult to explain how the victory to be won at such cost would permanently ensure their security in the face of Germany's obvious power, and even less how it would establish a better system of international relations. The detachment of this or that piece of German territory, or the destruction of the German fleet, or heavy indemnities did not seem to meet the case. Nothing less than Germany's elimination as a great power altogether— that is, its partition—seemed sufficient. This, however, was difficult to avow and scarcely less difficult to conceive, for the breakup of a national state (as contrasted to Austria-Hungary or Turkey) ran counter to the Allies' preconceptions of what was possible even in the event of complete military victory.

Their eventual solution was to assert that the overthrow of the Hohenzollern system in Germany would convert that country to a more pacific policy and enable it to take its place in the projected postwar concert of peaceloving states. This became the basis of allied policy when Woodrow Wilson, assuming the ideological as well as the economic and military leadership of the alliance at the beginning of 1918, reformulated and expanded its war aims in response to the many-sided crisis confronting it. Wilson was the first to suggest that the Allies could not make peace with the existing regime in Germany and to propound war aims with the explicit objective of stimulating the liberal and Socialist opposition in Germany to replace the existing system of government. Conservatives in Britain and France did not much like the idea of promoting revolution in Germany, not least because they feared that it might take the form of Bolshevism rather than something milder. But they had nothing better to offer and Wilson's program on this point became Allied policy.

That program, set forth in the Fourteen Points on January 8, 1918, contained much else, general and specific. Under the spur of the Russian defection from the war and the call of the new Bolshevik government at the end of 1917 for a democratic peace based on self-determination, Wilson and many others realized that the Allies too had to show that they were fighting for principles, not just interests, to rally the weary peoples of their countries to face the last year of the war; to hold the support of the left critics of the Allied governments, who demanded more from the war than mere victory; to prevent the Bolsheviks from winning support among the peoples of both the Allies and the Central Powers with their revolutionary principles; to keep the Central Powers from scoring a propaganda success by giving lip service, as they were doing at Brest-Litovsk, to the Bolshevik peace principles; and to present a program that might encourage the German opposition to challenge its own government.

Wilson presented his program when and as he did in response to the Bolshevik ideological challenge and the German response to it, but his proposals reflected more than expediency. He had advocated "peace without victory" before the United States entered the war and had called for a new postwar organization of international relations to replace the old system that had led to conflict. Once in the war he looked to total victory over Germany as the means to achieve these objectives, but the broad objectives themselves remained much the same as before.

The other Allied governments were far from sharing all of Wilson's views, but they were subject to domestic pressures to accept them and, above all, they desperately needed the United States at that moment. As Arno Mayer has put it: "In the dawning battle for the minds of men, all the governments had recourse to one and the same New Diplomacy gospel and practice."[2] The Allies thus pledged themselves to the ideological goal of fighting the war as a means to end war altogether by eliminating its most important cause, the German militarist regime, but also the broader evils of the balance of power system, secret diplomacy, and the denial of self-determination to subject peoples.

The French and Italian governments, however, gave only lip service to these broad objectives even during the war, and the British were by no means wholly committed to them either. The many pressures, internal and external, that had led to an apparent Allied consensus on Wilsonian policies in 1918 were far weaker in 1919. The Paris peace conference has thus often been seen, particularly in the United States, as a clash between Wilson's idealistic effort to frame a just and nonvengeful settlement and the sordid avarice of the European Allies as expressed in their "secret treaties"—a clash in which Wilson too often accepted unworthy compromises, inconsistent with his principles and dangerous for future peace.

This view is not entirely wrong but it is much too simple, for several reasons. Wilson's bargaining position with the European Allies was far weaker after the armistice than it had been during the war. The tide

2. Arno J. Mayer, *Political Origins of the New Diplomacy,* 1917–1918 (New Haven: Yale University Press, 1959), p. 276.

which had carried Allied public opinion and governments toward the
New Diplomacy in 1918 reversed itself once the war had ended and
flowed strongly toward conservatives who favored a severe peace with
Germany—and, hardly less important, severe measures to deal with
Bolshevism in Russia. This swing, which was interwoven with domestic
politics everywhere, was no less pronounced in the United States itself,
where the Republicans won the midterm congressional elections, than in
Britain and France and Italy, where "hanging the Kaiser" and "making
the Germans pay till the pips squeaked" were the order of the day.
Wilsonian principles retained supporters everywhere, but they were on
the defensive and proved frail barriers to the particular national demands of articulate opinion in each country.

Further, the Wilsonian principles themselves, whatever the Germans
believed in 1918–19 or came to believe later, did not promise that
Germany would emerge from the war intact, at least in Europe, except
for a change of regime. Once the Germans had changed their regime at
his call, Wilson did want to reintegrate democratic Germany into the
liberal world order he hoped to build—not least because he feared that
an embittered Germany would be propelled toward Bolshevism. As
Assistant Secretary of State Breckinridge Long said, in considering
the Bolshevik threat to Europe, "Germany cannot safely be annihi-
lated."[3] But Wilson also thought that defeated Germany should be put
under restraint until its new republicanism, established only at the last
minute before the armistice and beset by enemies on both right and left,
had been tested and demonstrated. As he said in February 1919: "until
we knew what the German Government was going to be, and how the
German people were going to behave, the world had a moral right to
disarm Germany, and to subject her to a generation of thoughtfulness." [4]

Wilson also recognized that devastated France and other Allies must
have both reparations and security guarantees, and he was strongly
committed on the merits of the case to the emergence of new Slavic states
in Eastern Europe. The Fourteen Points, on the basis of which Germany
had surrendered, contained many specific if not always precise territorial provisions, notably the concept of redrawing the frontiers of Central
and Eastern Europe on the basis of nationality—a policy which was
necessarily costly to Germany. Wilson's commitment to the Eastern
countries was reinforced by the conference's obsession with the Bolshevik problem, which made it difficult to resist the French argument
that these states, and above all Poland, had to be as strong as possible to

3. Quoted in N. Gordon Levin, Jr., *Woodrow Wilson and World Politics* (New York: Oxford
University Press, 1968), p. 135.
4. Ibid., p. 157.

serve as a barrier against the contagion from the East. Few, after all, were prepared to rearm Germany to play that part!

For all these reasons, Wilson found it difficult to use American economic pressure on the Allies to secure the kind of peace he wanted or even to formulate a clearcut issue on which to stand up against them in an appeal to public opinion. Lloyd George, Clemenceau, and Orlando knew what prevailing opinion in their countries demanded of them, and when Wilson finally tried to publicly resist Italy's claim to Fiume he found out, as he must have realized before, that he was in a weak position to challenge any of them on the particular issues of most moment to their countries, however unprincipled and dangerous he thought these claims. In addition, he dreaded an open breakdown of the conference and was not alone in thinking that a failure to preserve Allied unity and make peace as best it could be made would open the way for Bolshevism to spread westward.

In weighing the rights and wrongs of the Treaty of Versailles in these terms, it is often overlooked that German revanchism may have been exacerbated by particular provisions—notably the war guilt clauses, the open-ended reparations, and the loss of territory to the new Poland— but was in fact created by the defeat itself, coming after victory seemed so near and, what was worse for European peace, in circumstances that allowed many in Germany to think that there had been no defeat at all. It was not by chance or weakness that the Germany army, with the homeland still uninvaded by the enemy, allowed the new republic to shoulder responsibility and blame for accepting a defeat which the army knew it could not prevent. The many Germans who accepted this view of events at face value and the many who believed, as late as October 1918, that the war might end with the loss of no more than part of Alsace-Lorraine and perhaps the African colonies, were impossibly out of touch with reality. Whatever the details of the peace settlement, the Germans were bound to be bitter when their illusions were inevitably shattered. The Weimar Republic had a great burden to carry as the signer of the Versailles treaty, but an even greater one as the receiver in bankruptcy of a military defeat that the country did not accept as such.

Wilson's efforts in the Paris negotiations were not, in fact, entirely in vain, either in details or in a broader sense. The European Allies too knew that the peace had to contain something besides annexations and indemnities that would make future war less likely. To Clemenceau, it is true, the League of Nations probably meant no more than a means of binding the United States to the support of the postwar European power system. But he accepted it. To Wilson and many others, however, it offered a means eventually to ameliorate the less satisfactory parts of the settlement and a framework for superseding in time the imperial and military rivalries that they saw as the very causes of war.

As it turned out, the distinctive American contribution to the settlement, the League of Nations, which should have appealed to American moralism and messianism, led Wilson's own country in the end to reject the treaty, precisely because its opponents claimed that League membership involved an indefinite commitment to defend the peace settlement. Wilson's failure—or, rather, America's—left the European settlement, and the balance of power that underlay it, standing on one leg. The peace treaties themselves accurately reflected the power distribution of 1919: America stood beside Great Britain and France; Germany was beaten; Austria-Hungary had already dissolved; and Russia, though in everyone's thoughts, was far offstage as an actual factor in the power equation of that moment. But Britain and France had won the war only with American help, and neither their victory in those circumstances nor the peace settlement that followed made them powerful enough by themselves to outweigh Germany—even the Germany of the peace settlement. That is, neither the defeat of Germany nor the peace treaties restored the *European* balance of power that had already been undermined by the growth of German strength before 1914 and had been destroyed by the victory Germany so nearly won. The Americans no doubt believed the contrary when they chose to withdraw in 1920. The British and French knew better but had to go on as best they could.

The *internal* European balance of power might have been restored in 1919 only if the factor that had upset it was removed from the scene— that is, only if Germany, overpopulous and overpowerful in proportion to its neighbors, had been partitioned. But this was out of the question in a settlement whose keystone was the principle of the national state. The French, it is true, had secured Russia's agreement in March 1917 to separating the Rhineland from Germany (and in return had given the Russians a free hand to draw Germany's eastern frontier). Had imperial or even republican Russia survived until the peace negotiations, France might have pressed its Rhenish policy with some hope of success. Clemenceau did make a claim to set up a buffer state in the Rhineland. But in the face of American and British opposition he settled for short-term Allied occupation of the area and its permanent demilitarization, and, most important, treaties of guarantee with Great Britain and the United States. The expectation that the United States would remain at hand to enforce the settlement helped disarm those Frenchmen who dreamed of reversing Bismarck's work.

As it turned out, American rejection of the Versailles treaty also entailed rejection of the alliance with France, and that in turn released

Britain from its parallel obligation. But even without this aborted deal at the peace conference, partition of Germany would not have been seriously contemplated in 1919. Germany too was considered to have rights as a national state, and the very vehemence of Allied propaganda against the Hohenzollern empire led many to believe—or at least to hope—that only the policies of the imperial German government, and not the power of the unified German state, had upset the system. Democratic Germany was thus given its chance.

Germany was, of course, diminished and hobbled by the settlement. There was the loss of Alsace-Lorraine and of territory in the east to Poland; the loss of all colonies; heavy reparations; Allied occupation and permanent demilitarization of the left bank of the Rhine; and severe limitations on the size and the equipment of the armed forces. These were significant barriers to Germany's revival as a great power (though, in the event, only a fraction of the huge reparations bill was ever paid, and that to a large extent with foreign loans, and the disarmament clauses of the treaty were systematically evaded). But it was doubtful from the start whether the Weimar Republic or any other German regime would acquiesce in them indefinitely, or, if it did not, whether the Allies would preserve sufficient unity and determination to maintain them indefinitely. Most Germans were ready to believe from the beginning that their army had not been defeated on the battlefield and that, because of their last-minute switch to republicanism and their last-minute espousal of the Fourteen Points as the basis for peace, they had been promised by the Allies and were entitled to a settlement at little cost to themselves.

Few Germans, in 1919 or later, saw the irony in the fact that they berated the Allies for not living up in every particular to principles which had no part at all in the plans their own government had made for establishing German hegemony in postwar Europe. Even fewer gave the Allies credit for such compromises as the status of the Saar, Danzig, and the Silesian frontier and for their decision not to detach the Rhineland or, above all, not to partition Germany, the one effective bar to its revival as a great power and the one thing which all groups in Germany wished to avoid. More Germans, particularly in the 1930s, relished the fact that so many people in the victor nations, particularly in Great Britain, shared their own conviction that the "Carthaginian" settlement had been unjust and ought to be changed to Germany's benefit. The extent of this conviction *outside* Germany was perhaps the most important legacy of the failure of Wilson's New Diplomacy.

The power equation of 1919 on which the peace was based was thus ephemeral. Without American support, Britain and France could only try to believe that the "new" Germany would accept its diminished standing in Europe, or, if not, would be in no position to revise it. Their only prospective allies in maintaining the status quo were the new or strengthened states of Eastern Europe—the collective substitute for Russia in the renewed Entente—whose power potential, policies, and political future were all uncertain. Italy, dissatisfied with its gains from the settlement, became revisionist almost at once. Russia itself lay on the horizon, self-excluded from the postwar system and a sworn enemy of it, both territorially and ideologically. It is not coincidental that the 1920s were the high-water period for efforts to devise pacts and protocols to ensure peace—that is, the status quo. The lack of self-confidence of the defenders of the peace settlement, particularly France, is well reflected in their famous "pactomania"—the forlorn effort to conceal power relationships that they realized were unfavorable to them behind a thick foliage of paper guarantees. But the French knew, as Gerhard L. Weinberg has written, that

> Germany had emerged from the World War *relatively* at least as powerful if not more powerful than when it entered that conflict, with its erstwhile enemies relatively weaker than in 1914 and in any case divided among themselves.[5]

Nevertheless, with Germany defeated and Russia removed from the scene, Great Britain and France seemed in the early 1920s to enjoy a kind of joint hegemony over a restored European state system. Since this Indian summer of the old system was the "normalcy" to which those who fought World War II referred in thinking about the postwar world (an important point to which I will return when discussing the origins of the cold war in chapter 6), it is essential to understand the fundamental instability and impermanence which marked it from the start.

1. Great Britain and France were left as the only great powers in Europe (though Italy's claim to that status was more nearly accepted as real during this period than in any other, before or since). But France had lost nearly 1.4 million dead in the war, Britain about 750,000. Both had divested themselves of a good deal of their overseas investment to pay for the war. Both were heavily indebted to the United States. Both, as became clear almost at once, were even more wounded psychologically than economically or demographically by the war and increasingly reluctant to contemplate renewed hostilities. Finally, their policies in the 1920s and 1930s were usually at cross-purposes.

5. Gerhard L. Weinberg, *The Foreign Policy of Hitler's Germany* (Chicago: University of Chicago Press, 1970), p. 358.

From the start British opinion found the Versailles settlement unjustly harsh on Germany, and British policy, by some misplaced balance of power reflex, sought to check supposed French ambitions to hegemony with a certain revival of German power (and to make the settlement more tolerable to the Weimar Republic by ameliorating it). At first France tried to enforce the treaty to the letter. This policy reached its height when the French invaded the Ruhr in 1923 to assure reparations payments. The collapse of that effort in the face of German passive resistance and inflation led France, step by step, into dependence on Britain, its one reasonably sure major ally. The Locarno Pact of 1925 symbolized this new Anglo-French relationship, as well as the return of Germany to international respectability. Thereafter the French followed the British in an effort to conciliate Germany, albeit within the postwar status quo. What began with the Weimar Republic was continued, under the name of appeasement, after Hitler came to power in 1933.

2. Though amputated by the peace settlement of some 13 percent of its territory and some 10 percent of its population, and with its Western frontier demilitarized and army drastically limited, Germany nevertheless remained aware, along with the Allies, of the strength which had come so close to winning the war. This strength was not only a memory. The German population by itself threw a long shadow over all its neighbors except the Soviet Union. Despite wartime and postwar losses, it had grown to over 68 million by 1938 (not including Austria). In the same year Great Britain had about 48 million people and France had under 42 million.[6] Germany's preponderance, as before 1914, was equally marked in general industrial strength (see table 3.1) and steel production (table 3.2).

Germany was not able fully to translate its economic resources into political and military power as long as it accepted even some of the limitations of the Versailles treaty. And during the 1920s it did, in fact, conform broadly to those limitations (while evading some, particularly military) and tried to improve its position as best it could In this way, Germany achieved a practical reparations arrangement (the Dawes Plan, 1924), a guarantee from Britain and Italy against a renewed French invasion (Locarno, 1925), admission as a great power to the League of Nations (1926), a revised reparations agreement (the Young Plan, 1929), and early withdrawal of Allied troops from the Rhineland (1930).

All this left the main limits on German revival intact. But the Weimar Republic had reason to hope, by the end of the 1920s, that these too

6. Ingvar Svennilson, *Growth and Stagnation in the European Economy* (Geneva: United Nations Economic Commission for Europe, 1954), pp. 236–37.

Table 3.1   Net Value of Manufacturing Production of European Powers
(in millions of dollars, 1937 purchasing power)

	France	Germany	Great Britain	Italy	Russia
1913	2,366	6,093	3,858	1,015	767
1929	3,569	6,164	4,553	1,498	1,357
1938	2,905	8,225	5,881	1,647	6,549

Source: Basic Data of the Western European Economies (Washington, D.C.: Department of State, Division of Research for Western Europe, 1956), pp. 44–47.

might be modified or abolished in time, for Great Britain favored, and France could not forever oppose, this policy of reconciliation. Britain, indeed, was not hostile in principle even to some revision of Germany's Eastern frontier, and the Locarno arrangement was something of a triumph for German diplomacy—and a defeat for France's—in that it advertised the distinction which the British drew between the guarantee they would make in Western Europe and their refusal to make an equivalent guarantee to France's allies on Germany's eastern border. What will always remain unknown is whether the Weimar Republic, had it survived, might have been satisfied with the eventual ending of the unequal status imposed on Germany at Versailles, or whether, once these limitations had been removed, it would have begun to assert the country's strength in such a manner as to disrupt the basic postwar status quo. That is a question to which I will return in considering German foreign policy in the 1930s.

3. Between Germany and Soviet Russia lay a band of new or revived countries whose lands had for centuries belonged either to these states or to Austria or Turkey. There had been no independent Poland since

Table 3.2   Production of Steel Ingots and Castings of European Powers
(in millions of tons)

	France	Germany	Great Britain	Italy	Russia
1913	4.69	17.60	7.79	.93	4.8
1929	9.71	16.21	9.79	2.12	5.0
1938	6.22	22.66	10.56	2.32	18.1

Sources: For Russia, *Statistical Year-Book of the League of Nations 1938–39* (Geneva: League of Nations, Economic Intelligence Service, 1939), p. 147; for the others, Ingvar Svennilson, *Growth and Stagnation in the European Economy* (Geneva: United Nations Economic Commission for Europe, 1954), pp. 262–63.

1795, no independent Bohemia or Hungary since the early sixteenth century. The independence of these states, like the postwar aggrandizement of Rumania and Serbia (now expanded into Yugoslavia), derived not only from the Allied victory but from the peculiar circumstance that the war ended with the disappearance of Austria-Hungary and the enfeeblement of both Germany and Russia. Had Germany been victorious and the treaty of Brest-Litovsk implemented, all these states would have been under German control (some by way of Austria-Hungary). Had imperial Russia remained in the war to the end, it is likely that most of Eastern Europe would have been under its hegemony.

But Germany and Russia were both defeated in 1918, and Poland and the Austro-Hungarian successor states played a considerable part in interwar politics. Poland was considered almost a great power, and the Little Entente of Czechoslovakia, Yugoslavia, and Rumania had a similar status. All were allied to France in defense of the postwar settlement, though, in fact, some were mostly concerned with German resurgence, others with blocking Hungarian irredentism or restoration of the Habsburg monarchy.

4. The Soviet Union was not entirely isolated from the scene, emerging, for example, in 1922 at Rapallo to establish a kind of entente with Germany. But the USSR played a somewhat intermittent role in affairs until it became a member of the League of Nations in 1934, and the striking growth of its economy in the 1930s did not enhance its international weight. Soviet Russia continued to cast a shadow over all the countries of Europe and thus facilitated reconciliation between Germany and the victorious Allies, who feared that the two great "outcasts" might unite to upset the peace.

Apart from Italy, which played a lone and restless hand, the postwar European system was thus essentially four-tiered: Great Britain and France; Germany; the Eastern states; and the Soviet Union. The first and third tiers were in alliance to defend the settlement, though there was much disagreement among them about what to defend and how; the second and fourth were revisionist but went different roads in the 1920s—Germany toward accommodation with the Western powers, the Soviet Union toward relative isolation.

What were the chances for survival of this system? It did not, in fact, survive, but it is overly deterministic to be certain that World War II and its outcome and its sequels were all quite inevitable. Nevertheless, two things are sure: first, that both Germany and Russia were profoundly anti–status quo, and second, that the sum of their potential power was much greater than the sum of the power of those European countries that were pro–status quo (assuming the continued political abstention of

the United States). The situation was set forth simply and perceptively by
the Italian premier, Vittorio Orlando, as early as May 1919:

> . . . I cannot look forward without grave apprehension ʰ the future
> of continental Europe; the German longing for revenge must be
> considered in conjunction with the Russian position. We can thus
> see even now that the settlement to be arrived at will lack the assent
> of more than half the population of the European continent. If we
> detach from the block on which the new European system will have
> to rely for support forty million Italians, and force them into the
> ranks of the malcontents, do you think that the new order will rest
> on a firm basis?[7]

On the other hand, if the status quo powers were not only weak but
seriously divided, the revisionists were no less so. It was difficult for
Germany and Russia (and Fascist Italy) to make common cause. Further,
it was not so clear to contemporaries in the 1920s and even the 1930s,
population and economic statistics notwithstanding, that the actual
power equation was what it proved to be. France was respected for its
military showing in World War I, and Poland and Czechoslovakia were
thought to be military factors of some importance, while Russia seemed
extremely weak and Germany, of course, was under the restraints of the
settlement.

We may conclude, then, that in the long run the status quo was bound
to be changed, but when, how, and to whose advantage were less certain.

The key to the question concerns the might-have-beens with respect to
Germany. If the trends of the 1920s had not been cut short by the
depression and Hitler's rise to power, it is probable that the Allies would
eventually have agreed to drop one after another of the limitations or
burdens placed on Germany by the peace: reparations, military restrictions, demilitarization of the Rhineland. Would a prosperous Germany,
politically organized in the structure established by the Weimar constitution, then have been content with equality within the Versailles
system and frontiers?

A review of the history of the Weimar Republic up to the depression
suggests that this would have been unlikely. The wide acceptance of the
myth about the betrayal inflicted on Germany in 1919; the constant
drumfire of nationalist agitation and propaganda against the peace
settlement, even as it was being relaxed in the later 1920s, and against
the republic that had accepted it; the political weakness or frequent

7. David Lloyd George, *The Truth About the Peace Treaties* (London: Victor Gollancz Ltd.,
1938), vol. 2, p. 883.

exclusion from office of those forces most likely to accept a modified peace settlement; the influence within the democratic system not only of the army but of parties and social milieux which were only partly or provisionally committed to the republic and were militant opponents of the European status quo—all this suggests that in the best of circumstances the ending of the unequal restrictions placed on Germany by the peace treaty would not have sufficed.

The career of Gustav Stresemann, foreign minister of the Weimar Republic from 1923 until his death in 1929 and principal architect of the policy of "fulfillment," illustrates the ambiguities and limitations of that policy: his uphill struggle to carry his own conservative party along with his policy; his knowledge of and connivance at clandestine German rearmament, both inside the country and in the Soviet Union; above all, his care to keep Germany's claims and options open in the East for the day when freedom of action in that area would have been won by astute diplomacy in the West. For it was above all the Polish frontier which was the fixed target of German revisionists.

Revision of the German-Polish frontier was constantly in the minds of German policymakers even as they pursued reconciliation with Great Britain and France.[8] They were careful at Locarno, for example, to accept only their Western frontiers as final but not their Eastern. They were also careful to follow up the Locarno agreement with a neutrality treaty with the USSR and to enter the League of Nations on terms that excused them from taking part in future sanctions against that country. They thus maintained a relationship, begun at Rapallo in 1922, that was seen by one of its authors, General von Seeckt, the commander of the army up to 1926, as a means for bringing about the partition of Poland, and by others as the least allowing Germany to play off the Western powers against the Soviet Union to Germany's advantage.

No German government was likely to overlook the obvious facts that Poland and the other Eastern states were weak and that Germany was in a position to pursue revisionism in the East either in partnership with the Soviet Union (the Rapallo option) or with the acquiescence if not the support of the Western powers (and particularly of Great Britain), perhaps in the name of defense against Bolshevism. At its most accommodationist the Weimar Republic actively kept open its maneuverability

8. Their concern was to right what they considered a dangerous and intolerable strategic wrong, not to rescue lost or abused Germans. The question of the Germans in the Sudeten region of Czechoslovakia, which Hitler chose to deal with before tackling Poland, received little attention from German revisionists in the 1920s—partly because the area had belonged to Austria-Hungary rather than to the German empire, but above all because the Sudetenland was not a strategic "wound" like the Polish corridor.

in Eastern Europe. German acceptance of the Polish frontier as settled was out of the question. As Hajo Holborn said: "Revisionism was the program of all the German parties, including even the Communists, and one of the achievements of the Weimar Republic was that it undermined the moral validity of the peace settlement of 1919."[9]

It is not necessary to accept the "moral validity" of the Versailles treaty to note that this widespread and deep German determination to change it, when combined with the resources Germany could bring to that task, implied at the least a substantial shift in the postwar balance of power in Europe. Germany's gains, in the circumstances, could only be the losses of others—in power and status as well as in territory.

There is no reason to assume that Stresemann and many others who favored such revision expected to accomplish it by force (though they did not exclude that in suitable circumstances, such as a Russo-Polish war). But there is also no reason to assume that it could have been achieved with the willing consent of Poland. The phrase "peaceful revision" is deceptively mild when applied to a country in Poland's position. The Poles would surely have had to be coerced before they would surrender a substantial and valuable part of their Western territories and their access to the sea. Germany had neither the interest nor the means to compensate them, as was sometimes suggested, with territory to be seized from the Soviet Union. What would have remained of Poland after such revision would have become a dependency on Germany—the more so if, as would have been likely, the USSR took the opportunity to seize eastern Poland for itself with or without German sanction (and some German nationalists, as I have noted, favored such a deal).

Nor would that have been the end of the matter. Successful German coercion of an unwilling Poland would have implied acquiescence by Great Britain and France—like the way in which "peaceful revision" of the German-Czech frontier was brought about in 1938. Such acquiescence was, in fact, one objective of Weimar's Western policy. But Western acquiescence would have destroyed the entire postwar balance of power built around France and its Eastern allies. This is what happened when Czechoslovakia was peacefully dismembered in 1938, and the same thing would have occurred whenever Germany succeeded, as it aimed throughout the Weimar Republic, in revising the Polish border. All of Eastern Europe would then have become the object of German-Russian

9. Holborn, *Modern Germany*, p. 762. It is striking to note that many of the leaders of the internal opposition to Hitler who plotted to oust him in 1938 and in the July 1944 coup believed that Germany ought to hold on to Austria, the Sudetenland, and the Polish corridor. Hermann Graml et al., *The German Resistance to Hitler* (London: B. T. Batsford Ltd., 1970), pp. 1–54.

rivalry or cooperative partition, but in either case little would have remained there of French power, the sole prop of the independence of the Eastern states. There is much difference between peaceful change and war, but peaceful revision of Germany's Eastern frontiers was likely to have had much the same effect on the interwar power system in Europe as forcible disruption of it. Indeed, as events developed, that system had in fact been destroyed *before* war broke out in 1939.

At bottom, the Germans could not achieve even the seemingly limited aim of revising their Polish frontier without, by that very act, replacing the existing system with their own hegemony. Their population and resources gave them the means to aspire to such a role; the weakness confronting them in Eastern Europe invited them to play it; the reluctance from the start of the British, and in their wake of the French, to resist frontier changes in Eastern Europe removed the barrier to them; and the rancors of defeat, by no means assuaged during the few prosperous years of the Weimar Republic, pushed them on. The fact that the Soviet Union and the Western powers would have found it very difficult indeed to reform the Triple Entente would have allowed Germany, if instructed by its mistakes before 1914, to play off the two sides with great effectiveness and to achieve more than border changes. This would not necessarily have led eventually to war, but it would at least have established a dominant position for Germany in Europe commensurate with its actual power.

This line of conjecture is sobering but in the end irrelevant, because, if anything was inevitable in the postwar period, it was the impact of the great depression on Germany. Whether or not the deep and prolonged collapse of the American economy after 1929 could have been avoided, the spread of this collapse to Germany as U.S. lenders disinvested could hardly have been averted given the close creditor-debtor linkage between the economies that had grown up in the wake of heavy American investment in the so-called Dawes loan. U.S. policy—actions and nonactions—contributed mightily to the length and severity of the worldwide depression, without which Hitler almost certainly would not have come to power.[10] Too little attention has been paid in this context to

10. "Even with [U.S.] anti-cyclical capital movements, there would have been a depression. With a flow of international capital positively correlated with business conditions in the lending country, the depression was inevitably severe. Add to this position, which was perhaps beyond the power of policy to correct in the existing state of knowledge, beggar-thy-neighbour tactics in trade and exchange depreciation, plus the unwillingness of the United States to serve as a lender of last resort in 1931, and the length and depth of the depression are explained." Charles P. Kindleberger, *The World in Depression, 1929–1939* (Berkeley: University of California Press, 1973), p. 306.

the direct American contribution to the European crisis of the 1930s. In fact, the causal interlocking of events on the two sides of the North Atlantic goes back long before the last world war. The earlier war made the United States Europe's creditor. The economic interdependence of the 1920s led on, step by step, to crisis, war, and postwar political and military interdependence—a condition that existed long before that overused word became fashionable. Nothing is recent, fortuitous, or transitory about this. The United States has been involved in Europe's fate every step of the way.

The downward economic spiral that overtook Germany from 1930 on—fed by drearily conventional deflationary policies within the country as well as abroad—could hardly have failed, in the heated and divided state of German politics, to bring a right-wing regime to power. That group was most likely to succeed which seemed to the dominant economic and social forces and those who followed their lead best able not only to prevent the German communists and socialists from exploiting the economic crisis but to right the wrongs of Versailles—not the less complained about even in those years of domestic distress.[11] Hitler filled the bill on both counts: virulently anti-Communist and a nationalist, even if with bad manners, who spoke what many with better manners wanted to hear.

Hitler was not necessarily implicit in Versailles, and not even in Versailles plus the depression; had he never been born (which was not a historical necessity) he would not have come to power in 1933, and probably there would have been no National Socialist party waiting in the wings to do so either. But given the crisis, coming on top of the wounds inflicted on Germany by its 1918 defeat (however plastered over in the 1920s), a conservative and nationalist regime was practically inevitable. Frustrated nationalism alone, even when added to inflation and the congenital insecurity of the republic, might not have had that effect—the Nazis won only 12 seats in the 1928 Reichstag election—but the depression, coming on top of earlier disaster, was bound to.

If the nationalist regime brought to power in Germany in the early 1930s by economic distress was not inevitably Nazi, nor necessarily

11. It is pertinent that the last democratic chancellor of the Weimar Republic, Heinrich Bruning, judged that the best way to reinforce his weak political position after the September 1930 election was not to try to alleviate economic distress but to exacerbate it to persuade the Western powers to abandon reparations. When this proved impossible he turned to the project of an Austro-German customs union to gain that foreign policy success which seemed to him essential to his political survival. In both cases he was not looking for substantial economic benefits from these policies but for means to satisfy the surging nationalism of his countrymen. Holborn, *Modern Germany*, pp. 672–82, 695; Kindleberger, *The World in Depression*, pp. 174–77.

committed to all the domestic policies and foreign policy tactics which made the Nazi regime notorious, nevertheless it would almost certainly have pursued an assertive foreign policy. It could hardly have failed to exploit the weakness that surrounded it on every side—far more pronounced in the 1930s than in 1914—overawing the small countries in the East and the disspirited British and French in the West and playing the anti-Bolshevik card with all of them, and perhaps the revisionist card with the USSR as well. Such a regime would have ended the Versailles limitations more rapidly than Weimar could have done, and from there would almost certainly have moved on to press its territorial claims in the East.

The situation would not have been very different even if Hitler, once launched in power, had been overthrown before war broke out in 1939. There were moments of choice in the crises of the 1930s when German foreign policy might have been defeated and the Nazi regime possibly overturned at home. It is generally taken for granted that in such a case the European status quo would then have been preserved. But by 1936 or 1938 Hitler had already ended the Versailles limitations and reasserted German prestige and power—both very welcome to the Germany of the 1930s. The regime which succeeded Hitler's could hardly have been a restored Weimar Republic. Though it would have been more careful of flouting the Western Allies (whose resistance to Hitler in the Rhineland or Czechoslovakia would, on this hypothesis, have sparked his overthrow), it would still be ruling by far the most powerful state in Europe and would need not to thwart aroused and again frustrated German nationalism. Power has its logic. Such a regime would probably have adopted more prudent tactics but gone ahead with an active policy in the area of greatest weakness and greatest opportunity, Eastern Europe. Indeed, this more "respectable" German regime might have been better able than Hitler to assert German continental hegemony by dealing with the West against the USSR.

If at any point German expansionism led to a conflict with the Soviet Union, as would have been likely, British-French acquiescence in German victory would have consecrated Germany's hegemony. But if an alliance between the Western powers and the Soviet Union had been possible, would it have been strong enough to prevent war? If not, would it have led to a negotiated peace short of the *tabula rasa* in Germany that Allied victory produced in World War II and then to a Europe more balanced and secure than that of 1939, or 1978? None of these questions has a certain answer.

The Western Allies had opportunities in the 1930s which they could have used better, and they might even have succeeded in avoiding the war. But the countries that had failed to partition Germany in 1919, their moment of greatest opportunity could hardly have avoided the eventual consequences of German power, whatever the form in which it manifested itself. The course of events in the 1930s might therefore have been different, but the basic power facts in Europe would have made it more and more difficult for German power to be contained even if Hitler had never come to power or had been deposed before war began. The outcome might have been a very different kind of German hegemony than Hitler's—by no means a small difference to its victims—but there is no sign of the economic, demographic, or diplomatic revolution in Europe that would have been necessary to modify the fact of German supremacy. Germany, having lost the war, was ready and able to challenge the outcome; Britain and France, having won, were not ready to defend it. The one was nerved by defeat itself and a sense of power; the others were unnerved by the cost of victory and a sense of weakness. The joker in the game, the Soviet Union, was not only undependable but anti–status quo. These basic facts were bound to have consequences, however the situation developed in detail.

Leaving these conjectures aside, the actual course of events after 1933 was straightforward—to war. Great Britain and France had disagreed since 1919 on how and to what extent to preserve the peace settlement. From the peace conference forward the British had been skeptical about the prospects for Poland and the other Eastern states and had refused to commit themselves to defend France's allies against Germany. As long as the German army was small, French military predominance gave these states their chance to live. But in March 1935 Hitler renounced the Versailles limitations on the German armed forces and began to rearm on a large scale. Britain, France, and Italy entered a perfunctory protest, but in June the British signed a separate naval limitation treaty with Germany, thus clearly accepting the violation of the Versailles treaty.

As long as the German Rhineland remained demilitarized, the French were able in theory—whether or not their defensive strategy and their diplomatic dependence on Britain would ever have permitted them in practice—to sweep into the heart of Germany if Germany moved against Austria, Czechoslovakia, or Poland. But in March 1936 Hitler remilitarized the Rhineland, without response from the Western powers. This—and not Munich—was the crisis of the decade. From that moment the Eastern states could not be saved from German attack without a major war, which neither the British nor the French—wounded by memories of World War I, economic weakness, and demoralized public opinion—wanted to fight. The Germans could overrun those countries while the Western Allies, even if they decided to fight, could only sit in the Maginot line (the supertrench that had been built behind France's eastern border in the anticipation that World War I would be fought over again but with less blood) and wait for the United States again to help them conquer Germany. In these circumstances, even the prospect of an alliance between the Western powers and the USSR was no guarantee to the Eastern states—and Poland and Rumania feared Soviet Russia as much as Germany or more. The horror of their geographic position was glaring in these years, once Britain and France had let go whatever chance they had of a quick march through the Rhineland into Germany.

After 1936 the four-tiered European system became more rigid as the Eastern states lost ground and as Italy, self-alienated from the Western powers by its Ethiopian campaign and the Spanish Civil War, foolishly cemented an alliance with the strongest nation on the continent. But it still remained to be seen how the three remaining sides would align. Revisionism had been respectable long since in Britain and Hitler did not make it much less so, only more urgent. The British government continued to hope, into 1939, that an overall agreement might be reached that would satisfy Germany's "legitimate" grievances in Europe—including, in particular, the implementation of the Wilsonian principle of nationality in favor of the Germans residing in Austria, Czechoslovakia, and Poland. The German government, for its part, cleverly continued to feed such British hopes. The French did not share these hopes but after 1936 were incapable of an independent policy line. These circumstances led to the Munich agreement and, with Hitler's success, to the aborting of the most serious prewar plan made in Germany to depose him.

The Soviet Union, from 1934 on, offered alliance against Germany to the West. Britain and France feared, however, that the USSR might embroil them with Germany to its own advantage and that such an alliance, if victorious, would bring Russian soldiers into Central Europe. But the Russians themselves could hardly have thought it likely that the Western countries would be either willing or able to protect them against Germany and may have used these offers, first, to prevent a capitalist alliance against themselves and, second, to reach an understanding with Germany—the one country which threatened the USSR directly, and the one, therefore, with which peace had to be maintained if, as Stalin strongly desired, the USSR was to avoid war.

The crisis of the 1930s was brought to a climax by the German seizure in March 1939 of what remained of Czechoslovakia after Munich. This act galvanized the British into issuing a unilateral guarantee of Poland, obviously the next object of German policy. Conscription was reestab-

lished in Britain in April. But while the British did move toward rearmament, they apparently hoped that their actions would deter Hitler and
thus prevent war. They and the French pursued desultory negotiations
with the Soviet Union, but they balked at its territorial demands and
their allies, Poland and Rumania, still resisted military cooperation with
the USSR.

While these negotiations went on between the Western powers and the
Soviet Union, talks also began in the late spring between the latter and
Germany. These three-sided negotiations ended on August 23 when the
Russians signed a nonaggression pact with Germany including a secret
protocol providing in effect for the partition of Eastern Europe between
them. Hitler perhaps saw this agreement as likely to prevent war, judg-
ing that Britain and France would not dare to fight Germany without a
Soviet alliance. But Stalin appraised the reversal of British policy more
accurately and saw the agreement as involving Germany in war with the
Western Allies, whose forces, according to all expectations, would be
sufficiently strong to produce a stalemate; keeping the USSR itself out of
war at a particularly difficult moment of Stalin's rule; and permitting the
Russians to regain lost lands in Poland and Rumania and on the Baltic.

The brief twenty years of freedom for Eastern Europe which began
with Russian and German defeat ended, brutally and quickly, with their
agreement. Poland followed Czechoslovakia off the map, along with the
three Baltic republics, and in the next five years the rest of the countries
in that area fell first under German and then under Russian hegemony.
This restoration of the pre-1914 map of Eastern Europe (minus
Austria-Hungary) was a natural by-product of the alliance of the two
powerful states whose simultaneous defeat in 1918 had led to a sweeping
but transitory redrawing of frontiers at their expense. The alliance of
the two revisionist states, shortlived as it was, made quite clear where
power in Europe lay in 1939. Even if Britain and France could have
maintained their own independence, the European system based on
their victory was gone.

Within a year it was evident that the balance of power was upset not
only in Eastern Europe but in Europe as a whole. Great Britain's sudden
guarantee of Poland in the spring of 1939 did nothing for Poland, which
was overrun by Germany and the USSR within a month, but it sufficed to
bring Britain and France into war when Hitler moved east on September
1. There was no fighting in the West, however, until the spring of 1940.
Then Germany overran Norway, Denmark, Holland, and Belgium and,
to the surprise probably even of some Germans, defeated France in a few
weeks. Britain remained fighting, not for its postwar co-hegemony of

Europe or for the balance of power but for its existence as an independent state.

Germany's position at that moment seemed far more powerful than even at the beginning of 1918 when it defeated Russia and was poised to defeat Britain and France when the European state system was preserved by American intervention. In 1940, with France defeated, Germany faced only what was thought to be a weak Soviet Union and an embattled Britain, excluded from the continent. The ascendancy of German power in Europe was indisputable, augmented now by the resources of conquered territory; the quickness and completeness of its victory far more promising than in 1918 for its future hegemony; and the destruction of the old European balance of power undeniably evident.

What almost happened in 1918, but for American intervention, happened in 1940. This time the United States had either to live with these results or make a far greater effort than before, with far greater consequences for itself and Europe, to reverse them.

CHAPTER 4

World War II: From One System to Another

World War II completed the transformation of the European power scale that had been underway since 1870 and had come so close already in World War I. By 1940 Germany had become so powerful that it would dominate Europe unless prevented by a coalition of Great Britain, the Soviet Union, and the United States. It took the power of all three to defeat the Third Reich. Britain alone, even with American support short of intervention, could at best have maintained control of its home island and the lanes of communication to its overseas dependencies and friends. The Soviet Union, even with Britain still in the war and with help from the United States, could at best have maintained a core of the Russian state, Brest-Litovsk style, at the farthest eastern end of Europe. Britain and Russia together could not have defeated Germany or disrupted its European empire. As in 1918 only American entry into the war could tip the balance from German victory in Europe to German defeat.

This time, as a result of decisions made by the Allies during the war, the Germany created in 1871 was not merely weakened as a factor in European affairs, as in 1919, but was destroyed as a state. Its disappearance left all of Europe subject to the three countries which controlled decisive power when the war ended. Their relations, in turn, were conditioned by two closely related factors: first, the actual military course of the war itself—that is, the physical transformation of one system of power relationships in 1939 to another in 1945; and second, the arrangements they had made during the war for the future. The military and diplomatic events of World War II were not simply the prelude to what came after; they were the determinants of postwar Europe.

For this reason the might-have-beens of the war, like those of the prewar period, raise tantalizing questions of how Europe might have developed after 1945 if the victorious Allies had done things other than those they did. The most important of these contentious issues have been much debated: unconditional surrender, the Mediterranean strategy, the failure of the Western Allies to seize Berlin and Prague in the spring of 1945, their willingness at the end of the war to withdraw from advanced positions in Germany to the predetermined zonal borders. There were also diplomatic "alternatives," particularly concerning the way the United States during the war handled—or avoided—the oncoming problems of Eastern Europe. For all the discussion, it remains very uncertain what would have followed had some of these developments gone otherwise. In the end, what matters analytically is what happened during the war.

Germany's conquest of almost all of continental Europe west of Russia was swift and complete. After gaining control over Western Europe by defeating France in June 1940, the Germans then extended their rule over the Balkans (Hungary, Rumania, and Bulgaria became satellite allies; Yugoslavia and Greece were conquered) as a prelude to their attack on the Soviet Union in June 1941. The USSR was not defeated, but vast stretches of its territory were occupied by the German army. The Reich thus added the resources of almost the entire continent to its already formidable power machine. Even when its own advance was stopped in Russia in 1942, it defied its enemies from that position of strength to regain what had been lost.

The United States gave extensive assistance to Britain and Russia but did not enter the war itself until attacked by Japan. Even then it did not declare war on Germany until Hitler came to the assistance of his Japanese ally a few days later. Despite very heavy Allied setbacks in the Pacific and in Russia during 1942, American entry into the war meant that neither Britain nor the USSR would be defeated as France had been. But it was still far from clear when and how—and perhaps whether—Germany would be dislodged from its position of mastery in Europe.

The Soviet leaders persistently and urgently pressed the Western Allies to relieve the pressure on their own army by opening a second front in Europe. The American and British leaders committed themselves to this plan, but the date for a full-scale offensive was constantly put forward. One reason was the enormity of the military problems involved in mounting a landing that could establish a foothold on the continent without unacceptable casualties. Another was the diversion of effort, first to North Africa, then to Italy. It took the Allies two and one-half years after the United States entered the war to land in France.

The timing of the second front became a serious source of wartime friction between the Western Allies and the USSR. This is not to say that the Russian leaders would have looked with kindly eyes or confidence on the Western powers but for the dispute over the second front. On the contrary, their experience and outlook as rulers of the only socialist country in the world could not but lead them to see the capitalist United States and Britain, whatever they did, as at best temporary allies of convenience. That fact is fundamental to any examination of how the wartime alliance was so quickly transformed into cold war hostility. But the delay in opening a second front obviously did not quiet inevitable Russian fears that the United States and Britain might wish to see Germany and the USSR fight on indefinitely in the East, nor did it obviate Western concern that the Russians, believing this, might contemplate a separate peace. Many in the West recognized that the Red Army was bearing the brunt of the major fighting against the Germans during 1942 and 1943, that its losses were heavy, and that a Bolshevik government, of which Stalin had been a member, *had* made a separate peace in 1918, not to mention the 1939 deal with Germany.

Little evidence indicates that Stalin ever seriously contemplated negotiating another such deal with Hitler. It is true that the Russians delayed accepting the unconditional surrender formula adopted by Roosevelt and Churchill at Casablanca. Perhaps they did not believe at first that so total a victory would be possible. There are signs that in mid-1943, when German victory was no longer possible but Allied victory was not yet assured, the USSR saw advantage in playing with the idea of a separate peace, or letting the Western Allies think that they did (the parallel to the multiple goals of Soviet policy in the triangular diplomacy of 1939, including pressure and reinsurance, is obvious).[1] But as the fortunes of war improved they put aside such prospects and accepted unconditional surrender and its implications for Germany.

In November 1942 the Western Allies took the offensive in the Mediterranean by attacking French North Africa, which had remained under the control of the dependent government the Germans had permitted to rule southern France and the French empire from Vichy. This effort fell far short of satisfying the demand of the Russians—then engaged in the turning-point battle of Stalingrad—for a second front in Europe. Indeed, the diversion of supplies required putting off the second front even farther. But the operation did get American troops into battle in the European theater in 1942 in the only way that was possible then and led within a few months to an important Allied success.

The Allies, finding that their preinvasion intrigues with local French officials did not secure the surrender of North Africa, tried to avoid fighting by striking a deal with Admiral Jean Darlan, the Vichy vice-premier who, apparently by chance, was then in Algiers. The decision to leave Darlan in power in North Africa created a storm of protest in the United States and Britain which was not quelled when he was assassinated at the end of 1942. Critics of the Darlan deal raised the question

1. Vojtech Mastny, "Stalin and the Prospects of a Separate Peace in World War II," *The American Historical Review* 77 (December 1972), 1365–88.

whether the Allies might one day choose to negotiate, in the name of military expediency, with some Nazi leader—a prospect not very helpful to the ideological basis on which they were fighting the war.

As it turned out, the Allies did not find it easy to secure control of North Africa even with Darlan's help. German and Italian forces that had been fighting in Egypt, and were then driven into Libya, retreated in early 1943 into Tunisia and held out there until May. The Allied resources needed to deal with this helped delay the second front in Europe into 1944.

While the fighting in North Africa was still going on Roosevelt and Churchill met at Casablanca in January 1943. Among much other business, they decided to ask unconditional surrender of the Axis powers for several reasons, some related to the current situation, others to longer-range considerations. First, unconditional surrender was meant to be an explicit reassurance to those who feared that the Darlan deal could serve as a model for an arrangement with some unsavory group that might take power in Germany when the war began to go badly for it.

Second, relations between the two Western Allies and the Soviet Union were never so good as to preclude suspicions on either side that the other might try to make an advantageous separate peace with Germany. The delay in the second front and Western refusal to accept Stalin's postwar territorial demands in Eastern Europe—the 1941 frontier—fed these suspicions, and fears of them. Unconditional surrender was seen as a self-denying ordinance against the possibility of a separate peace, as well as a public pledge by the Western powers that a second front in Europe—without which total victory was inconceivable—would be launched.

Finally, and probably most important, the Allied leaders of World War II remembered that Germany had surrendered in 1918 within the framework of the Fourteen Points and had then complained that the Allies had not honored that commitment. Many in Germany, as I noted earlier, even claimed that their country had not been defeated at all but had been "stabbed in the back" by treason at home. Unconditional surrender was seen, particularly by Roosevelt, as preventing a repetition of this situation. The Allies, while announcing that they did not seek the destruction of the enemy peoples, admitted that they reserved the option of imposing Carthaginian terms on Germany, including drastic changes in its government and social system and even its unity. This surrender formula was intended to make clear to the Germans in advance that the Allies intended to deal with Germany after the war, and with the problem its power represented, with a free hand.

Unconditional surrender has been the subject of much criticism on the grounds that it prolonged the war by strengthening German resolve to fight and discouraging dissident groups that might otherwise have been willing to overthrow Hitler and make peace. This is an unrealistic kind of *realpolitik*. Potential German opposition groups could see that in Italy, only a few months after the Casablanca declaration, the king had dismissed Mussolini and the Allies had permitted the Badoglio government and the House of Savoy to remain in office. (Just as in Japan, later, unconditional surrender was bent to permit the survival of the imperial institution.) If that opposition acted only in the last year of the war, the reason was not its fear of unconditional surrender but the fact that the German army and people remained obedient to the state to the end, whether from expectation of victory, patriotism, discipline, or terror. When a few well-placed persons finally saw an opportunity to act in the prospect of defeat, the unconditional surrender formula did not prevent their July 1944 plot against Hitler, nor can it be blamed for their failure.[2]

If, however, the plot had succeeded, the new regime would have tried to reach an agreement with the Allies which would have maintained the continuity of the German state and its own survival. It would have been more difficult for *three* Allies to reach such a decision than it was for Britain and the United States to do so with respect to Italy or for the United States to do so, virtually alone, with respect to Japan. If the joint attempt failed, either the Western powers or the USSR might have pursued it on their own. If, in any case, the war had been ended with a negotiated peace which left intact a still-united German state led by the anti-Nazi but largely conservative plotters of July 1944, would that have contributed to postwar European stability?

Had the plotters of July 1944 succeeded in their plot and made peace with the Allies, Germany would obviously have been better off for being spared the traumas of dissolution and total occupation. The West as a whole might also have been stronger in the early years of the cold war competition with the Soviet Union. But the price would have been an assertive, powerful, and by no means acquiescent Germany within the West and within Europe. Would that have been better than the strong, stabilized, and stabilizing West Germany that emerged after 1949, purged of its internal demons and no longer able, even if it wished, to pursue disruptive goals? *That* Germany, the most benign since 1870 from the point of view of European stability, is the outcome of three things: Allied victory, unconditional surrender, and the cold war. It is

2. Hajo Holborn, "The German Opposition to Hitler," *Germany and Europe* (Garden City, N.Y.: Doubleday, 1970), pp. 250–51.

difficult to imagine how that result could have been achieved without all three.

As it turned out the plot did not succeed, and was not repeated even as the Allied ring closed tighter around Germany. The Allies thus did not have to face the problem of dealing with Hitler's heirs or successors, and the war proceeded on to produce a political *tabula rasa* in Germany. Such an outcome, which was the object of the Allies in adopting unconditional surrender, reflected their conviction that the war was being waged not just against the Nazi regime but against the power of the German state, which, experience had shown, was not compatible with the independence of the other nations of Europe. The Casablanca formula, unlike the Fourteen Points, opened the door to the possibility of settling the German problem once and for all—and that, after all, was what the war in Europe was about.

The Bismarckian state therefore ceased to exist. There has been no "stab in the back" myth to bedevil the political life of the Federal Republic of Germany. The very failure of the July 1944 plot has helped the Germans keep the record clear. There could be no such myth, no belief that the country had been robbed of victory, no later complaint of Allied violation of the armistice terms. It is easy but wrong to overlook the fact that the *tabula rasa* created in Germany in 1945 played no small part in making the Federal Republic a very different—and better—polity than the Weimar Republic.

Since the unconditional surrender formula was designed to fit the German case, it is not surprising that it was applied less than literally against the other two major Axis powers. When the Allies invaded Sicily after their victory in North Africa (July 1943) King Victor Emmanuel dismissed Mussolini and formed a new government under Marshal Badoglio. The Allies then accepted the surrender of this regime while allowing it to remain in office. The Germans, however, were in firm control of Rome and the north of the country and Badoglio could not procure the surrender of those areas. The Allies invaded the mainland in September but were not able to advance much beyond Naples in the face of strong German resistance. The war in Italy remained stalemated for many months.

The circumstances of the Italian surrender set an important precedent, not only for the interpretation in practice of unconditional surrender but for the way in which the Allies were to organize control of occupied territory. Since the invading army was a British-American force under the command of General Eisenhower, those two governments handled the negotiations for Italian surrender, informing Russia as they went along. But Moscow made clear that it wanted a three-power Allied commission established to supervise the occupation through the commander-in-chief. The Western Allies successfully resisted this proposal. In the end a purely advisory body was set up which the Russians joined but found of little interest. In effect, therefore, control of Italy remained in the hands of those whose armies, as Churchill put it, "are doing all the fighting."

The principle thus established in Italy was next applied by the Russians themselves in Eastern Europe. In the summer of 1944 the Red Army, which had steadily pressed the Germans back after its victory at Stalingrad in January 1943, began to move across the 1939 frontiers of the Soviet Union and into the territory of Poland and of the German satellite states—first, Finland and Rumania, then Bulgaria and Hungary. The first of these Axis satellites to call it quits was Finland. For reasons that are far from clear, the Russians gave Finland moderate armistice terms which did not include Soviet occupation.

Why the USSR should have been so lenient toward a country which had humiliated the Red Army in 1939–40 and had then attacked it again at Germany's side is unknown. Perhaps the Russians still respected Finland's powers of resistance, even in defeat. Knowing that the United States had been particularly pro-Finnish in 1939–40 and had never declared war on Finland, perhaps they did not want to stir up a new controversy with Washington. Perhaps they thought that the Finnish Communist party, which had substantial local roots, might come to power after the defeat without the presence of the Red Army. Whatever the Soviet reasons, Finland lost some territory but escaped both occupation in 1944 and communization later—a fact to ponder in trying to understand the goals and tactics of Russia's postwar policy in Eastern Europe.

The Russians were much less gentle with the other countries they occupied. Passing over Poland—an especially important case treated in greater detail chapter 6—the Red Army entered Rumania and Bulgaria in the summer of 1944 and dictated armistices to both. Rumania had sent troops to fight in Russia against the Red Army; Bulgaria had not even declared war, but the USSR declared war on it just a few days before the Soviet army, coming across Rumania, reached the Bulgarian border. In both cases occupation machinery was set up in which all effective power was vested in the Soviet military commander. The American government had foreseen, apparently with equanimity, that the Russians would follow the Italian precedent in this way. Later, when it and the British attempted to assert some influence on Balkan affairs, the Russians, whose troops were "doing all the fighting" in these countries, explicitly cited the Italian armistice regime as the precedent for their own unilateral proceedings.[3] By early 1945 governments were set up in Rumania and Bulgaria which were clearly headed toward eventual domination by the Communist parties (hitherto very small in these countries) and those allied with them.

Watching this Russian advance into the Balkans, Churchill decided to try to get Soviet ratification for what he hoped would be the balance of power in the area by making a frank spheres of influence deal with Stalin. Knowing the strong American objection to the name and the concept of spheres of influence, Churchill claimed to be concerned only about short-term military arrangements, which would be superseded later by free elections in those countries and the overall security system of the new world organization. These professions did not convince the State Department, which seemed to fear Anglo-Soviet agreement as much as disagreement. Churchill obviously hoped to strike a deal based on power realities which, if recognized and accepted by both sides, would govern postwar relations in that part of Europe.

Roosevelt sanctioned a three-month trial of the proposed arrangement. Churchill went to Moscow in October 1944 and made his proposal to Stalin on a slip of paper. Stalin at once accepted it. It provided this:

> In Rumania, the USSR was to have 90 percent influence, the United
>   Kingdom (and the United States) 10 percent.
> In Greece, the situation was to be the reverse: 10 percent and 90
>   percent.
> In Bulgaria, it was to be 75 percent Soviet, 25 percent Western.
> In Yugoslavia and Hungary it was to be 50–50.
> Poland, the most difficult case, was not included.

We can wonder what Churchill, not to say Stalin, thought these percentages meant. Ostensibly they dealt only with wartime and immediate postarmistice circumstances. But they clearly reflected the existing military facts of life in Rumania, Bulgaria, and Greece (then under British occupation), and it must have been clear that the immediate would have a strong influence on the postwar period. Presumably the British and

3. The Russians would not have acted differently in Eastern Europe had the Western Allies acted differently in Italy, though they would not have been able to charge the Allies with a double standard (a charge to which the Allies at the time paid no attention). Relations with Poland and some of the other Eastern European countries were top priority items in Soviet postwar policy, not likely to have been much affected by whatever happened elsewhere (see chapter 5).

American representatives were to have somewhat more influence in
Bulgaria than in Rumania, or non-Communist parties were to have a
larger role in the cabinet. Perhaps Churchill hoped the Russians would
treat traditionally pro-Russian Bulgaria leniently from the point of view
of the domestic social and political order. On the other hand, the Greek
Communists were to have only a minor role, like the Rumanian anti-
Communists. Churchill in effect wrote off Rumania and Bulgaria to the
Russians in exchange for their recognition of British dominance in
Greece. He was probably more optimistic about Yugoslavia, where the
British had as assets not only the exiled royal government of King Peter
but also their contact with Tito. Hungary was farther west, non-Slavic,
and traditionally outside Russia's sphere of interest. Here too Churchill
may have hoped that Western power might be held in some kind of
balance vis-à-vis Soviet.

It is interesting to consider Soviet policy in Eastern Europe against this
agreement. In Rumania and Bulgaria things went as Churchill had
expected and sanctioned. At the same time, Greece was beginning to fall
into civil war between Communist and anti-Communist forces. Churchill
then and later gave credit to the Soviet Union for keeping its distance
from this conflict—which, thanks to British political flexibility, in 1945
ended its first phase with pro-British forces in control. In Yugoslavia negotiations on a coalition government were carried on between the Yugoslav government-in-exile and Tito. After Yalta these went largely Tito's
way, thus seeming to belie the 50–50 agreement of October 1944. It is
not as clear now, however, as it seemed then that Tito was under Soviet
control. Indeed, there is some evidence that Stalin urged caution on the
Yugoslav Communists. But their position did not depend on the Red
Army and, seeing their chance to consolidate their power, they took it.
In Hungary, which the Red Army had to fight over more slowly, a
government was set up with less Communist influence than those in
Bucharest and Sofia and elections were held. Finally, in Czecho-
slovakia—which of course was a liberated ally, not a German satellite
—President Benes included seven Communists in his twenty-five-
man cabinet but remained more independent of Moscow than the
Rumanian or Bulgarian governments.

Churchill's late attempt to preserve some Western influence in the
Balkans by direct negotiation with Stalin looks at first sight like a fallback
position arrived at once his attempt at a "Mediterranean strategy" had
failed. During the cold war guilt debates of the 1950s Churchill was
widely credited—by Roosevelt's detractors—with having tried to get the
Western Allies to move militarily into the Balkans and from there into
Central Europe to prevent the Soviet Union from establishing control.

As it happens, there *was* an Anglo-American debate about the Mediterranean during the war but the issue was not saving the Balkans from Russia. This mythical might-have-been of the war has commanded so much attention in discussion of cold war origins, however, that it merits some examination, if only to suggest how little attention the Western Allies—the perspicacious British as well as the naive Americans of mythology—gave to Eastern Europe while the fighting went on.

Farsighted concern about the future of Eastern Europe played a significant part in Churchill's strategic arguments only for a few weeks in the summer of 1944, when he wanted the British-led army of Italy to march on from Rome through Yugoslavia to Vienna—an idea whose practicality was more than questionable and which, in any case, was vetoed by Washington because it would have distracted effort from the front in France.[4] During the debates over strategy in 1942–43, Churchill had quite different reasons for promoting military activity in the Mediterranean area and doing what he could to put off an Allied landing in France. For one thing, he—and not only he—feared that an invasion of France would exact a fearful toll of Allied casualties. For another, he seemed to have an intellectual dislike for the idea of the clash of mass armies and to seek, instead, ways in which the enemy might be defeated by flank attacks. This preference reflected a debatable reading of British military history. But it was natural that the leader of the weakest of the Big Three would think in such terms, both to save men and to have a theater where Britain could use its resources to greatest advantage for its particular national interests and even for its glory. The Mediterranean in general, and Italy in particular, became that theater.

This did not mean that Churchill had a preconceived Mediterranean strategy. Rather, he took advantage of the situation created by the American desire to go into action in 1942 in the European theater and the U.S.–U.K. decision that North Africa was the only feasible place to do so. Nor does it mean that he aimed to avoid an invasion of northern France altogether. But some Americans came to believe that he did, and certainly the further buildup of the Allied armies in Italy in 1943–44 or other enterprises in the Mediterranean area would have drained off

4. "[T]he chances of overcoming the sub-Alpine logistics of Slovenia in the autumn or winter of 1944–45 were so slight that the likelihood of arriving anywhere in the Danube region before the Red Army was almost nil." Trumbull Higgins, *Soft Underbelly* (New York: Macmillan, 1968), p. 220. On this general subject see also Trumbull Higgins, *Winston Churchill and the Second Front 1940–43* (New York: Oxford University Press, 1957); and Michael Howard, *The Mediterranean Strategy in the Second World War* (London: Weidenfeld and Nicolson, 1968).

forces and supplies needed for the cross-channel attack, just as the needs of the North African campaign did in 1942–43.

The American military leaders, however, thought of North Africa, Italy, and the Balkans as sideshows compared to the main business of landing in France and marching to the heartland of German power. They were strongly committed to this strategy as early as 1941. They deferred to Roosevelt's decision to get American troops into combat in 1942 in North Africa. Once in the Mediterranean, they agreed with the British to invade not only Sicily but mainland Italy. But they suspected the British of favoring operations in that area to buttress their own imperial interests at the expense of the agreed strategy of a cross-channel invasion. They therefore insisted that the Italian campaign be viewed essentially as a means of diverting German strength from Western Europe and that the Allied commitment to an invasion of France be reaffirmed.

This in effect blocked the British attempt to reinforce Allied efforts in Italy, not to say the eastern Mediterranean or the Balkans. Churchill had to accept these terms, and he never pressed the issue to a decisive showdown on the grounds of heading off the Soviet conquest of Eastern Europe, or any other. Indeed, he seemed content with the Teheran decision to continue the Italian campaign even as a diversionary effort and as a springboard not toward Yugoslavia but for an invasion of southern France in support of the priority cross-channel invasion. Italy, not the Balkans, seemed to be his military preoccupation in late 1943, and not for any reason connected with stemming the Soviet tide.

Roosevelt has been criticized for rejecting what has since been described simplistically as Churchill's attempt to carry the war into the Balkans, and the "loss" of Eastern Europe has been laid to that decision. It seems clear, however, that the real debate about the role of the Mediterranean in Allied strategy was not between a Western and a Balkan strategy. Of course Roosevelt and most Americans thought more in terms of expeditiously defeating Germany than of the detailed postwar settlement of Europe. In their view, there seemed no alternative to challenging German power at its heart, and they held to this despite British attempts to build up the importance of the Mediterranean theater. All this had little or nothing to do at the time with consideration of the postwar fate of Eastern Europe.

Even so, it is worth considering further what might have happened if Churchill's position had been what it has been represented to be and if his alleged counsel had been followed. How would the Russians, for example, have responded to yet another postponement of the long-promised second front, particularly if the substitute for it was an Allied drive into or toward areas of special interest to the Soviet Union? It is interesting that Stalin, at Teheran, still pressed for the cross-channel invasion. Was it to keep the Western Allies out of the Balkans, or did he want to defeat Germany as soon as possible? Then, the course of the fighting in Italy suggests that the Allies might well have bogged down in Yugoslavia, or in Austria or Czechoslovakia or Bavaria, even had they made a priority effort to reach Germany by this difficult route. Meanwhile, the Germans would have remained in control of the resources of Western Europe. And the Russians might well have advanced farther into Germany than they did. Would the postwar situation in Europe have been more satisfactory if the Western Allies had reached Vienna or Prague while the Russians were advancing to the Rhine or Paris?

Much of the discussion of this issue, as of the whole question of cold war origins, seems to take for granted that the United States could do anything it wished whereas the Russians, though aiming to conquer as much of Europe as they could, were weak. Such assumptions are absurd. The United States was very strong at war's end but not omnipotent. The Soviet Union had definite policy goals, like every other combatant, and the victorious Red Army was a formidable instrument for achieving them. It must be said here, because it underlies so much of what follows, that the Soviet Union won the war too.

Ironically, some members of the American new left, refuting the contentions of the old right, have argued that Roosevelt rejected Churchill's alleged policy not because he was ignorant of or complaisant about Soviet designs in Eastern Europe, but because he thought it more important to save France and Germany than Poland and Yugoslavia from advancing Bolshevism. Both schools of critics overlook the fact that the American government set first emphasis on defeating Germany and was right in believing that the place to do so was in the German heartland, which was most readily reached through France and the Low Countries.

Further, the Americans understood the implications of this decision for Eastern Europe. When ex-Ambassador William Bullitt urged in 1943 that the United States and Britain plan to introduce military forces into Eastern Europe to prevent Soviet domination, the European Division of the State Department expressed this view to Secretary Hull:

> Where? Presumably he means with the view to reestablishing boundaries as of September 1, 1939 in Eastern Europe. Our friends in the War Department tell us that such an attempt would be sheer military fantasy; that the United States and the United Kingdom are not in a position successfully to oppose the Soviet Union in Eastern

Europe if Germany is defeated. In short, the only way Mr. Bullitt's suggestion could actually be implemented would be by means of a coalition between the United States, United Kingdom, and the German military forces.[5]

Knowing this, the American government proceeded with its plans for a landing in Western Europe. What can be validly criticized is not its strategy for the defeat of Germany but its failure to act on its own insight into the prospects for Eastern Europe and follow Churchill's example—or at least support his effort—and try to work out what terms it could get for the area from the Russians. But Roosevelt purposely tried to keep American hands free of specific postwar territorial agreements, particularly in Eastern Europe, and as far as possible to keep Britain free also. There were several reasons for this: a tendency to concentrate on military over political problems; a wish to avoid straining wartime unity with divisive issues; a belief that such issues would become less important when the postwar security machinery was put in place; and a conviction that American power to affect events would be at its height at war's end. As it turned out, American power was very great when the war reached its end, but by then the Soviet Union was on the way to creating a fait accompli in the area which Washington then found unacceptable and to which it reacted as if it had not foreseen the problem.

When the British and Americans finally landed on the coast of France on June 6, 1944, they did so in such power that their initial advance was very much quicker and less bloody than had been expected. France was practically cleared of the Germans by year's end. In December the Germans succeeded in counter-attacking in Belgium—the Battle of the Bulge—and the Allied position was in jeopardy for some weeks before it was stabilized and, after a pause, the advance into Germany resumed. Germany was gradually occupied by the armies advancing from east and west, and the two met on the Elbe on April 27. Hitler committed suicide in his Berlin bunker. The phantom government that succeeded him tried to surrender only to the Western Allies. After their refusal, it surrendered unconditionally on May 7.

The United States, Great Britain, the Soviet Union, and France thus found their armies in complete physical control of Germany. Their authority replaced that of the vanished German state. In those circumstances they begun to implement their plans for the occupation and government of Germany.

5. Quoted in Lynn Etheridge Davis, *The Cold War Begins* (Princeton, N.J.: Princeton University Press, 1974), pp. 79–80, from Records of the Department of State, Decimal File 840.50/2521.

The Allies had long taken for granted that, consistent with unconditional surrender, they would occupy Germany, and they began to
negotiate about the relevant problems soon after the Casablanca conference. The idea of joint occupation was ruled out almost from the start,
and in October 1943 the Big Three appointed a special group, the
European Advisory Commission, to lay out three occupation zones and
make other plans to be referred to the governments for decision. It was
always understood that the USSR would occupy a zone in Eastern Germany, the area where its armies would presumably find themselves when
the war ended. This zone was eventually defined to include about 40
percent of Germany's 1937 area, 36 percent of its population, and 33
percent of its productive resources. The rest of the country was to be
divided into a northwestern and southwestern zone.

The British laid claim to the northwestern zone, including the German
industrial heartland, the Ruhr valley, with the thought that France might
eventually take over the contiguous southwestern zone when the Americans, as they often stated, withdrew their forces from Europe. But for
various reasons Roosevelt did not want the southern zone (though that
was the area where U.S. troops would be when the war ended) and
haggling went on between the British and Americans for many months
after the plans were ready, thus delaying signature of the occupation
agreement by the three powers. Roosevelt yielded at the second Quebec
conference with Churchill (September 1944) on condition that the
United States would also get the port of Bremen as an assured entry to
Germany. Further haggling then went on for several more months about
the terms of American control of Bremen and access from there to the
U.S. zone.

In January 1945, however, the Russians were advancing so rapidly
across Poland and Germany—250 miles in three weeks—while the Western Allies were tied down by the Battle of the Bulge, that it seemed
prudent to the Americans and British to settle their dispute and be sure
that the zonal agreements were ratified before the Red Army occupied
territory not assigned to it. When the Yalta conference opened, the
Russians were less than 50 miles from Berlin; the Western Allies were
not yet on the Rhine. The zonal agreement and occupation plans were
thus finally approved by the Big Three at Yalta, on February 6. They
provided for military occupation in prescribed zones, joint occupation of
Berlin in three sectors, and an Allied Control Council to make policy for
all of Germany, composed of the commanders-in-chief and operating by
unanimous agreement.

One other important decision was made in this connection at Yalta:
the inclusion of France in the plans for the occupation of Germany.
General de Gaulle had gone a long way between June 18, 1940, when

almost alone he had raised the banner of Free France, and August 1944, when he returned to Paris in triumph as head of the French provisional government. But the Allies had not included France in their planning for Germany, nor invited it to their summit conferences. The Yalta conference, like those before it, was replete with references to the exclusive club of those with 5 million men under arms—a standard to which restored but weakened France could scarcely aspire. Nevertheless, de Gaulle had steadily pushed his claims to France's great power status, and with some success. By the time of Yalta the British, thinking that the Americans would not stay on in Germany for very long, had become convinced that France should take part in the occupation. Roosevelt was reluctant but yielded, and so did Stalin after it was agreed that the French zone would be carved entirely from territory assigned to the other two Western powers. After further discussion, with Roosevelt again reluctant, it was agreed that France would also join the Allied Control Council as an equal member—that is, with a veto on its decisions. This was, of course, a major triumph for French status and security. But it was due less to France's diplomacy, and even less to its military claims, than to Britain's desire to have a partner in postwar Germany when, as was expected and predicted by Roosevelt, the United States cut back its direct participation.

As it turned out, the Western armies regained their military momentum in March, just as the Russians lost theirs, and moved east into Germany beyond their zonal boundaries before the war ended. They might have taken Berlin but for General Eisenhower's concern that the Germans might be establishing a military redoubt in Bavaria. Churchill, after the fighting stopped, urged the American government to let the Western Allies hold their ground and not implement the occupation agreements until the Russians made concessions on disputed matters in Eastern Europe. Allied relations over Poland and the setting up of the United Nations, among other things, were at a low point in May 1945. But the United States, notwithstanding the tough line it was then trying to follow with the Russians (see chapter 6), was eager to implement the control machinery in Germany and concluded that it was necessary to abide by the agreed zonal lines. This was done, providing further material for later disputes.

It is an open question what would have happened had the Western powers tried to bargain over implementing the zonal boundaries with the Russians or simply held their ground. The likely failure of such a bargaining attempt would most probably have meant that the Allies would have held on to their extra mileage in central Germany, would still have had no more impact on affairs in Eastern Europe, and, since they were not yet in Soviet-held Berlin, would probably never have been admitted to it by the Russians—for better or worse. If the joint occupation machinery had then never been implemented, the partition of Germany between East and West would have been clearly visible some years before it was.

Because of the American decision the withdrawals did take place and the zonal boundaries were implemented (including a quickly drawn set for a small French zone in southwestern Germany). The four commanders-in-chief, on June 1, issued a declaration assuming supreme control of Germany. In July the three Western powers occupied their sectors in Berlin, and a series of hastily worked out military agreements defined their rights of access to the former capital by road, rail, and air. By the end of July the occupation of Germany and of Berlin by the four powers had been put into place. Only then, at Potsdam, did the Big Three make their first systematic attempt to decide what to do with the country—no longer a state—whose sovereignty they had jointly assumed.

CHAPTER 5

Entrance of the Superpowers

The dissolution of the German state in 1945 signaled the restoration to independence of all the European nations that it had seized since 1937. But while Germany's conquests could be undone, all the effects of its work could not be. Germany had long since undermined the old European balance of power by growing too strong to be contained. Had Europe been left to itself, Germany would have ended the old system in 1918 and established something else: its own hegemony. This—and more—it achieved in 1940, and in the next few years it organized Europe for the first time on a continental scale, creating a proto-superpower able to stand up at least for some years against Great Britain and the two true continental states, the Soviet Union and the United States. But once again Europe was not left to itself. As Germany by 1914 had broken beyond the scale of the nineteenth-century European states to something greater, so by 1945 its own power—even augmented by its European conquests—was overshadowed by a transformation of scale to a still higher level.

The power of the two great peripheral states that had taken a less than central part in European affairs before 1939 was revealed, if not in a sense created, by the war. By mid-1945 they (along with Britain) were in control of all Europe. This time there was no attempt to resurrect the old state system, which Germany had finally destroyed along with itself. In this sense Hitler was indeed a Wagnerian figure, his role in history out of *The Twilight of the Gods*. His part, however, was not that of Siegfried the hero, slayer of dwarfs and dragons, but of grim Hagen, whose pursuit of absolute power brought down not only his own house but the very order of the world.

In life as in myth, however, the old order perished but the world survived. Though Hitler finished off not only the Bismarckian state but the old European system while trying to transcend it, he did not destroy the states of Europe. The revived European states at once found themselves invoived in a new power system, and their main business as international actors thereafter has been to try to preserve their security and independence in the circumstances imposed on them, to work out responses to the situations created by the agreements and conflicts of the superpowers in physical control of the continent at the end of the war.

Even Great Britain, though at the start still one of the Big Three and considered to be a world power for many years afterward, was in fact not a member of the new club. Only two states were organized on the new power scale in 1945, the United States and the Soviet Union.

The new European system that was inadvertently created by the superpowers after 1945 as a by-product of their rivalry had its roots in events of the preceding sixty or seventy years, but it had no resemblance at all to the óld multipolar, Europe-centered system. The shape of this new bipolar system was already clearly visible in mid-1945. International political allegiance everywhere in Europe was gravitating toward those whose armies were occupying one or another country. Italy and Greece, France and the Low Countries, were heading west; Poland, Rumania, and Bulgaria were heading east; the alignment of Finland, Czechoslovakia, Hungary, and, above all, Germany, seemed to be in suspense. It has turned out to be self-evident that nothing is as effective in orienting a country as an occupying army.

Europe has visibly changed out of recognition since 1945, but the most important and persistent theme in its affairs from then to now has been the continuous interplay between the United States and the Soviet Union. As a result of World War II, these two great states, alone of their kind in the world, were left face to face in Central Europe with a starkness, from the point of view of *power*, that was not fully grasped then and is still not fully grasped now. On the one hand, their situation was unique, not least in that they were so unprepared for it by their national experiences. On the other, their meeting was like that of other great powers in history in that concord and mutual trust have not been the normal state of affairs between powerful nations—quite the contrary. The weakness of all others invited, perhaps imposed, the competition that followed. There should have been no need to postulate demon motivations on either side to account for the friction which developed between them as they undertook to define their relations with each other. At best that was bound to be a slow, tense, and difficult process even had there been no preexisting ideological framework at hand to inflame the confrontation. It remains, still, the paramount issue in world politics.

There were several theoretical models for the behavior of the two superpowers. They might, for example, have pursued various contradictory aims but within an overall framework of basic cooperation for more overriding ends such as economic development, or preservation of peace, or quiet domination of their respective spheres in Europe. Or their competition might have assumed such sweeping form, geographically or in terms of the issues which the protagonists believed to be at stake, as to lead to war. As we know, there has been no war between them—perhps the single most remarkable phenomenon of the cold war. But their clash did in fact take a most extensive form, geographically and ideologically, starting in Eastern Europe and eventually spreading from Korea to Cuba to Katanga.

The problem is not to explain why there was friction between the only two great powers left in the world in 1945—in itself a most probable phenomenon—but to understand why their relations took the particular contentious direction they did at the start, rather than some other. To do this, it is essential to consider both the circumstances in which they met in 1945 and the way in which each saw its own and the other's role in Europe.

In a sense both countries were looking at each other seriously for the first time. They had not been either traditional antagonists or allies; indeed, their prior contacts had been sporadic and distant. Such political contact as there had been had usually been defined in relation to third powers. Thus, there was a curious U.S.–Russian entente during the American Civil War aimed at Great Britain. They were distant allies during the months in 1917 when both were at war with Germany. The establishment of diplomatic relations between Washington and Soviet Russia in 1933 was connected with the Japanese move into Manchuria two years before. On the other side was the brief incursion of American soldiers into Russia at the end of World War I, when the United States played a part in the Allied intervention that tried to overthrow the Bolshevik regime.

All of this is marginal. However much Americans decried Bolshevism and Soviet Russians decried American capitalism, neither country had been particularly concerned with the other's policies until 1945. Thenceforth they have been obsessively concerned with each other. Perhaps the earlier distance made the conflict more acute, because less familiar, when it came.

America and Russia had one thing in common since the eighteenth century: an ambivalent attitude toward Europe. Americans had turned their backs on the old country and gone west; Russians had been forcibly europeanized in the eighteenth century by strong-willed rulers but had debated ever since about who and what they were in relation to Europe, for all the important role they played in European affairs. Both the United States and the Soviet Union had been self-exiled (and the USSR had been more or less exiled by the other European countries besides) from the spurious revival of the European system after 1919. It was entirely consistent with their pasts, as well as with the situation they confronted, that each came back into Europe in 1945 not as a participant in an ongoing system but in some sense as the conscious architect of its successor.

Both the new superpowers brought to Europe not only specific policies for the postwar period but designs for the new international system that would have to be built on the ruins of that destroyed by the war. While their particular policies were new insofar as the problems and possibilities they faced were new, their grand designs were rooted in ideological frameworks and, what is more, a mutual ideological rivalry that were much older. It was of critical importance that there had been a sweeping ideological conflict between the United States and the Soviet Union thirty years before there was any conflict between them over political specifics. As early as 1917 Lenin and Wilson stood out above warring Europe offering new designs for a better world, both cast in ideological terms, both explicitly proclaimed as alternatives to the discredited old European system, and both worked out in 1918–19 in a dialectical process of which the two leaders were conscious.

Both Lenin and Wilson called for democratic control of foreign policy, an end to secret diplomacy, and a peace settlement to be based on the self-determination of peoples—all radical departures from the theory and practice of prewar Europe. But Lenin's design, based on the Marxist analysis as adapted by him, also called for a revolution that would utterly sweep away capitalism and all its institutions, which were seen as the universal source of misery, injustice, and war. Wilson, on the other hand, for all his condemnation of the old balance of power and imperialism, raised no challenge to the basic structure of economic relations or nation-states in the West but aimed to reform both in a drastic though nonrevolutionary way:

> In political terms, the President envisaged a worldwide order of liberal states, free of traditional military alliance systems, in which an unstable balance of power system was to be superseded by a stable and inclusive community of power embodied in a League of Nations. In economic terms, freedom of the seas and non-discriminatory trade arrangements would replace a war-engendering system of national commercial barriers and permit thereby the natural processes of an inherently peaceful international capitalism to bring about universal progress and prosperity. In other words, the backbone of the Wilsonian postwar ideology was the political economy of liberal-capitalist internationalism. The President interpreted America's national interest as being one with the maintenance of international liberal stability.[1]

1. N. Gordon Levin, Jr., *Woodrow Wilson and World Politics* (New York: Oxford University Press, 1968), p. 126 (footnotes omitted).

In this context Leninism was not particularly directed against the United States but against all the capitalist countries. Wilsonianism, on the other hand, was defined at first, before the United States entered the war, as a challenge to all the imperialist powers of Europe whose actions collectively had led to war; then it was directed particularly—but still not exclusively—against Germany, whose militarism was seen as worse than the practices of the Allies; and eventually, after the Bolsheviks launched their call to world revolution, against that appeal. None of these factors crowded out the others. Confronted suddenly by Bolshevism, Wilson saw his program as a "third-force" between old-style imperialism and new-style socialist revolution, and as such even more important than before because the two extremes reinforced each other and one or other would prevail if he did not.

Both the United States and the Soviet Union approached the postwar world in 1945 with distinctive ideas about how to organize it. Both found ready to hand, only intermittently muted since 1917–20 for all their political isolation from each other, an ideological framework for their own policies and an ideological rivalry between them which could explain what they themselves and their rivals were doing with respect to the specific political conflicts which arose between them.

So strong and noisy was this, the oldest facet of their clash, that it was widely taken to be the conflict itself. But in fact the quarrel of ideologies, while real, was at the start only one aspect of each country's approach to the problems and possibilities presented to it by the disappearance of German power from Europe. Each approached the postwar world with definite policies in which ideology and more conventionally defined interests were blended in their usual complex mixture. The development of the policy aims of each in face of those of the other makes up the most important strand of what has happened in Europe since 1945. That story properly begins, therefore, with the attitudes, goals, and policies which the new masters of Europe brought with them to the victory.

The Soviet Union

If analysis of American foreign policy is made difficult by the abundance of data, which provides material to support almost any thesis, objective understanding of Soviet policy is severely hobbled by the scarcity of relevant documents. The Soviet Union does not publish many diplomatic papers, its archives are not open to researchers, its leaders produce few memoirs, its press does not contain leaked or independently developed material. In scholarly terms, this situation obviously requires the utmost prudence in drawing conclusions.

Unfortunately, the importance of the subject has produced the op-

posite result. Western analysts—governmental, academic, and jour-
nalistic—have tended to seek the essence of Soviet policy rather than
closely study the details of Soviet behavior. Worse, they have often
claimed to find it, while in fact their work tendentiously interpreted
Soviet foreign policy according to the international—and domestic—
temperature of the moment. The mainstream of analysis in this country
during the cold war period saw Soviet policy as deeply purposeful,
devious, and expansionist. The two main models of the Soviet Union, in
William Welch's agreeable typology, were the Great Beast of Revelation
and the Mellowing Tiger.[2] There was, it is true, a third stream whose
model Welch calls the Neurotic Bear, but it had little impact on mass or
official thinking.

Soviet policy was thus widely thought not to be susceptible of analysis
in terms comparable to that of others. As late as 1963 Marshall Shulman
found it useful to call for an approach to Soviet behavior as "an explica-
ble human phenomenon."[3] The Great Beast has had a long life and its
ghost lurks about even now.

There are also myths of another sort. The critical reexamination
which has painted American policy as more purposeful, devious, and
expansionist than had previously been believed has tended—by omission
or indirection or simple and sometimes passionate reversal of cliches—to
treat Soviet policy as passive and conservative. Without serious reexamination of Soviet policy itself, the Soviet Union has sometimes emerged
from between the lines of American revisionism as an Injured Lamb.

The model of Soviet policy which I suggest here might be called
simply the Other Superpower. It assumes that Soviet policy has been the
work of men who were politicians and diplomats as well as ideologues,
that they pursued discrete and finite goals as well as others that were less
so. But anyone reading about Soviet foreign policy is well advised to
approach all interpretations (including what follows) with some skepti-
cism, while anyone trying to write about it with detachment must recognize that most judgments have to be tentative and that on some important points the only sound conclusion that can be reached in light of
grossly deficient data is the Scottish verdict of "not proven."

Within these limits, some things seem clear.

In the case of the Soviet Union as of every other country foreign policy
is colored by geography and history. Those who rule in Moscow must
have Russian history in mind, just as their subjects do—not so much the

2. William Welch, *American Images of Soviet Foreign Policy* (New Haven and London: Yale
University Press, 1970).

3. Marshall D. Shulman, *Stalin's Foreign Policy Reappraised* (Cambridge, Mass.: Harvard
University Press, 1963), p. 3.

details of the record, of course, as learned attitudes toward it. In the case of the Russians, the past cannot be seen as anything but a dark, bloody, and tumultuous tapestry of success and failure, conquests and staggering defeats, occupations and losses of blood and land. This is not only the legacy of the distant past but of recent times: invasion and massive defeat in World War I; invasion, the loss of over 15 million lives, and hard fought victory in World War II. From all this Russians can have acquired no confidence that the political order of the world is intrinsically benign, whatever official Marxism maintains as to the meaning of history. They see, as do most Europeans, that conflict is constant, order precarious, and security transitory and subject to attack.

In particular, any Russian government would be concerned with its frontiers and the power of its neighbors. Military technology since 1945 has made it much less important, from a military point of view, whether a border is some miles one way or another. But that is a recent and not yet absorbed phenomenon. No Russian government in 1945 would be oblivious to where its frontier was fixed. Nor would any Russian government overlook Russia's historic frontiers, brutally changed between 1918 and 1920 in one of the country's darkest hours. In this sense, any Russian government would see 1945 as vengeance for 1918, or, rather, belated justice. The victims of Brest-Litovsk, once victorious over the same enemy after a second terrible war, would not be likely to accept again the frontiers imposed on them by that dictated peace and its sequels.

All of this would be true whether Russia was ruled by Bolsheviks, democrats, or Romanoffs.[4] It is both strange and unfortunate that informed analysts could consider that Soviet foreign policy after 1945 was inspired entirely by Marx and Lenin and not at all by Peter and Catherine and their heirs.

At the same time, the regime in Moscow in 1945, and now, *is* a particular kind of regime and as such has its own particular outlook on and insights into the world. In this sense the characteristics of the regime are the middle link between the "national interest" as broadly defined by concepts based on geography and history and the individual policymaker with his own private visions and penchants. There has, of course, been a continuous debate in the West about the mix in Soviet

4. Arno Mayer writes that the allies in 1919 took it for granted that any Russian regime that was admitted to the peace conference would press for most of the old frontiers if not also for the promised spoils of war: "A tsarist autocracy, a constitutional monarchy, a bourgeois republic, or a social democratic regime—each in its own way could be expected to reclaim Russia's imperial heritage." *Politics and Diplomacy of Peacemaking* (New York: Knopf, 1967), p. 285.

policy of elements stemming from the Russian heritage of the rulers and of those derived from their Communist heritage. Without materials on the personal thinking of the leaders or of the policymaking processes, it is not possible to analyze the mix with much precision, the more so as it obviously varies from time to time and man to man, just as it does in other countries (and few policymakers anywhere are not motivated by multiple considerations). The most useful judgment in the Soviet case is that the ideological background of the Russian rulers is an important input into their foreign policy, not so much in setting their current operational goals as in coloring their thinking about and interpretation of events and the policies of others. Following on a suggestion of Adam Ulam, it is useful to think of Marxism-Leninism as giving the Soviet leaders not a plan for changing the world but a prism for looking at it.[5] That is important, for perception can matter as much as goal-setting in policymaking.

Besides their general experience as Russians and as Marxist-Leninists, the rulers of Russia in 1945 and since have also had before their eyes the very specific experience of their own regime since 1917 and the lessons they have drawn from that as guides to policy. The Bolshevik leaders of 1917–18 believed that their success was only the first phase of a general revolution which would soon sweep over war-ravaged Europe. According to their doctrines this had to be so because they did not think that a revolutionary regime could survive in a single country, and certainly not in backward Russia. So their foreign policy, including the Treaty of Brest-Litovsk, was seen as a holding action, buying time for their diminished state until the revolution spread elsewhere. They had no notion of having to carry on permanent relations with other states. When Trotsky became commissar for foreign affairs, he said that he would issue a few proclamations and close up shop.

By 1920 or 1921, however, the Soviet leaders were disabused of these hopes. Finding themselves in control of the one and only "socialist" country in the world with little early prospect of there being more, they improvised the new doctrine of socialism in one country—an inevitable adaptation to their circumstances. Abroad, they had to accept the fact that they were going to live for awhile in a world of capitalist states. It then became a question of establishing normal relations and even, as at Rapallo in 1922, closer than normal relations.

Political reality thus imposed itself on ideology and ideology then adapted itself to reality. Peaceful coexistence began in practice in 1920

5. Adam B. Ulam. *Expansion and Coexistence: The History of Soviet Foreign Policy, 1917– 1967* (New York: Praeger, 1968), p. 30.

but Soviet theory took forty years to catch up. Later Soviet leaders were well aware that Lenin himself gave them a license for flexibility and improvisation as part of his heritage. Still, ideology did adapt and therefore survived, its integrity and the hopes it held out for the future both seemingly intact. For, though these adaptations began to be made very early in the history of the Bolshevik regime, they did not mean that its leaders gave up their basic view of the world. This was provided by Marx's familiar economic analysis, Lenin's contribution on the conflicts engendered by imperialism, and, above all, a clearcut notion that the USSR lived in a world of states with which relations of various sorts were necessary but which, nevertheless, were profoundly hostile. The 1919–20 intervention of the allies—including the United States—in an effort to undo the October Revolution only confirmed in practice what the Bolshevik leaders knew in theory. This concept of a two-camp world, seen as a place of danger and struggle, was hardly strange to Russians.

At some point, of course, those who believe in a two-camp world but also have to live in it insensibly abandon their more extreme hopes and, while maintaining their formal claims to virtue or mission, however defined, nevertheless gradually become a part of the game among others. Were the Soviet leaders conscious of this by 1945? Probably not. The time since 1917 had been too short, the personnel too continuous, and, above all, the expectations of their official doctrine too well confirmed by events (give or take a little reality) to have invalidated their fundamental outlook. Stalin almost certainly did believe that his regime represented a historically determined wave of the future, and his successors probably still think so, though the moment of the desired consummation continues to recede. Thus, fear and suspicion of the outside world were balanced by confidence, and confidence in some sense and to some degree bred patience and flexibility.

The Communist rulers of Russia had very definite expectations of what was going to happen in the world after 1917. Their immediate hopes were disappointed, and they adapted their policies and their ideology as best they could. But they had other hopes too. For one thing they expected a great economic collapse in the capitalist world. And, indeed, it took place in 1929. They also expected war among the capitalist powers. While the United States did not go to war within Britain, or Britain with France, as they had expected, yet World War II could be seen by Communists as confirming their analysis of the inevitable struggles within the capitalist camp.

The Soviet leaders in 1945 surely looked forward to another economic collapse and further quarrels and even wars in the Western camp. They thus expected greater weakness and division than turned out to be the case. But their expectations were relevant, of course, to their own policymaking. The Soviet leaders may thus, in 1945, have taken for granted greater hostility to themselves and greater fundamental weakness in the West than existed. But though their policy might have been aimed to parry the hostility and exploit the weakness, they would have had sufficient confidence in the rightness of their analysis of the world situation to proceed with both confidence and caution in face of the obvious economic and military power of the United States. There would be no need for excessive haste or risk-taking. Hitler thought that he was working with destiny because of the might of the present German state; the Soviet Communists believed that history was on their side whatever the immediate constellation of power in the world. Very different policies followed from these beliefs.

As I noted above, the political outlook and interests of the ruler or rulers cannot be discounted from the policymaking equation, whatever the strength of the forces, supportive or hostile, they are dealing with. In the case of Stalin, his system of government as it developed during the great purges of the 1930s immensely heightened those characteristics of suspicion and inwardness which have marked so much of Russian history. It seems clear that Stalin, whether or not some clinical tag is hung on him, was to say the least very jealous of his own power and ruthlessly vigilant in defending it. This obviously affected his foreign as well as his domestic policy. The first Bolsheviks to rule Russia proclaimed an aggressive and self-confident doctrine and no doubt believed in it, but their actual policy had to be the defense of their state, and of their power within it. Of course Soviet means of action vis-à-vis prospective enemies were much greater in 1945 than in 1918. But neither this nor the official content of their doctrine—the eventual communization of the world as a result of the laws of history—is sufficient to prove that Stalin in 1945 was immediately aggressive in a broad sense.

It is unlikely that Stalin, who had been at or near the top in the Soviet state since its creation, would have abandoned even in the intoxication of victory all the caution that had been used for thirty years in the defense and expansion of his own and Soviet power. He was well aware in 1945 of the losses inflicted on his country by the war and its weakness in economic power—a factor no Communist would overlook—vis-à-vis the United States. This sense of weakness may not have bred passivity or cooperativeness—quite the opposite—but it did breed caution.

Nevertheless, the tone and turn Stalin gave to Soviet society, and to foreign policy, had an important impact on other countries and, thus, on Soviet relations with them. The repressive measures he thought necessary to assure his rule at home—implying at the least a minimum of

contact and quite possibly a high level of tension with the outside
world—were similar enough to those of the well-remembered Nazi system
to lead many to think that the foreign policy was also Hitlerian, a natural
though illogical conclusion. In addition, Soviet policy was often expressed in the late 1940s with an extraordinary vituperativeness. This
may have been meant to conceal weakness, but it had important effects
in the West to the extent that statesmen and, *a fortiori*, peoples take their
antagonists as they present themselves—again, a not necessarily accurate
identification but one that came naturally enough to people who regretted dismissing *Mein Kampf* as having no bearing on Hitler's actual policy.
Then, the process by which Soviet control was asserted over the countries of Eastern Europe was brutal and repellent, again reminiscent of
Nazi practice. And the fact that the USSR had an extra instrument of
policy at hand in the foreign Communist parties gave Western societies a
feeling of externally induced internal instability (usually exaggerated),
comparable, again, to the Fascist Fifth Column.

Taking Soviet postwar policy as a whole, however, it was probably
mistaken to conclude that the regime which seemed to resemble Hitler's
in these ways was as disposed as he was to risk war in pursuit of its goals.
The USSR after 1945 was a severely weakened state, which did not find
it prudent or feasible to attack even deviationist Yugoslavia in 1948, not
to say any area under the military occupation or influence of the United
States. Yet with so little known then of Soviet policymaking and with the
Nazi experience so recent, it is not hard to see that Western contemporaries of Stalin overlooked the practical prudence behind the harsh
rhetoric which filled the air in those years, the forced communization of
the states of Eastern Europe, and the activities of the Western Communist parties from 1945 on. The benefit of the doubt is given in law to
the defendant, but when one does not know much about other people's
purposes in politics, it is at least as human to expect the worst as the best,
and even more so in proportion to the power of the other. Analysts after
the fact can have the detachment to say "not proven," but contemporaries are likely to do so in inverse proportion to the stakes as they see
them.

Drawing together these tendencies in Soviet policy, its main specific
elements in 1945 and therafter may be summed up in this way:

1. The first requirement for security, which victory made possible, was
to establish what were then thought to be secure frontiers—an already
obsolescent but obviously powerful consideration after such a war as
World War II. In this case security meant many things: moving the
Finnish frontier a few miles to the west; absorbing three tiny Baltic
republics which were seen as historically though not ethnically Russian;

occupying territory in Poland containing mostly ethnic Ukranians and White Russians, thereby removing a foreign irredentist threat and pushing the military frontier substantially westward; annexing Carpathian Ruthenia for ethnic and security reasons, and Bessarabia and Northern Bukovina for historical and security reasons. This was not the 1914 Russian frontier because Finland and Poland survived as independent states. But it was close, and represented to the Soviet leaders their coming back into possession of those Russian lands of which they had been despoiled in 1918 and, after a brief reoccupation, in 1941.

It is interesting to observe in this connection how nationalist these Russian Communists were. Assuming that they then foresaw (because they were planning) the communization of Poland and Rumania, their first concern throughout the war and after it was nevertheless to secure classical frontier and territorial advantages at the expense of those very countries. This obviously did not make the new pro-Russian regimes more popular in their countries. Is it possible that the Soviet leaders were not at first certain that they would choose or would be able to communize those countries? Did they foresee (having had little relevant experience up to that time) that the process might at least be difficult, and even reversible? Did they not trust Polish and Rumanian Communists? Were conventional strategic, historical, and nationalist considerations primary to the Soviet Bolshevik leaders in any case?

Whatever the answers to these questions, certainly any other Russian regime would have done much the same thing once the power balance in Eastern Europe made these annexations possible. Any Russian government, after such a war and the defeat of Germany, would have annexed border territory which it had lost only twenty years before, just as it would have restored the pre-1905 status quo in the Far East once the defeat of Japan made possible the recovery of its colonial position in Manchuria and northern Korea.

2. Similarly, we have but to imagine what a Brest-Litovsk in reverse might have been, imposed in 1918 by a victorious Romanoff or republican government, to grasp the continuity of Russian policy with respect to the weak states across the new Western frontiers. Any victorious Russian government would have wanted "friendly" states across the border, but of course there could be many political definitions of that term. Did Stalin think any state could be friendly with respect to Soviet interests that was not Communist? Did he see any alternative to an anti-Soviet *cordon sanitaire* other than satellization? The answers appear to have been affirmative in the case of Finland, a fact to which too little attention was paid in the West in weighing Soviet policy, negative in the cases of Poland and Rumania, to which much attention was paid. These two

countries were strongly anti-Russian between the wars and it is difficult
to believe (or to think that Stalin believed) that any freely elected government in either after 1945 could have been very friendly to the USSR,
the more so as both had just lost much territory to it—a particularly
painful and extensive loss in Poland's case. It is therefore plausible to
think that Stalin had decided early on an orginal solution of the Polish
problem (as seen from Moscow): namely, the forcible imposition of a
regime which would be friendly to the USSR not only because of
ideological ties but also because of its weak domestic support. The same
kind of motivation pointed to the same solution for Rumania.

These policies did not flow from any act of omission or commission by
the Western powers. They were, as nearly as that can be said of any
policies, absolutes for the Soviet government.

The cases of the other countries of Eastern Europe are less clear.
Unlike the countries bordering on the USSR, Bulgaria was Slavic and
not anti-Russian (though anti-Soviet in the interwar period). Its satellization must have seemed less necessary but nevertheless a natural and
easy revival of a Russian policy dating from the 1870s and a means
of bringing added influence to bear on Turkey (an even older Russian
policy), and perhaps also on Yugoslavia. That country, as we have
learned since, was in Tito's hands at the end of the war, not Stalin's, and
the course of events there is not really relevant to this discussion.

As for Hungary and Czechoslovakia (the former traditionally anti-
Russian, the latter traditionally pro-), their communization took several
years longer than that of the countries bordering on the USSR. It can be
argued, of course, that the Russians proceeded according to an advanced plan there but only as fast as they judged internal and Western
resistance would permit. On this interpretation, the Stalin-Churchill
50–50 deal on Hungary does not indicate Soviet caution or uncertainty
but only duplicity. It can also be argued, however, that the communization of these countries came about because of a process of interacting
events between the USSR and the Western powers in the 1945–48
period, or, at least, that it occurred as a *part* of such a process. This, as
in reverse the Finnish case, may be regarded as one of the issues of
postwar Soviet policy that remain "not proven."

3. To the west of their sphere of dominance in Eastern Europe, the
Soviet leaders wanted to make sure that Germany did not renew its
aggression again, either alone or as part of an anti-Soviet bloc organized
by the United States or Great Britain. Their historic obsession with
Germany long remained, and still remains, out of proportion to the
threat posed to the USSR, now a global superpower, by divided—or even
united—post-1945 Germany. But they were not alone in the 1940s in

fearing a revival of German power, as after 1918, and looking for ways to prevent it.

The Russians gave high priority in the early postwar years to drawing reparations from Germany to help rebuild the devastated USSR. As I discuss in a later chapter, it is unclear just what their overall policy toward Germany consisted of. On the one hand, Germany's most important industrial resources were in the zones occupied by the Western powers. That implied that the USSR had to cooperate with them if it was to gain substantial industrial reparations in the short term and to have a voice in the disposition of Germany in the long. But, on the other hand, the Russians also became increasingly committed, if they were not so from the start, to keeping control of the resources—and the future development—of their own zone of occupation. We do not know when their priorities with respect to the clash of these objectives became clear to themselves—that is, when they decided to sacrifice whatever share of influence they thought they might have in the western part of Germany rather than risk loosening their control in the eastern zone. The same question can be asked about American policy. As events were to show, the policies of each, whatever their points of departure, conditioned if they did not control the policies of the other.

4. The question of whether and on what terms the Soviet Union might have pursued cooperation with the other major Allies in Germany is, of course, part of a larger question concerning their overall relationship. This problem is examined in detail later in this chapter and in those which follow. Looking ahead to the conclusions of this examination, there is reason to think that the Soviet leaders did not exclude such cooperation a priori and in fact saw certain benefits in it, but also that there were policy goals that took priority if they had to make such a choice. The Russians on the whole played along with the West in building the United Nations organization. They reached a modus vivendi with the United States on Far Eastern questions. They would not have disdained economic aid had it been forthcoming without political strings. They seemed willing to bargain over Germany (though not necessarily in such a way as to ensure an outcome compatible with Western interests as these came into focus). But their sine qua non for this kind of cooperation, if it can be called that, was Western acceptance of the priority goals of Soviet policy I have discussed. When that was denied, the possibility of maintaining even a facade of cooperativeness, if not something more, disappeared.

5. Beyond its territorial, hegemonic, and security policies, the Soviet Union had a wider goal: to have its frontiers and sphere of influence recognized by the other great powers, particularly the United States.

This was a major preoccupation throughout the war, when it ran into the U.S. policy of deferring territorial decisions and refusing to sanction spheres of influence in Europe. It remained a preoccupation long after.

An even broader Soviet goal was to be treated by the Western Allies as a great power. Such a policy goal might seem both superfluous (in light of Soviet power) and contradictory (in light of the fact that the Soviet leaders denied the existence of an overarching world system that included both themselves and the capitalist countries). But they acted as if it suited both their interests and their pride—after the outcast years of the 1920s and 1930s—to be accepted as an equal participant in world affairs. In this, as in other things, Russian nationalism was at work. It led the Russians, for example, to claim trusteeship over a former Italian colony in Africa. Partly, no doubt, this claim was to be used for bargaining on other things; but quite probably it was also a demand to be treated as an equal in the making of the postwar world.

This Soviet demand for a trusteeship struck the Western leaders as highly peculiar and sinister; after all, Russia had never had colonies or interests in Africa. This small episode—the Soviet demand and the Western response to it—highlights the deeper and long-lasting problem of Soviet claims to, and Western reluctance to accept, the full implications in status terms of the USSR's position as a *world* power. The Russians, in their view, had borne the main brunt of the war against Germany and had lost millions of dead and untold material wealth in the effort. What did the victory won at such cost amount to, the Russians might have asked, if not recognition of Soviet claims and interests by those powers which had sacrificed less? If the United States could establish outposts in Central Europe and Japan, and even challenge Soviet policy in Poland, why could not the Russians express their interest in areas beyond their traditional sphere of interest?

As a matter of fact, the USSR was slow to penetrate areas of the world outside that sphere. It was only after 1955 that the power of the Soviet state began to be felt in Africa and the Middle East; only after 1965 that its proximity to the Mediterranean was translated into an assertive naval role there; only in the 1970s that its fleet became a factor in the Indian Ocean. These Soviet activities of course ran athwart the established interests of other powers in these areas and were resisted for that reason. Western reaction to them, however, has reflected not only such normal considerations but also surprise and even indignation that the Soviet Union was developing interests of its own in areas of the world habitually dominated by others. The West continues to find it not only disquieting, which is natural, but odd, which is less understandable, that the co-victor

of World War II asserts global interests and, far behind the United
States, has gradually developed a global reach.

In some respects the Soviet Union has stirred up the feelings that
German assertiveness in Africa and Asia and at sea had met before 1914,
and in some respects Soviet motives have probably not been so different
from those of Imperial Germany. Chancellor Bethmann-Hollweg defended Germany's expanding navy as being necessary "for the general
purposes of her greatness." Whatever else has gone into Soviet policy,
there was a good deal of that. The USSR, like pre-1914 Germany,
realized that its power ran ahead of its status. Despite the seeming
incompatibility of such considerations with the outlook of a state committed to a two-camp view of the world, it appears that the Russian
leaders in practice wanted the other great powers to treat them according to the standards applied in the *other* camp to a great power.

6. One means by which the Russians hoped to exert influence in areas
outside their military control was the Communist parties of the West,
which in 1945 shared power in many European countries. As long as the
Communists remained in Western governments—up to mid-1947 in
France and Italy, for example—such countries could not take part in a
bloc hostile to the USSR. Even out of office the Communist parties might
hope to prevent these countries from becoming actively anti-Soviet. The
defensive objectives of this policy closely resembled those of the Popular
Front in the 1930s. Whether the Russians saw the Communist parties as
having serious prospects of taking over control of these Western countries is less certain. In all cases except Greece the local Communists in
1944–45 gave up the weapons they had used in the underground and
agreed to the dismantling of the resistance organizations as separate
political entities. This does not prove that the Communists thereby gave
up all thought of achieving power in these countries. Everywhere the
parties of the left—particularly but not only the Communists—played a
much larger role than prewar, and the Communists may well have
hoped to take power later by legal means and by Popular Front tactics,
whereas a premature attempt in the face of Anglo-American armies
could not but fail. But it became clear quite soon that, even apart from
the presence of those armies, Western Europe was more numbed than
revolutionary and that the institutions established or reestablished
there, weak as they seemed in some cases, were still too strong to permit
Western European Communist parties to take power, legally or otherwise. It seems likely that both they and the Russians realized this.
Whether their behavior reflected respect for a more or less long-term
Anglo-American sphere of influence in Western Europe or a calculating

deferral of hope until the Anglo-Americans might be gone remains uncertain.

The United States

The Vietnam war stimulated—and prepared an audience for—a serious reexamination of American foreign policy since World War II, the thinking that has underlain it, and the national attitudes and economic and social structures that have conditioned that thinking. It will hardly ever again be possible, as it was through much of American history, for us to look on our country's activities in the world without some degree of critical detachment. Others, we find, have not seen us as we have seen ourselves, and at last neither do we.

Our new self-consciousness and self-insight have brought a better understanding of American foreign policy but have also created new misunderstandings. Some of the revisionist historians, moved by indignation over Vietnam and eager to challenge the black-and-white clichés of the postwar period, have turned the traditional tables completely and laid the main or exclusive blame for the cold war on the doorstep of the United States. Plenty of documentation exists from which an American design for the postwar world of one sort or another can be woven, whereas so little is known of Soviet policy aims that they are often relegated to a minor or passive role. In its most extreme reductionist form American foreign policy has been explained as nothing more than an outward projection of internal problems that are insoluble in the established economic structures of the society.[6]

Between these new simplifications and the older ones is the fact that both the superpowers have pursued many goals, of varying degrees of importance, with less than perfect consistency and success.[7] Above all, they have done this in a process of often confused interaction with each other. But before this concept can be given its due as a framework for understanding the origins and evolution of the cold war it will be necessary to demystify both Soviet and American foreign policy, and at the

6. See, for example, Gabriel Kolko, *The Roots of American Foreign Policy* (Boston: Beacon Press, 1969), in which the United States is depicted as struggling desperately but in vain to maintain its markets and sources of raw materials in a third world that is throwing off the shackles of a colonial past of which America is the last defender. The Soviet Union plays no part at all in this picture.

7. For example: "The United States was capitalist, but it was also arrogant, Christian, militarist, racist, highly technological, chauvinistic, and industrialized. It should be kept in mind, truism though it may be, that the US had become a world power of uncommon dimensions, not just a capitalist power, and behaved like other great powers through history—it exploited opportunities." Thomas G. Paterson, *Soviet-American Confrontation* (Baltimore and London: The Johns Hopkins University Press, 1973), p. 263.

same time. A good start has now been made at casting the devil out of our understanding of Soviet policy, but at the cost of introducing him onto the other side. The further study of the cold war in context will eventually correct that. In the meantime, we can now examine the policies of the United States toward Europe and the attitudes behind them, as well as those of the Soviet Union, with a good deal more objectivity than we could a decade ago.

The United States, like Russia, has long had ambivalent feelings toward Europe, a sense of being linked to but also separated from the countries of Europe. Joined to these attitudes has been a belief in its own uniqueness and, until very recently, in its own innocence. Most Americans had come to the New World with distaste for what they had left behind in the Old and a desire to build a different and better life. The nation itself was born in an act of revolution against a European country, and it is to the point to observe that the American national consciousness has not remembered that independence was gained with the help of other European countries in a context of the balance of power system of the Old World. Fortunately for the United States, it was able to become detached from this system after a third of a century of close involvement with it. From then on it was easy to believe that the country had been uniquely self-generated as the first large-scale nonmonarchical political system in the history of the world. As such, it was seen as a unique experiment in human liberation, both by Americans themselves and by nineteenth-century European liberals. It is to the point that the United States dates official proclamations not only with the Christian year but with the year of its own independence—the beginning, presumably, of that "New Order of the Ages" proclaimed on the national seal.

This historical experience, and Americans' consciousness of it, had several important, implications for the way in which the country looked at the world after World War II. For all its continuous involvement with European civilization, there has been a kind of national impatience with the tiresome and dangerous complexities of European history and politics. During the war President Roosevelt and Secretary of State Hull, following closely in the steps of Woodrow Wilson, were explicit in their belief that the old system of spheres of influence and balance of power had failed and should and could be replaced by something else— presumably a new order of the ages on an international scale. If the United States could not stand clear, then it would have to change the old system into something better; it could not simply become a player in the bad old game. This impatience with the many states, parties, and rivalries of the old Europe is remarkably persistent, recurring most recently, for example, in the fervent belief of so many otherwise lucid Americans that European nationalism and nation-states were dead or dying and would shortly be replaced by a new federal state—like their own, of course.

This rooted distaste for the politics of the old countries was reinforced by the happy fact that the United States had been able to develop at a long distance from powerful neighbors and had thus been spared having to take part in a balance of power system and the ordinary vicissitudes and exasperations of international relations. Separated from the major powers by a broad ocean and with only weak states as neighbors, it was able to take its own hemispheric sphere of interest so much for granted, because that was practically uncontested, as to be unaware of the existence of such a sphere. American good fortune came to be seen as a reward for virtue, contrasted to the wars and clashes bred by the contentious vices of the European experience. Americans could feel surprise and indignation when foreigners saw as hypocritical their deeply held conviction that their sphere of influence in Latin America and the Pacific was nothing of the sort and had nothing whatever in common with other people's spheres of influence in other regions.

Because the United States has had weak neighbors and was distant from Europe, it has had a history of only sporadic conflict with other countries, and that always in a good cause (what could be more manifest than manifest destiny?) and always victorious (except, perhaps, for what New England called Mr. Madison's war). It is true that this created the problem of which president would be the first to lose a war, a difficulty that no European statesman need ever face. But it also had the more important consequence of inculcating the idea that military and political rivalry among nations need not be the law of life, that the adjustment and readjustment of power relations are not habitual, and that order and security are the normal course of things unless they are wrenched from their channel by wicked men. All this, of course, is the reverse of the European experience—not least the Russian. So deep a divergence in outlook on such fundamental issues never facilitated a meeting of minds between the United States and either its allies or its enemies, and the American view has tended to breed both conspiratorial notions of the causes of problems and simplistic solutions for them.

This concept of inherent international orderliness has been reinforced by a similar self-understanding of American national history. It has been thought in the mainstream that there was a basic consensus on institutions and goals and that politics had to deal only with, so to speak, details—negotiable things. Americans have therefore downplayed what there has been of violence, coercion, and disorder in their history, which have been no worse than most other people's, and better than many, but which have been far more important than the national myth has allowed. This concept of consensus at home reenforced the implications of long isolation from normal international relations and inculcated the belief that the international order too, wicked as it has been for centuries, is nevertheless inherently consensual or, at any rate, is susceptible of being redeemed if the problem is approached in the right way.

A further implication of several of these ideas has been the long-held notion that the United States was not a usual, regular participant in world affairs but intervenes only in great emergencies and that, in those cases, its purpose is to set the machinery in motion again, to restore or, better yet, bring into being a latent order of consensual relations, while limiting its own future role in keeping the machine going properly. This view of the ideal or natural international system is closely analogous to that concept of an economic system moved by an "invisible hand" which has been a most sacred American article of faith.

Woodrow Wilson, of course, tried to change this outlook and to engage the United States in the running of new international machinery, but he was defeated by the traditional view, which then persisted for another quarter-century. Roosevelt took up Wilson's effort and succeeded. But the old ideas have lurked about in unexpected places. The United States has been a normal day-to-day participant in major international affairs only since 1945. It is not surprising that this novel situation did not come naturally, had to be buttressed at home with arguments about urgent external threats developed for the occasion (which have then had their own consequences), and is in periodic jeopardy of being reversed as the country is tempted by a powerful historical tug to cut back on its vast commitments with as little discrimination between the essential and the marginal as it sometimes showed in undertaking them.

The sense of playing only a fireman's role in international affairs,[8] combined with the sense that U.S. activities are qualitatively distinct from the ordinary wear and tear of European power politics, has tended to lead Americans to set their foreign policy goals in high and abstract terms. The American government announced two policy aims in 1917: to protect the rights of neutral shipping, and/or to end war and make the world safe for democracy. One of these was very specific, and too small for the occasion; the other was very grand indeed. Between them was the

8. One of Roosevelt's most effective—and most revealing—arguments in support of the lend-lease bill in 1941 was his image that, if your neighbor's house is on fire, you should let him use your garden hose. Roosevelt, an old Wilsonian, of course believed that cooperative measures would have to be taken once the emergency was over, but he also knew how to speak to his fellow citizens.

useful and attainable purpose of restoring a shattered balance of power and preventing Europe from falling into the control of a hostile nation. But this was something which the Americans of 1917 and other times have not found it easy to say or to hear or to believe in.

World War II was no exception to this practice, nor was the cold war either. Once engaged in a foreign enterprise, American purposes were proclaimed to be the building of a just and lasting peace, resisting aggression and change by force, assuring democracy and self-determination everywhere, building a new peace order, and the like. Is not this passage a fair summary of the American state of mind, popular and official, in this century?

> There was one people in the world which would fight for others' liberties at its own cost, to its own peril, and with its own toil . . . ready to cross the sea that there might be no unjust empire anywhere and that everywhere justice, right, and law might prevail.

Such rhetoric has a contemporary ring, but revisionists will not be surprised to know that it was Livy who thus described the Roman view of the Roman conquest of the Mediterranean world.[9]

Such objectives are also proclaimed by others, of course, but—until recent years—Americans have probably been more inclined to see them as attainable policy goals than as pious hopes or propaganda. Indeed, they have been not only goals but modes of thought and analysis—or substitutes for them, which is more serious. Universalism of this sort can become a simplistic nightmare, obstructing understanding of the particular—that is, of the real world. In a sense, such policy goals are a projection outward of what is understood to be America's internal order, which is a profoundly ideological exercise. Americans have wanted the world to be like themselves, have thought it would be better off if it were, and have believed this transformation was not only attainable but the natural order of things if only certain specific obstacles could be removed and certain institutions, rather like their own, constructed.

The unfortunate consequence of pursuing unrealizable objectives is failure to achieve them, then disappointment and frustration at the failure (the more intense because the goals are seen as virtuous and natural), and, finally, reaction, impatience, and drawback—cycles of doing too much and too little. It is noticeable in the foreign policy of the United States that periods of pursuit of high goals are often followed by a spell of cynicism or defeatism.

---

9. Quoted in Chester G. Starr, *A History of the Ancient World* (New York: Oxford University Press, 1965), p. 491.

All these concepts and attitudes, and a consciousness of its own power and of the needs of a war-ravaged world as the American government conceived them, fused together to make up an explicit and extensive design for ordering the postwar international system. The Soviet Union's vision of the postwar world was vast in a historical sense but much narrower and more regional in the here and now. That of the United States was ideologically less articulated but worldwide in scope and concrete in details that reflected a conscious commitment to advance planning. This is not to say that all American leaders agreed at all times on a detailed set of policies. The processes of the American government were not then—and are not now—neat, tidy, or precise. But there was broad agreement on essentials. In their widest terms these included two things: replacing the old system of balance of power and spheres of influence with a worldwide security structure, the United Nations, that would be the first step toward an eventual system in which change as a result of the use of force would be abolished and the rule of law would be established; and establishing an economic system based on a worldwide open door—that is, lowering all barriers to trade and abolishing discriminatory barriers.

The American leaders who thought in such terms saw these goals as meritorious in themselves but also as entirely consistent with the interests of the greatest power on earth, whose well-being would be best preserved and advanced in a stable, orderly, and open world organized according to universal legal principles. Indeed, they thought this new order of the world, including its open door to American exports, was essential if the country's prosperity, social, and economic system, and democracy itself, all challenged in the thirties, were to be maintained. In their view, a system in which American interests coincided so well with those of everyone else could be brought into being on the basis of a combination of its self-evident merits (the long delayed natural order of international relations) and the suitable use of American power. The failure of the United States to implement some such design after 1918 had led straight to World War II, in their view. Now that the opportunity had come to try again, the same mistakes would not be made. American leadership would not fail again. For who else could lead? As Gaddis Smith put it, describing Dean Acheson's view in the early postwar years, "only the United States had the power to grab hold of history and make it conform."[10]

So obvious did all this seem to the American leaders that they failed to notice that their design might be seen by others as *theirs* and not the

10. Gaddis Smith, *Dean Acheson* (New York: Cooper Square Publishers, 1972), p. 416.

whole world's. Perhaps the main achievement of the revisionist reexamination has been to replace the earlier view of American policies as either self-evident truths or responses forced on us by others with a greater consciousness of interest, design, and the planned linkage of economic and political goals.

The American design for the world of 1945 closely resembled Wilson's. Roosevelt was an old Wilsonian, however much he had departed from Wilson's policies in the 1920s and 1930s for reasons of both conviction and expediency. He, along with Hull and many others, shared Wilson's antipathy to traditional European politics, to alliances and balance of power, to militarism and colonialism—all the things which they thought, not without reason, had led to war. They believed, like him, that the historically unique "liberal-exceptionalist" virtues of the free American political and—not least—economic system could Lockeanize a hitherto Hobbesian world and that, in the "stable liberal confines" of the new system, "a missionary America could find moral and economic pre-eminence."[11] What they assumed to be exceptional about this preeminence, in contrast to hegemonies of the past, was that America's good was good for all men and that America's interests were naturally the same as those of all nations. Thus, the world would be liberalized and americanized (in the broadest and best sense) at the same time, to the benefit of both the world and America.

Many of these ideas antedated December 1941 but they did not lead the United States to enter the war before it was attacked. Indeed, they probably did not have much to do with America's prewar policy. Rather, the Roosevelt administration moved along a slow path from the isolationism of the mid-thirties to policies of aid to Britain which were little short of acts of war against Germany because it believed that a German victory in Europe would at the least require converting America into a permanent garrison state, incompatible with its traditional way of life. Roosevelt recognized the importance of the German threat early but did not feel able to lead the country to act on his insight. He therefore moved with caution. It is not clear just when he decided that U.S. entry into the war was inevitable or when his policies passed over from helping Britain short of war to creating a situation likely to force the United States into war. In any case, once he decided that the United States must prevent a German victory, he understood that a U.S.–British victory would have to bring more than a return to the status quo ante.

The framework of Wilsonian goals came readily to hand, despite

11. This summary of the Wilson policy is drawn from the work of N. Gordon Levin, Jr., cited in footnote 1. The final quotation is on p. vii.

earlier neglect, reinforced by the specific experiences of the 1930s. The American government did not intend to leave the achievement of these goals to chance or improvisation. Official planning for the postwar world began in the Department of State as early as September 1939 and became more structured and comprehensive as time went on. Serious attention was given first to economic problems because, as the historian of the effort has said, "It was thought that the common interests of nations were more generally recognized in the economic than in the political field."[12]

Whether or not this was true, the interests of the United States were certainly more clearly defined in the economic sphere. For all the obvious uncertainties about when and how the war might end, the planners had a solid foundation of experience and policy on which to build. The Wilsonian objection to discriminatory economic arrangements was now powerfully reinforced for American leaders by the experience of the 1930s. It was widely accepted in the United States and elsewhere that an important underlying cause of German and Japanese aggression—perhaps even the main cause—was the economic depression and the policies that had both contributed to it and stemmed from it, and not least American protectionism. High and preferential tariffs; bilateral and barter trade; competitive devaluations; attempts to develop economic autarchy; colonial and cartel agreements to divide up markets, restrict distribution of raw materials, and control prices all were seen as impediments to full employment and the economic development, foreign trade, and prosperity of both the United States and others; fosterers of dictatorship; and main contributory causes of the war.

The American wartime policies directed to keeping down postwar international trade barriers, tariff and nontariff, followed on what had eventually become the main thrust (only partially realized in practice, as in the reciprocal trade legislation) of the New Deal's foreign economic policy. Similarly, the policies which led to the blueprinting of a new international monetary system at Bretton Woods reflected the experience of the thirties in the form of reaction against its practices, including American unwillingness in those years to take up the economic leadership which Britain was no longer able to continue. These policies were no mere rationalization of a quest for markets and raw materials, nor even a means to maintain full employment through exports. Nor were they deliberately chosen as preferable to domestic economic reform and redistribution, the alternative use for American "surplus" production

12. Harley A. Notter, *Postwar Foreign Policy Preparation 1939–1945* (Washington: Department of State, 1949), p. 23.

proposed by recent critics of wartime and postwar U.S. economic policy. American policymakers were internationalists as well as capitalists, and for political as well as economic reasons. Their policies reflected the whole of American experience, a powerful and persistent ideological and practical thrust which was seen as benefiting both the United States and the rest of the world indistinguishably. Nor were these policies thought to serve only economic purposes. Freer trade meant greater prosperity for all, prosperity meant—eventually at least—democracy, democracy meant peace.

Others, of course, did not see the matter in the same way—not least the British. They found American objections to special economic spheres of interest directed squarely at imperial preference. They were right. American leaders, liberal and conservative, not only objected to British colonialism in general but agreed before, during, and after the war that imperial preference was unjust to the British dominions and colonies, unfair to American trade, prejudicial to international prosperity, and therefore to peace.

These ideas on international trade and finance were invoked with— and against—the British during the war, usually in the context of broader policies. Thus, a qualified pledge of cooperation by the two governments to promote equal access by all countries to trade and raw materials was included in the Atlantic charter (August 1941). More specifically, as part of the lend-lease agreement (February 1942) American diplomacy forced the British to agree in principle to work for the reduction of tariffs and the elimination of trade discrimination (such as imperial preference) between the two countries after the war.

A third step in building the postwar economic order was taken at Bretton Woods in July 1944. There, forty-four countries followed up on long U.S.–U.K. negotiations and agreed to establish the International Bank for Reconstruction and Development and the International Monetary Fund. The former was to provide capital to war-impacted areas. The latter was designed to prevent a recurrence of the disruptive monetary disorder of the thirties by establishing, for the first time, conscious international control of the monetary system. To that end the fund was given a certain authority—not very clearly defined because of British reluctance as creditors—to address the economic policy of member states that turned to it for help in adjusting short-term balance of payments difficulties (by borrowing foreign exchange from it) or "fundamental" disequilibrium (by changing their exchange rates beyond the narrow range permitted by the agreement). Both institutions embodied American multilateral goals and would be, if not under American control, under preponderant U.S. influence. The Soviet Union sent delegates to Bretton Woods but did not join either organization.

The fourth step was the U.S. loan to Britain, signed after the war ended (December 1945) but a direct (if unforeseen) outgrowth of wartime thinking. In return for this and the writing-off of lend-lease debts, the British promised early partial convertibility of sterling (which was essential sooner or later for the eventual implementation of the Bretton Woods agreement) despite the Labour Party's fear that this would hobble economic planning and full employment. They also joined in pledging action toward assuming "the obligations of multilateral trade." To that end the two governments simultaneously issued proposals for expanding world trade and employment which were the outcome of several years of British-American negotiations.

These American policies laid the long-term foundations for the postwar world, or at least for the large part of the world susceptible to American influence. But they had little to do with the origin of the cold war. First, the United States and Great Britain had reached at least a working agreement before the end of the war on relevant institutions and goals if not on policies and timing. Second, and more to the point, Anglo-American relations, important as they were for postwar economic planning, were not the focal point of the postwar global balance of power. Soviet-American relations were. Universalistic as was the American economic plan in theory, it is most unlikely that Roosevelt could have seen it as the touchstone in itself of postwar relations with the Russians, if, indeed, he even expected the Soviet Union to join. Economic issues (notably aid) were an item, but a secondary one, on the agenda of wartime U.S.–Soviet relations. Roosevelt almost certainly saw the postwar relationship as turning on political issues. So did the Russians. And he and they were right.

The political side of the American design, which was developed more slowly than the economic, came to be centered officially on the United Nations organization. Like American economic planning, it was tailored as a matter of course to American conceptions. Deliberately but almost instinctively, the United States made sure that a large majority of the General Assembly were nations likely to follow its lead (including many Latin American countries that had taken no part in the war) and that its voice was likely to be preponderant also in the Security Council (supported among the permanent members by the British and by China, that fictitious great power imposed by the United States on its doubtful allies).

But the formal Wilsonian structure of the United Nations was not the whole or even the core of Roosevelt's design. For the world security system was to be built in reality on the continued harmony of the principal wartime allies, those that Roosevelt called the four policemen: the United States, the Soviet Union, Great Britain, and China. (France was a marginal member in his eyes, though it obtained nominal "great power" rank at the San Francisco conference, and China was certainly marginal in the eyes of both the British and the Russians.) Peace in the future would depend on the prompt use of force against peacebreakers, and only the great powers possessed such force. The permanent members of the Security Council, therefore, were armed with a veto. They could not be coerced by the organization as such; all others could be coerced by them in the name of the organization. The system was clearly seen to depend on the consensus of the main victors. Without that the organization could not work and peace could not be assured.

This plan shared some characteristics of Wilson's but the roles of the great and small powers were quite different. For all its idealistic, moralistic, and legal embodiment in the complex apparatus of the UN, to the detailed perfection of which American policymakers devoted so much attention in 1944 and 1945, it was by no means unrealistic. If the main wartime allies could hang together—as the victors over Napoleon did manage to do in large part for forty years—then peace probably could be assured on the basis of the postwar distribution of power. If not, not.

In seeking to revive Wilson's League of Nations on this basis, Roosevelt was perhaps too ready to assume that the considerations that bound the major allies in wartime would carry over into peace, and that all of them would then behave as status quo powers, more interested in defending the postwar settlement (but against whom?) than in changing it. The widespread disorder that followed the war and the subsequent breakup of the colonial empires provided obvious temptations to those who might want and were able to benefit from such changes. Perhaps, however, Roosevelt was confident that American economic and military power could lead the Soviet Union and other possible recalcitrants, by one means or another, along the right path. Or perhaps he was not confident at all that this plan could be made to work but saw no acceptable alternative to trying. In any case, the historians of the new left have not succeeded in clearing Roosevelt of the heinous charge, leveled by the old right of the 1950s, that he tried to get along with the Russians.

For the design had fundamental validity then, and has it still. The international organization itself had several symbolic purposes, including that of conspicuously committing the United States to continuous participation in world affairs in a form that was alleged to be very different from the old balance of power system which Americans, leaders and people, decried. Behind it, nevertheless, was a realistic attempt to achieve some degree of world order by concertation among the major powers, at least to the extent of preventing major war. That attempt has not been one that could be safely abandoned forever. It may have been bound to fail on the first try because Germany had been much more completely defeated than Napoleonic France and there was no parallel in the world after 1945 to the fear of a French revival, which to some extent held the allied coalition together long after 1815. The world was too clearly in the hands of the victorious superpowers for them to set limits on their rivalry for that reason. And each saw an ideological threat in the other rather than, as after 1815, in a defeated but still powerful enemy. Curiously, however, the military uses of atomic energy emerged just then to provide the common threat that in due course prompted the beginning of a new phase of Soviet-American détente and even cooperation—but only after a long detour of hostile confrontation.

Even during the war there were many Americans, not excluding many in the government, who remained fundamentally anti-Communist in ideology and anti-Soviet in policy and who were skeptical or worse about the chances for U.S.–Soviet cooperation when peace came. After all, official relations were established between the two countries only eight years before they became allies and following fifteen years of cold war in miniature. The very scope of the Red Army's success, though it commanded admiration, gave new fuel to fears held throughout the inter-war period about the uses to which Soviet power would be put. This distrust was made up, in different proportions for different people, of fear of Soviet military expansion into Europe and China once German and Japanese power was removed; doubts that the USSR would accept integration into the American political and economic program; concern that postwar disorder would let local Communist parties, assumed to be under Soviet control, take power; and plain all-out ideological anti-Bolshevism, which was older than any specific quarrels with the Soviet state and had roots in considerations of domestic policy, even in the absence of any such differences. All these elements were visible in the American response to developments in Eastern Europe from 1944 on, discussed in the next chapters, and they eventually became the dominant theme in U.S.–Soviet postwar relations.

But they became so as a result of a series of events in which both Soviet and American actions figured and of the way each saw and responded to the other's actions. They were not dominant in Roosevelt's wartime approach to the problem of postwar relations. On the contrary, he remained faithful in this respect to the earlier and more fundamental formulation of Wilsonianism, before the October Revolution and its sequels made Bolshevik Russia an enemy to the American design for the world. Unlike many other American leaders of World War II who were inspired by the Wilsonian vision, Roosevelt's view of the world did not include the ideological and political anti-Bolshevism which became an important part of Wilson's policy in 1918–19 (and, again, of Truman's after 1945). Stalin was not on his list of incorrigible evildoers. Though a dictator at home, he was not seen as an aggressor abroad. To Roosevelt the ideological division of World War II was simpler than that which faced Wilson at the end of World War I and forced him to adapt his policies accordingly. There was militarist Germany and its allies on one side, all its enemies on the other. Business could be done with the latter but not the former.

This led Roosevelt in 1941, cautiously and slowly, to decide to extend massive military aid through lend-lease to the USSR. He rejected counsel to extract political concessions in return. In his view the Soviet military position was too weak, the understanding between Washington and Moscow too tenuous, to risk pressing the Russians as he did not hesitate to press the British on other matters. Roosevelt no doubt hoped that wartime aid might improve the prospects for postwar collaboration. But that was not a major motive for giving aid. Russia could help win the war with maximum speed and minimum cost to the United States. Its defeat or a separate peace with Germany—he thought of 1917 and 1939— would be catastrophic. That was motive enough for Roosevelt to provide the utmost help possible and to do so with the utmost accommodation to the demanding and secretive Russians.

Once the tide of war had turned Roosevelt held to this basic line of dealing with the Russians, with respect to continued military aid but also to other issues as they emerged. In his view the Soviet Union was needed for the peace just as it had been needed for the war. Hard *quid* for *quo* bargaining would not achieve what he wanted and he continued to resist that policy, increasingly urged by many advisers, until the end of his life.

It is tempting to believe that Roosevelt at his most pessimistic thought of the USSR much as Wilson had thought of Japan in 1919: as a country which was inclined to resort to the bad old policies but which, by careful handling, might be brought along to see the benefits to itself of entering the new system. Colonel House in 1918 asked the Japanese ambassador to Washington whether his country intended to follow the path of German or American civilization—that is, the old order of international life or the new.[13] Roosevelt must have thought about the Soviet Union

13. Levin, *Woodrow Wilson and World Politics*, p. 118.

during the war in just that way, concerned about some of its policies but hopeful that basic agreement compatible with American interests might be achieved on the large issues if the United States dealt fairly with the Russians, refrained from demanding a concession in return for every benefit, and gave them a respected place in world affairs.

One important tactic of Roosevelt's strategy for dealing with the Russians, his policy of putting off decisions on territorial questions until the end of the war, was challenged by the Russians, who wanted acceptance of the frontiers they sought in Eastern Europe, and also by the British, who understood much better than the Americans did that their own relative power would wane rapidly after the war ended. The policy was also questioned within the U.S. government. Isaiah Bowman, serving as a member of a special committee advising Secretary Hull on postwar problems, wrote in March 1943:

> Russia has need, first, for a western border strengthened by the tangible additions that improve Russia's position militarily. Without adjustments on that border she will neither disarm, nor guarantee postwar boundaries, nor enter a general security system. . . .
>
> I would begin by serving Soviet interests on the assumption that if we cannot force her either now or later to our desired course of action, or stop her if she resorts to force at Petsamo, or on the Baltic shore, or in Bessarabia, we must come to terms with her and terms will be lighter now than later. I would begin with agreeing with her on the western border and make the best terms possible. . . .[14]

This sensible view got nowhere in Washington in 1943, nor in 1944 when the Polish problem became acute (see the next chapter). Those who hoped to cooperate with Russia after the war reversed Bowman's logic, believing that these matters would become less important for Soviet security and therefore less difficult to resolve once the new international system was established. Those who were skeptical about such cooperation thought American bargaining power would be greater at the end of the war. No one at the decision-making level saw the merit, as Churchill did, of striking the best deal possible with the Russians as the preface to establishing the postwar order. Certainly no one thought of an understanding on spheres of influence as a prerequisite to doing so. On the contrary, such an approach was seen as the most basic challenge to the American vision of the postwar period. Even conservative State

14. Lynn Etheridge Davis, *The Cold War Begins* (Princeton, N. J.: Princeton University Press, 1974), pp. 80–81, quoting from the Bowman memorandum in the papers of Cordell Hull.

Department officials seemed to see the problem of Eastern Europe in 1943–44 as being, not Soviet policy, but the reappearance of power politics. Not only Russia but also Britain, whose postwar power was overestimated by Americans during and after the war, was seen as a sinner in this respect.

Just before he died Roosevelt began to express concern about Soviet policies, particularly in Poland, which seemed to be the old power politics at its worst, hegemonic and unilateral. He was also shaken by the brutal expression of Soviet mistrust evoked by the U.S.–U.K. negotiation over the surrender of German forces in Italy. Partly for these reasons, but also because of the political delicacy of the whole question of postwar aid to the Allies, his response to Soviet requests for such aid were reserved.

It cannot be known whether he, like his successor, would have permitted Eastern European issues to become the rock on which prospects for Soviet-American cooperation foundered, or whether he would have persevered in his earlier approach. Even if he had done so, we cannot know whether his idea of cooperation with the USSR could have been made compatible in the long run with Soviet policy priorities or what the Soviet response to such an effort would have been. Certainly Roosevelt did not lack confidence in the rightness and beneficence of American plans for the postwar world, economic and political; could not have failed to see that the Soviet Union would probably be an isolated member of his projected world directorate of four or five powers; and gave no clear sign before his death that he grasped the full implications for his own plans of the fact that the Soviet Union emerged from the war as a co-victor with the United States and a state that could be expected to have policy goals of its own with which America's, at best, would have to be compromised (in both senses) if the alliance was to be preserved. Roosevelt may well have had so much faith in his own ideas and in his ability to persuade the Russians of their correctness that, if he failed, he might have turned strongly against them and, like his successors, consigned them to the camp of evil men with whom no business could be done.

On the other side of such speculation, however, are the facts that he did go some distance during the war toward accepting—or at least not rejecting—certain Soviet policies, and, above all, that he had a basically sound view of postwar power realities, of the newness of the postwar world. His grasp of the implications of the war for the European colonial empires, for example, was much nearer the mark than Churchill's or de Gaulle's (as his prewar appraisal of the German threat had been clearer than those of the British and French leaders of the thirties). His espousal of China's role as a great power, however self-interested his motives, has turned out to be, perhaps ironically, prophetic. His emphasis on the practical importance of great power cooperation was analytically sound and might also have been constructive policy. Addressed squarely to the Soviet Union, it offered the Russians cooperation along with global responsibility.

As Roosevelt became increasingly aware of the scope of the Soviet victory, he might have become more and not less convinced, in light of the stakes, of the necessity of pursuing the attempt to cooperate with the USSR. This, after all, was inherent in the institutional structure of the American political plan for the postwar world, which Roosevelt saw as only the first step in the process of making and keeping peace. He did not have to be certain of success to judge it worthwhile to persevere in trying to reach an agreement with the USSR on the fundamentals of the bilateral relationship, if not on all aspects of it. He was an optimist, to begin with, and a realist. He believed in the effectiveness of personal diplomacy, both in principle and in his own practice. He also had reason to know that an American administration could powerfully lead public opinion, that policy did not have to be the prisoner of presumed popular attitudes. Besides, what foreseeable alternative to trying was there but conflict, and perhaps war?

Whatever Roosevelt might have done about the situation the United States confronted at the end of the war in Europe, we know that his successor and the Soviet government together participated in a series of events which led, in fact, to the cold war. Wilson in 1918 did not like what the Japanese proposed to do in China and Siberia but found it prudent to acquiesce in what he could not prevent and to work along with his ally where their policies seemed to coincide. The American problem with the USSR was far more serious, for it was a much more important ally in 1945 than the Japanese had been in 1918 and its actions in Eastern Europe were far more visible to the world, and to the American public, than Japanese actions had been in the Shantung peninsula. The American government under Truman proved unwilling to accept the stern implications of a policy of seeking cooperation with the USSR on a realistic basis.

Certainly an elaborate international structure where some deference was paid to the sensibilities and even the interests of lesser states was not the Soviet vision of the future. The Russians could not have been expected to take the formal framework of the UN very seriously, nor to have been unwary of a body which, at its inception, was bound to be under the control of capitalist states. Their concern would grow as American emphasis shifted (even before Roosevelt's death) from the great power directorate to insistence on certain rights for the smaller countries. Nevertheless, they were willing to enter the organization at American prompting, and to take enough interest in it to put considerable effort into trying to shape its procedures to suit themselves while not rejecting realistic compromises—notably in the matter of the veto. Their willingness to take part in a structure so likely to be under the control of hostile states no doubt followed from a willingness to take part in the great power directorate which lay behind the UN as Roosevelt expounded it to them. But to them both the organization and the directorate, if they were to work at all, had to be based on a great power concert which would not supersede but reflect the respective spheres and interests of the main powers. And this, in turn, required the mutual respect by the great powers of each other as such, and of each other's interests.

Here was where the American design as Roosevelt's successors applied it came into immediate and fatal conflict with the highest priority Soviet policies. The United States for many reasons did not accept that its conception of the postwar world would have to be adjusted to the interests of a powerful co-victor. It did not accept the manner or the outcome of Soviet policy in Poland and Rumania. It did not accept the creation of a closed economic bloc in Eastern Europe—not because of significant commercial interests there, past or future, but because *any* such bloc not only signified the exclusion of American influence but challenged its postwar security, political, and economic design, which was universalistic and hostile to special blocs, whether economic or political. Above all, the Americans refused to accept that the United Nations and its great power directorate might be built on a system of spheres of influence.

Few American leaders in 1945 would agree with foreign cynics that the United States had its own sphere of influence in Latin America, not to mention China, Italy, and the rest of Western Europe, and perhaps hoped to extend it by the use of its great economic power. Secretary of War Henry Stimson could refer in all innocence to "our little region over here which has never bothered anybody."[15] It is true that Stimson, almost alone among American leaders, could wonder at the same time whether it was politic for his government to object so strongly to the spheres of others. After all, Great Britain as well as the USSR had signed the Atlantic Charter with reservations to protect its special interests, and there was official American hostility to British imperial policies too. But he overlooked the difference in American eyes between American

15. Quoted by Richard Barnet in Lynn H. Miller and Ronald W. Preussen, eds., *Reflections on the Cold War* (Philadelphia: Temple University Press, 1974), p. 150.

methods in Latin America and Soviet methods in Eastern Europe. He also overlooked that the Russians could not see the American presence in Latin America as a threat, while his countrymen could easily see Eastern Europe as a Soviet springboard westward.

Stimson's approach therefore did not find any greater favor with Truman than with Roosevelt. Faced by the reality of an emerging Soviet sphere of influence in Eastern Europe, the American government refused to accept the form this took—and, perhaps as important, the means used to bring it about—as compatible with Russian participation in the postwar peace order. Since such acceptance was a *necessary* condition of Soviet cooperation—it is impossible to know whether it would have been a *sufficient* condition—whatever chance there was for that system was doomed.

Before the implications of the incompatibility of American and Soviet policies were fully grasped, however, the United States made an effort to change, not its own design or its attitude toward what the USSR was doing, but Soviet policy. That is, it tried to bring the Soviet Union into the American design for the postwar world on American terms. The Polish problem was the occasion for this effort. Its failure launched the cold war to come.

CHAPTER 6

The Cold War Begins

Louis J. Halle correctly observed that "There is a sense in which the Cold War, like World War II, began with a Western attempt to rescue a Poland that was beyond its reach."[1] If the Big Three had not fallen out in early 1945 over the Polish question they might well have done so on some other issue, particularly the disposition of defeated Germany. But in fact their first great quarrel was about Poland, and the circumstances of that quarrel colored their relations thereafter in a particular way. The cold war began between the Yalta and Potsdam conferences with respect to Poland; the more important deadlock of the Allied effort to devise a common policy toward Germany was a consequence and not a cause of the conflict that was already underway.

Poland was almost certain to be a major topic of Allied discord. It was the Soviet Union's most important neighbor in Eastern Europe. As such, and because of the centuries-long history of bad relations between the two countries, Poland's frontiers and postwar regime were at the top of the list of Soviet policy preoccupations. Great Britain also continued to take an interest in Poland's fate, having gone to war, together with France, to defend it in 1939. The Western powers might have prevented the outbreak of war had they been willing to make the kind of deal with Stalin at Poland's expense which Hitler had no hesitation making. They were not and war came. Poland was then lost, France was lost, Great Britain was driven from the continent, the Soviet Union was invaded and ravaged, and at the end of it all the issue which the grand-alliance-to-be could not resolve in 1939 was still waiting for solution—but in very different circumstances.

The United States, of course, had *not* gone to war in 1939 to save Poland. One scholar has said that, if we could understand why the United States wanted to deny to the Russians in 1945 what it conceded to the Germans in 1939, we would be near to explaining the origins of the cold war.[2] In fact, the question is not so difficult to answer. By 1945 the United States had been through more than three years of war fought in the name of principles it took seriously with respect to Allies as well as

1. Louis J. Halle, *The Cold War as History* (New York: Harper & Row, 1967), p. 57.
2. Norman A. Graebner, "Cold War Origins and the Continuing Debate," *Journal of Conflict Resolution* 13 (March 1969), p. 131.

enemies; had designed plans for a better postwar world on a scale proportional to the effort made in winning the war; and had become a global power that was unwilling to be excluded from presence and influence in any part of the world, including Eastern Europe. It is not surprising, therefore, that the Polish question became for the United States a touchstone of Soviet cooperativeness in settling problems in common and, in general, of the Soviet Union's willingness to take its part and find its security in what I have described in chapter 5 as the American design for the postwar world.

It is even less surprising that the Russian leaders saw this very important matter as a touchstone of Western attitudes toward *them*. Poland had been partitioned between Germany and Russia in 1939, but when war broke out between them in June 1941 the Germans quickly overran the rest of the country. The Soviet government established diplomatic relations with the Polish government-in-exile in London, but in the darkest days of the war Russian leaders emphasized to their allies that they expected to regain that part of Poland which they had seized in 1939 and to which, in their view, they had both ethnic and historic claims. The Russians made much of the fact that most of the area they claimed had been assigned to them by an Allied commission in 1919 but then was forcibly seized by the new Polish state. Stalin said that he could not explain to the Russian people why, after a victorious war, they should accept a less satisfactory frontier than Curzon and Clemenceau had been willing to give them in the dark period of defeat and civil war after World War I.

The Polish government-in-exile, however, would not agree to these Soviet demands, even when they were joined with promises of Russian support in annexing much German territory in compensation. Polish nationalism had long been bitterly anti-Russian, and the authoritarian regime that ruled Poland between the wars was strongly anti-Bolshevik as well. The London Poles, like the prewar leaders of their country, feared alliance with Russia almost as much as conflict with Germany.

The underlying rancor between the exiled Polish government and the Russians came to the surface when, in April 1943, the Germans announced that they had found a mass grave in the Katyn Forest in the Ukraine which contained the bodies of 10,000 Polish officers. They accused the Soviet Union of the crime. The London Poles, who had been trying without success to discover what had become of the many Polish officers taken prisoner by the Russians in 1939, asked the Red Cross to investigate. The Russians, taking this to mean that the government-in-exile gave credence to the German charge, broke diplomatic relations with it. They were never reestablished.

Even before this break the Russians had set up a Moscow group called the Union of Polish Patriots, mostly but not all Communists, which put itself forward as a future political force in Poland. The Russians may have intended from the first that this group would eventually rule Poland. At the least they intended that it would play a much more important role there after the war than the Polish Communist party had played before 1939. When the Red Army entered eastern Poland in January 1944 this group came with it and in July was established in Lublin (west of the Curzon line) as the Polish Committee of National Liberation. On the last day of 1944 the committee retitled itself the provisional government of Poland, and on January 5, 1945, the Soviet Union recognized it. Two weeks later the Red Army entered Warsaw with the provisional government in its train.

Churchill, seeing how the land would lie in Eastern Europe once the Red Army entered Poland, urged the London Poles to reach an accommodation with Moscow. He did not succeed. He himself was ready in May 1942 to recognize the 1941 Soviet frontiers. But he was restrained from doing so by the United States, which did not want frontier questions to be raised at that time. At Teheran, however, in December 1943, Churchill agreed to accept the so-called Curzon line of 1919—to which the Russians had reduced their demands—as the eastern frontier of Poland. Roosevelt did not agree, on the ground that he did not want to make such a commitment before the 1944 presidential election. Nothing was put in writing but from Stalin's point of view the matter of the frontier must have seemed settled. At the same time it was understood that Poland would annex most of East Prussia and a large (but undetermined) slice of eastern Germany.

By then the question of frontiers had given way to the more important issue of who was to rule Poland. Throughout 1944 Churchill continued to urge the London Poles to accept the Curzon line and to reach an agreement with Moscow, but still without success. The American government, faithful to its policy of avoiding territorial commitments, and with an eye to the presidential election and the Polish vote, did not exert such pressure. The effect was to give the London Poles reason to hope that they might look to Washington for support against Moscow. It would have been odd if the Soviet government did not reach the same conclusion.

It must remain uncertain, at least until the Soviet archives are opened, whether there was any possibility that the Russians might have refrained from setting up a pro-Communist regime if the London Poles, as Churchill urged, had courted Moscow's benevolence by keeping quiet about the Katyn Forest massacre and settled the frontier question as best they could. As events turned out, the stubbornness of the London group on the frontier question allowed the Russians to claim that it clearly could not be the desired "friendly" government which they thought themselves entitled—and enabled—to see established in Warsaw.

But even if the London Poles had fully understood the hard realities of their country's postwar situation adjacent to a victorious Soviet Union, it is still difficult to believe that any more or less representative government chosen in Poland could have allied itself with the USSR after giving up a third of the country's territory. The Russians were probably not displeased that the Katyn quarrel and the frontier question provided occasions for rupture with the London Poles and for setting up a government bound to depend on themselves. The bitterness on both sides of the ancient Russian-Polish quarrel makes it unlikely that anything any group of Poles might have done could have saved Poland from Soviet satellization in the European power structure of 1945. There is less ambiguity about Soviet policy toward Poland than toward any other country in Eastern Europe.

The broader importance of this issue is that tacit American support for the London Poles in 1944 opened up a decisive quarrel with the Soviet Union. Once the Red Army was in control of most of Poland, and the Lublin committee was administering the country under Russian authority, the painful question arose of what relations were to be worked out, if any, between the Warsaw group recognized by the USSR and the London group recognized by the Western powers.

By the principles of *realpolitik*, it should have been obvious from the start that, unless the Western Allies wanted to fight the Soviet Union to save Poland, power there would go to the protégés of the Red Army, then in control of the country. Churchill appears to have seen this clearly throughout the war, and to have told the London Poles in no uncertain terms, and with increasing brutality as 1944 drew to a close, that Allied cooperation was more important to him than they were. Since the Soviet Union was in possession and willing to risk a crisis with the Western Allies to have its way in this essential case if in any, the only options left open to the Allies were either to swallow the *fait accompli* in the hope of maintaining some degree of postwar cooperation with the USSR or to challenge what the Russians were doing, at whatever cost to postwar relations. In neither case could they expect to have any appreciable impact on events in Poland, as their impotence during the Warsaw uprising (August-September 1944) clearly advertised.

At the Yalta conference Roosevelt and Churchill leaned toward the first course. Both disavowed any great national interest in Poland, the former citing face as a basis of his concern, the latter citing honor. They

tried, however, to mitigate, perhaps with some hope of eventually modifying, the stark Soviet control that had already begun to fall over
Poland. The fact that the Russians already occupied the country and
were less than 50 miles from Berlin when the conference took place,
while the Western Allies had not yet crossed the Rhine, no doubt colored
the discussion. Much of the conference was taken up with haggling
about how to put the London and Warsaw Polish groups together in one
provisional government which all the Allies could recognize and which
would conduct "free and unfettered" elections, in the language of the
Yalta agreement. The legislative history and the actual wording of the
understanding finally reached after much debate leave no doubt that the
Big Three intended that the provisional government then functioning in
Warsaw (which was named in the agreement) was to be reorganized into
a new Provisional Government of National Unity by the addition of
other Poles from inside and outside the country, including some from
the London government-in-exile (which was not named). How new this
government would be depended on how many non-Lublin Poles it
contained and in what positions. But the balance clearly lay toward
Lublin and away from London.

It is hard to believe that Roosevelt and Churchill, after this long and
involved discussion, did not know how widely different were their intentions from Stalin's. But they also knew what they were doing when they
settled for the enlargement of the Lublin government. Though Churchill had said that those who conducted elections in certain countries
tended to win, presumably he and Roosevelt thought that the promised
Polish elections (which Stalin said might take place within a month)
would permit something other than a purely Communist government to
emerge, and that, but for the Yalta agreement, there was no hope at all
for such a result. This did not reflect naive optimism but was, as Churchill said, the best they could get.

The same hope-against-hope reasoning applied to the rest of Eastern
Europe no doubt lay behind their support of the vague Declaration on
Liberated Europe. This embodied the American attempt to prevent the
emergence of spheres of influence and undemocratic regimes in Eastern
Europe and to obtain a voice in the affairs of the area without commit-
ting itself to any concrete line of action. The specific problems of the
Eastern countries were not addressed.

The Yalta agreement with respect to Poland, however, proved no
easier to implement than to negotiate. Even before Roosevelt's death, on
April 12, a good deal of conflict had arisen about how the Warsaw and
London Poles were to be brought together. Some American officials
came to doubt that Yalta would in any way mitigate Soviet control of

Poland. Several other issues also soured Allied relations at that time: a Yugoslav attempt to seize the area of Trieste; almost continuous wrangling at the San Francisco conference about the structure of the United Nations; increasing Soviet control of the areas occupied by the Red Army in Eastern Europe. In these circumstances the new Truman administration quickly adopted a firm attitude toward what it saw as Soviet violations of Allied agreements. In this spirit Truman delivered a stern lecture to Molotov in late April, demanding Soviet adherence to the application of the Yalta agreement on Poland as the latter was interpreted in Washington. This quarrel erupted openly at the San Francisco conference where the United States not only blocked the seating of the Warsaw government but took part in a fierce and wide-ranging confrontation with the Russians.

Yet the American government's new firmness was erratic, more probably tactical than strategic. Thus, Truman did not accept Churchill's proposals that the Western armies should seize Prague or hold on to the territory in the Soviet zone-to-be in Germany that they had occupied. Then, alarmed by the war of words at San Francisco and by the cautionings of Henry Stimson, Joseph Davies, and others, he sent the russophile Davies on a mission to Churchill (a clear signal in itself of Truman's desire to distance himself from British policy) and Harry Hopkins on a mission to Stalin. There the United States (in Britain's absence) practically abandoned its case on Polish affairs as part of an arrangement which also included Soviet concessions on United Nations issues. The United States agreed—again—that the Warsaw government would be the core to which other Polish leaders would be added. After further negotiations some London Poles joined the Warsaw regime, which the United States then recognized, but the Communists retained control. American policy did not let go of the shadow of the Polish issue even after the Stalin-Hopkins agreement. But, after swinging from firmness in April to compromise in June, its intermittent recriminations were increasingly irrelevant to events in Poland.

There was a curious postscript to the Polish affair. The American government had paid little attention during the war to Eastern Europe except for Poland. It had acquiesced in the armistice agreements the Soviet Union imposed on Germany's satellites. Though it had not liked the Churchill-Stalin spheres of influence agreement of October 1944, it had made little fuss in early 1945 about the progressive imposition of Soviet control over Rumania and Bulgaria. Even Vishinsky's brutal actions in Bucharest in March, coming so soon after the Russians had signed the Declaration on Liberated Europe at Yalta, had produced only shock, not action. Clearly the U.S. government wanted to adhere to its

principles while avoiding involvement and commitment in these countries.

But in June 1945 Washington suddenly took up the cudgels against
Russian policy in Rumania and Bulgaria. It complained that the Soviet
Union was violating the Yalta agreement and that, in particular, the
Russian commander-in-chief in those countries had openly relegated the
representatives of the other two Allies to the sidelines (as the Americans
and British had done to the Soviet representative in Italy—a fact which
gave the Russians an argument with which to defend, though not the
motive for, their own actions). The United States refused to recognize or
sign peace treaties with these two countries until their governments were
reorganized.

This American effort in the summer of 1945 was even more badly
timed than the Polish campaign and had even worse prospects for
success. If in the Polish case the United States seemed, at least at first, to
be trying to lead the Soviet Union to accept the principles of a cooperative, non–sphere of influence postwar order, in the subsequent episodes
its motive seems to have been to assert the right of a great power not to
be excluded from the affairs of any part of Europe. But the United
States had even less leverage in southeast Europe than in Poland.
Perhaps, however, it was mainly a case of piling up grievances as bargaining counters with the USSR, because the United States gave up
active interest in these countries as part of a comprehensive agreement
with the Soviet Union concluded in December at a three-power meeting
in Moscow. After agitating the Balkan issues at Potsdam and the London
foreign ministers meeting that followed, and constantly reaffirming the
Yalta principles while doing nothing about them, in Moscow the United
States traded a promise to recognize the Rumanian government—its one
card—for Soviet acceptance of a trivial broadening of it. What Washington got in return was much more important to it than the Balkans: in
addition to an understanding on how the peace treaties for Germany's
ex-satellites would be prepared, the Russians acquiesced in American
domination of the occupation of Japan and accepted the U.S.–U.K.–
Canadian plan for United Nations' handling of the atomic energy
question. James Byrnes, the American Secretary of State, was much
criticized when he came home for "appeasing" the Russians. Even so,
Moscow marked the end, for all practical purposes, of the American
effort to change Soviet policy in the Balkans, just as the Hopkins mission
had marked the end of the attempt to change Soviet policy in Poland.

Throughout the development of the Polish issue Soviet purposes are
clear with respect both to frontiers and to the overriding importance
the Russians attached to the nature of the postwar Polish regime. They

had probably predetermined that that regime would have to be Communist-dominated; if they initially had any flexibility on this point, it was canceled out early by the attitude of the London Poles. This primordial security objective, as events showed, took clear precedence over relations with the Western Allies. The Yalta agreement on Poland must have seemed to Stalin a mere figleaf to conceal Soviet control, and he must have thought that the Allies also saw it as such.

The British position also was quite clear. Churchill saw no point in quarreling with the Soviet Union over an issue on which the Western powers had so little leverage—or at least that was his position until, in the spring of 1945 when the Polish problem was practically settled, he began to favor taking a firmer line toward the Russians across the board.

For all the great importance of the Polish case in determining the postwar attitudes of the wartime Allies toward each other, it is nevertheless hard to get a fully satisfying grasp on the American position. A precise definition of American interests in Poland—obviously negligible before the war—was never made. In this case as in others Roosevelt tried to avoid all commitments on frontiers because he believed that such issues divided the Allies and, in any case, were of marginal importance compared to the question of setting up the postwar security system. Apparently he was not concerned that irreversible *faits accomplis* might be created by others while his government deferred decisions. Nevertheless, he tacitly accepted the Curzon line and the principle of compensation for Poland at Germany's expense. But he continued to put up a struggle for the London Poles, and the longer the quarrel lasted the more important it became, whatever its origins and merits, as a test case of Soviet-American relations.

Roosevelt at the start was concerned with Polish-American opinion, as he admitted at Teheran. Besides, he was sympathetic to the London Poles. Whatever their weaknesses and the deficiencies of the prewar Polish regime, they were the spokesmen for men who had fought heroically in Poland in 1939 and in various other theaters during the war and had a good press in the West. This consideration mingled with concern for the rights of the Poles under the Atlantic Charter to control their own fate—that is, with the ideological component of wartime and postwar American policy. It is sometimes forgotten that American ideology was much more than anti-Communist at the start of the cold war. It had a positive side as well as a negative. This was shown, for example, when Harry Hopkins told Stalin in May 1945 that the United States wanted Poland to be friendly to the Soviet Union but also to have a representative parliamentary regime and such accoutrements of a free society as a bill of rights and habeas corpus. This, with respect to a country which had rarely if ever enjoyed such institutions, was more nearly naiveté than disingenuousness. But these were among the things for which America had fought the war. They reflected a genuine and important strand of American thinking about Eastern Europe, potentially contributory to but distinguishable from crude anti-Sovietism.

It is absurd to dismiss such thinking as window dressing or hypocrisy on the ground that policymakers, unlike everyone else, are moved by nothing less tangible than economic calculations, and even more absurd to dismiss to the wings of policymaking those who, like Roosevelt and Hopkins, clearly took these things seriously. All American policymakers were children of the whole American system, not only its economic aspects. For many of them Soviet infringement of the principles of the Atlantic Charter was a serious matter, and not only because they believed that a new international organization could not be made acceptable to the American people unless it was based on those principles. So serious, in fact, that the official response to Soviet actions in Eastern Europe can better be described as an attitude than a policy—an attitude, as Hans Morgenthau called it, of "moral disenchantment" in face of the persistence of practices the war had been fought to eradicate.[3] Certainly there was little case-by-case and step-by-step calculation in what they did, or coherent joining of ends and means.

This ideological reflex became increasingly connected from late 1944 on with another consideration, the American objection to the Soviet Union's imposing the Lublin government on Poland by a unilateral act. This return to power politics was not only sharply at odds with the Atlantic Charter and the non–sphere of influence basis of Roosevelt's proposed postwar order but excluded the Western Allies from their due share of postwar influence in Eastern Europe. Even though Roosevelt went far at Yalta to sanction that act, he apparently thought even then that the promised elections would prevent total satellization and the total elimination from Poland of non-Soviet influence, two elements of the situation that were linked. The position he took on the problem just before his death suggests that by then he felt deceived in hopes which he had taken seriously, however little reason he may have had to do so.

Such talk as there was in the American government about economic interests in Poland, as in the later disputes over Romania and Bulgaria, more likely reflected a hope of establishing some basis, however minor, for balancing Soviet political preponderance than serious economic considerations as such. An American economic presence seemed to offer the

3. Hans J. Morgenthau, ed., *Germany and the Future of Europe* (Chicago: University of Chicago Press, 1951), p. 80.

best opportunities for minimally balancing the Soviet Union's preponderant political presence—that is, preventing an exclusive Soviet sphere of influence. Roosevelt saw no inconsistency between efforts to establish an entente with the USSR and refusal to accept complete American exclusion from the affairs of any part of Europe. On the contrary, he saw inconsistency in the reverse. This objective of obtaining at least a minimal role in Eastern Europe inspired much of American policy toward that area through 1945. It did not necessarily contradict Soviet predominance but it refused to accept Soviet exclusivity.

The Truman administration was even more resentful of Soviet unilateralism in Poland, linking it, in the discordant spring of 1945, with what seemed to be comparable acts elsewhere and adding them all up into a pattern of actual and potential Soviet expansionism to which American firmness was seen as the only reply. This view was strongly pressed on the new president by Ambassador Averell Harriman. From mid-1944 Harriman had been disturbed by the Soviet policy of establishing control over Poland and other neighboring states by force in the name of security. He increasingly urged that the United States should deal firmly with the Russians, not because he despaired of a U.S.–Soviet understanding but because he thought it had to be based on American policies which the Russians would respect and accommodate. His policy views were seconded by Navy Secretary Forrestal, Admiral Leahy, and the State Department professionals, headed by Undersecretary Grew. Most of these had remained highly skeptical even during the war of the possibility of a cooperative relationship with the Soviet Union, and events in 1944 and 1945 strengthened their doubts and concern.[4] Truman, uninformed and inexperienced, was far more receptive than Roosevelt to these men and ideas.

The change in American leadership, the end of the war and of the constraints it imposed on interalliance differences, the American realization of what the Russians were up to in Eastern Europe—all these combined to provoke the shift in the U.S. approach to the Soviets. The new president did not give up Roosevelt's policy of seeking to cooperate with the Russians but he was ready to change tactics and respond to

4. "(O)ne must explain the turn in American official attitudes toward the Soviet Union in small part by the prejudices of U.S. leaders, in larger part by occurrences in Europe and the Middle East, and in perhaps still larger part by the manner in which those occurrences were described and interpreted by the American bureaucracy." Ernest R. May, *"Lessons" of the Past: The Use and Misuse of History in American Foreign Policy* (New York: Oxford University Press, 1973), p. 31. For a summary of the sudden change in American personnel dealing with foreign affairs, see pp. 20–31. Secretary of War Henry Stimson was one of few who urged Truman in the spring of 1945 to proceed cautiously with the Russians.

Soviet behavior as he saw it. For one thing, he wanted to assert his own leadership, abroad and at home. For another, he and his advisers had a profound sense of the strength of their country at war's end. This consciousness had two main facets: the atomic and the economic.

The shift in American policy coincided, among other things, with the final development and first use of the atomic bomb. It has been argued that the Americans carefully planned to use their possession of the bomb to intimidate the Soviet Union, loosen its control in Eastern Europe, and roll back its power. This case has not been made convincingly. Even if the intention was there, as it was for some, the performance was lacking.

It is true that the British throughout the war thought of postwar possession of atomic weapons as a diplomatic tool vis-à-vis the Soviet Union and made this concern clear to the Americans with whom they argued to continue full U.S.–U.K. nuclear cooperation. It also seems to be true that Roosevelt had the problem of postwar British strength and Anglo-American cooperation in mind when he overrode his atomic advisers and in effect maintained the cooperative partnership. This, of course, meant excluding the third of the Big Three from the inner partnership of the other two. Certainly he, as well as Churchill, turned aside the suggestions of scientists and others that the Russians at least be informed of the existence of the atomic bomb project to avoid confronting them with a surprise use of the weapon against Japan, thus risking an increase in their suspicions of the West and reducing the chance that they would cooperate in a postwar atomic control system. Perhaps the way the issue was handled at Potsdam—Truman casually told Stalin that the United States had developed a new weapon of great power—did reduce that chance and make inevitable an already probable nuclear arms race.

But it is a long step from these considerations to the conclusion that American leaders were in a position to plan their strategy toward the Soviet Union with the certain knowledge that the atomic device would work, that Japan was on the verge of surrender in any case or could be brought to it by modification of the unconditional surrender formula, and that the U.S. decision to use the bomb (which was scarcely debated) turned as much or more on political considerations respecting Eastern Europe than on the problem of ending the war as early as possible and with the least cost in blood. The record does not sustain these conclusions.

But even if there were more compelling evidence for them, the lack of results of this allegedly carefully laid strategy would raise doubts as to whether it ever existed. Truman and others may have been cheered at Potsdam by news of the successful test at Alamogordo. They may have thought demonstration of the bomb's power would have salutary effects not only on Japan but on the Soviet Union too. But we cannot overlook the fact that the American leaders, if they had a diplomatic strategy based on their new weapon, played this master card with a lack of skill incredibly out of proportion to the supposed subtlety of the prior preparation. For, with all their atomic monopoly in 1945, they accomplished nothing in Poland or, later, in Rumania and Bulgaria. Nothing took place at Potsdam to American advantage concerning these issues, or at the London meeting of foreign ministers that followed, which would not have taken place had there been no bomb. Certainly the possibility of actually using atomic power to change Russian policy in Eastern Europe was never considered. Nor, whatever hopes some may have had, did the American government find any way to make a usable diplomatic tool of its new weapon. By December 1945 the U.S. government had written off Poland, Rumania, and Bulgaria.

Possession of the bomb may of course have strengthened the American tendency to be firm with the Russians (although again it should not be overlooked that the wartime American policy of postponing important decisions to war's end took for granted, quite apart from the bomb, its unique postwar power position). But the bomb had no discernible impact in 1945 on Eastern Europe, unless—as can be argued with some plausibility—its possession led the American government to yield to domestic pressures for demobilizing in Europe more promptly than might otherwise have been the case, thereby weakening rather than strengthening the U.S. diplomatic hand with respect to specific European issues.

More realistically, it has been suggested that the new American administration took for granted that the Soviet Union desperately needed economic help for reconstruction and would pay a high price with respect to Eastern Europe and other issues to get it. As early as March 1944 Harriman began to argue this case, and in the autumn he proposed signaling U.S. displeasure with Soviet policy in Eastern Europe by requiring, for the first time, strict accountability by the Russians of the lend-lease assistance they received.[5] Roosevelt refused, believing that an attempt to use aid in this way would not affect Soviet policy in the desired direction but might jeopardize the war effort in Europe as well as Asia.

5. "I am impressed with the consideration that economic assistance is one of the most effective weapons at our disposal to influence European political events in the direction we desire and to avoid the development of a sphere of influence of the Soviet Union over Eastern Europe and the Balkans." *Foreign Relations of the United States, 1944* (Washington, D.C.: Department of State, 1966), vol. 4, p. 951.

But the Soviet request in January 1945 for a $6 billion credit raised other issues, and other possibilities. Roosevelt hesitated to make commitments to help any of the Allies after the fighting ended (except the limited aid to be provided by the UN Relief and Rehabilitation Administration) because he knew that Congress at that time was cold to the idea. But apart from this inhibition, his position on the merits of the case was less clearcut than it was on the idea of using lend-lease for political leverage. Most of his advisers, with the exception of Henry Morgenthau, were moving in early 1945 toward the view that whatever aid was provided after the war should be linked to Soviet behavior, of which they were increasingly critical. Roosevelt died before coming to grips with the issue.

With the end of the war Truman had to deal with it as soon as he took office. On the one hand, he knew the congressional situation very well. Congress was not ready to consider substantial postwar aid to the Allies, and above all was hostile to stretching the lend-lease act for this purpose. On the other hand, Truman was confident of American power and was determined, following the lead of most of his advisers, to get tough with the Russians for their failure, as he saw it, to keep their agreements. These considerations, with roots in both domestic politics and international affairs, led to decisions which, whether or not Truman and others saw them as parts of a coherent whole, the Russians had reason to see, and to resist, as attempts to use economic leverage to induce them to modify their policies, particularly in Eastern Europe.

The first of these decisions was to cut off immediately lend-lease to the Soviet Union after V-E Day. Truman, Harriman, and others appear to have seen this as both compliance with the congressional will on lend-lease (the USSR was not yet at war with Japan) and a signal to the Soviet government that the United States would henceforth deal with it (as Harriman wrote in August) only on a "realistic reciprocal basis."[6] But there was no consultation with the Russians in advance and the decision was probably implemented down the bureaucratic line more abruptly than Truman intended. Ships destined for the Soviet Union were not only unloaded in port but actually called back from sea. The implementation was softened a few days later and shipments were resumed, though aid was disbursed with an increasingly tight hand.

It should be noted that the British were also affected. Far more dependent on lend-lease than the Russians, they were very bitter at the final sharp turnoff when Japan surrendered. But Anglo-American rela-

6. *Foreign Relations of the United States, 1945* (Washington, D.C.: Department of State, 1967), vol. 2, p. 1024.

tions were incomparably stronger than Russo-American. However much the actions of the new administration were based on political realities at home, the Russians were not likely to believe that its methods of doing business had nothing to do with its policy intentions. At the same time the signal, such as it was, was too diffuse to have been effective. It had no direct relation to any of the contentious issues of the spring of 1945.

The second decision concerned reparations from Germany (discussed in context in chapter 8). The United States (but not Great Britain) had agreed at Yalta that the sum of $20 billion should be the "basis of discussion" for reparations and that around half the sum agreed on would go to the Soviet Union. But when the reparations commission met in June to take up the matter the United States backed off from this agreement. The compromise worked out at Potsdam fell far short of Soviet expectations.

The third issue concerned the Soviet application for a $6 billion loan from the United States. The matter came to a head in Washington only when Molotov, on May 30, asked about the five-month-old application. In August the Russians were advised to apply to the Export-Import Bank and they promptly did so, this time for a loan of $1 billion. Throughout the autumn negotiations on the U.S.–British loan went forward but approval for the Soviet application languished in the State Department as relations between the two governments worsened. The Soviet loan was obviously hostage to Soviet behavior. But no discussions took place, no quid pro quo was asked for.

After the foreign ministers' conference in December, and as the British loan began its way through Congress, the Russians, who had been silent about their loan application during the autumn, began to ask questions. On March 1, 1946, the State Department announced that the Soviet loan application of August, which had not been in proper form in any case, had been mislaid but that negotiations might then begin. Whatever one may think about this explanation, the American government apparently had decided that the moment was ripe to try to use the loan application as explicit leverage on a wide range of Soviet foreign policies, economic and political. But the Russians refused to accept much of the agenda proposed by Washington—which included practically the whole of their policy—and no negotiations took place. This active phase of American economic diplomacy had no more positive effect than its preceding passive phase. Perhaps it was not expected to have. Whether a loan could have been negotiated and gotten through Congress is questionable; whether, if it had, it would have made much difference in Soviet policies in Eastern Europe is doubtful. But the handling of the issue, along with the reparations question, could not but have confirmed the Soviet policies to which the United States objected.

The assumption that Soviet need for help could have pried meaningful concessions from the Russians might have been correct in the early years of the war, though acting on it then might also—as Roosevelt feared—have precipitated a Soviet defeat or separate peace and in either case made an Allied victory over Germany impossible. But such an assumption, even in 1944, and certainly in 1945, was simply wrong. For one thing the Russians had their own illusions on the subject, believing that the United States needed them as customers to avert a depression and would therefore provide credits on easy terms and with no strings. In any case, the assumed American leverage was wildly inadequate to the objectives set for it. The Soviet government put its control of Poland, and much or all of Eastern Europe, ahead of entente with the United States or economic aid, and had the means to enforce its choice. In the process, the Russians secured that control but failed the test of cooperativeness set for them by Washington.

The record indicates that American policy between Roosevelt's death and the Moscow conference went through several phases of firmness and détente with the Soviet Union. This cycle suggests in turn that while many of the Truman administration's *acts* pointed in a different direction from Roosevelt's, these acts were periodically balanced by others whose thrust implied that Truman's *intention* during this period was still to seek agreement with the Soviet Union, but by other means. Thus, American agitation of the Polish issue was practically closed out in the agreement Hopkins negotiated with Stalin in June 1945. Agitation of the Rumanian and Bulgarian problems was similarly ended as part of a broad agreement reached at Moscow in December. It was only after 1945 that firmness became less and less a tactic to maintain the wartime alliance, more and more a very different policy, which in 1947 would be named containment.

For the United States, however, the most important result of the year-long wrangling with the Soviet Union about Poland and the Balkans was to sensitize American opinion, both official and public, to what the Soviet Union was doing in Eastern Europe—proceedings which were depicted as not only brutal and antidemocratic but also aggressive and in violation of wartime goals and agreements. These events, building on latent anti-Bolshevism, gave a powerful impetus to the oncoming cold war psychology in the United States.

We can be much less clear about what effect they had on Soviet policy. In this case as in others it is absurd to suppose that American policies had no impact on the Russian leaders. We can therefore set aside the once popular notion that they followed some kind of blueprint or timetable for expansion which took no account of what others were doing except when barriers were erected to Russia's inherent aggressiveness. On the other hand, there is no reason to assume, and much reason to doubt, that the Russians were ready for an openhanded postwar partnership with Britain and the United States but were turned aside from it by some particular act or acts of Western policy. Soviet thinking about the West was not a *tabula rasa* waiting to be filled in by British and American policy.

The Soviet regime, as discussed in the last chapter, took for granted the hostility of the capitalist world even though it was quite capable of collaborating with capitalist countries for particular objectives that furthered its own interests. Moreover, we have too little direct information on Soviet decision-making to warrant such conclusions as that the Grand Alliance might have been preserved if the United States had not cut off lend-lease deliveries in May 1945, or had been forthcoming with respect to postwar economic aid or the early handling of the atomic bomb or the acceptance of the Soviet sphere of influence in Eastern Europe. U.S. policy in these areas surely had some impact on Soviet behavior but we have no basis for determining precisely what or how much or with what consequences.

This said, we are entitled to speculate about the way American policies may have interacted with what seem to have been the priorities of Soviet policy as the war ended. Because the Soviet government attached overriding importance to Eastern Europe, it seems reasonable to believe that American policy there had the greatest impact on Soviet attitudes and behavior, within the limits I have suggested. In light of the Churchill-Stalin spheres of influence deal and the handling of the Polish question at Yalta, Stalin had reason to think that his grip on Poland and much of Eastern Europe had been recognized, or at least acquiesced in, by the Western Allies, just as he himself had accepted their own ascendancy in Greece, Italy, and Western Europe (at least temporarily—and the evidence does not allow more to be said with confidence, or less, than that). Subsequent Allied efforts to influence the affairs of the area, though intermittent and sterile, probably seemed to him to reflect a shift to a more hostile position toward the Soviet Union. Such a shift may not have surprised Stalin, once the compelling bonds of a common war effort had been dissolved, but he may not have been certain that it would take place just at that time and in that form. The significance of the change may have seemed the greater in that it coincided with a new American administration which, whatever its exact objectives, was exercising economic pressure on the Russians and, above all, had created and used the atomic bomb without any but the most perfunctory notice to the Soviet government.

Just as the Americans at the end of the war were conscious of their great strength even apart from the bomb, so the Russians were well aware of the weakness of their ravaged country on almost every count. Even so, the atomic weapon, however maladroitly used as a diplomatic tool by the Americans, was a fearful if ambiguous addition to the calculus of power familiar to the Soviet leaders. At the least these American actions meant that the Russians would have to be careful not to seem to be intimidated.

These considerations do not prove that the Soviet leaders were driven by American policy from a course of likely cooperation with the West to one of cold war. They do indicate that whatever chance there was that the Russians might have continued to find it in their interest to collaborate with the West for certain purposes in the postwar as in the wartime period was reduced by the policy interactions of 1945.

I suggested in the preceding chapter that the American design for a postwar world order based on the concert of the three major powers broke down when the Soviet Union, as ought to have been expected but was not, gave first priority to building a sphere of influence—or, more accurately, absolute control—in Eastern Europe and the United States refused to acquiesce in this policy. It cannot be known now what would have happened had the United States closed its eyes to what went on in Poland and elsewhere—that is, had bent its own broad policy goals to accommodate this priority Soviet preoccupation. The Americans might next have had to sanction the incorporation of the Soviet zone of Germany into the Eastern sphere, and perhaps other areas as well, and thus to permit their notion of a concert of great powers acting *in common* and without openly arrogating specific spheres to themselves to be converted into a very different kind of great power concert, that of mutual acquiescence in established spheres of influence. This the United States was unwilling then, and long afterward, to countenance.

Critics of American policy, then and since, have pointed to the double standard of maintaining U.S. hegemony in Latin America and elsewhere while refusing to accept an analogous Soviet policy (admittedly pursued by different means) in Eastern Europe. In some respects this American dilemma reflected, as I observed in the last chapter, a very selective reading of history. The Monroe Doctrine, by 1945 over a century old, seemed to Americans—not excluding policymakers—almost a law of nature, so little challenged as to seem unchallengeable. On the other hand, prewar Eastern Europe had consisted of states for whose independence from Nazi Germany the war had been fought. How could Americans acquiesce in a new enslavement of the very areas the West (if not the United States itself) had gone to war to keep free?

In this, of course, no attention was paid to the historical circumstances in which the countries of Eastern Europe had won and held their precarious independence after 1918. As I noted in chapter 3, the inter-war "normalcy" in Eastern Europe had been a freak happening, arising from the defeat of both Russia and Germany in 1918. The revival of both these powers in the interwar years had placed Poland and the rest in jeopardy; World War II had led to their conquest by Germany; Germany's defeat led to their occupation by Russia.

History gives no binding moral or even prescriptive right to the power and status of nations, but it does give information about what the balance of forces in a given area has been over a long period of time. In 1600 Poland stretched from the Baltic almost to the Black Sea. Russia was cut off from both, so that, when Boris Godunov's young son points to "the sea" on a map of his country, he means the Caspian. By the peace of Andrussovo, in 1667, Russia after a long war made firm its conquest of much of the Ukraine and replaced Poland as the preponderant power in northeastern Europe. For whatever reasons, this relationship was never reversed. These facts had profound implications for both countries once the other powers that impinged on the relationship—Sweden, Turkey, Austria, and finally Germany—had been eliminated from the power game in that area.

This does not mean that the historic Polish nation had no right to exist as an independent state. But it helps explain why contemporary observers of Poland's resurrection in 1918 had few illusions about the implications of its permanently precarious situation, already so con-spicuous in the eighteenth century. Marshal Smuts wrote in May 1919:

> It is reasonably certain that both Germany and Russia will again be great Powers, and that sandwiched between them the new Poland could only be a success with their good will. How, under these circumstances, can we expect Poland to be other than a failure, even if she had that ruling and administrative capacity which history has proved she has not? . . . I think that we are building a house of sand.[7]

And the French historian Jacques Bainville wrote:

> to contain Germany on the slope opposite ours, there is need for a greater Poland, a greater Bohemia, and a greater Rumania. These three states can have no consistency, cannot support each other

7. This quotation is in Arno J. Mayer, *Politics and Diplomacy of Peacemaking* (New York: Knopf, 1967), p. 797.

without annexing Russian territories or Slav populations traditionally under Ukrainian or Muscovite influence.

Accordingly, such a settlement will last only as long as Russia can be
ignored or continues to be asleep. The establishment of this "barrier" postulates an eternal sleep. The day the Russian state reawakens
and is again capable of having a foreign policy, it will automatically
team up with Germany against the nations formed at their mutual
expense. As in the past, Poland will unfortunately be caught in a
crossfire.[8]

There is also a story that someone warned Thomas Masaryk that the
greater Bohemia he wanted to create would surely fall prey, once the
Austro-Hungarian empire was gone, to either Germany or Russia. And
so it did.

Thinking of this kind, rooted in historical reality, was unknown to the
Americans of 1945. Henry Stimson was almost alone in the high places
of the administration in suggesting that Eastern Europe might not be
worth a rupture of the alliance. The war had been thought of by most
policymakers as the means to roll back and defeat German power and
then to restore what had existed before in this area. It was not realized
that the prewar system, which provided the American frame of reference, was artificial and unstable, that it had been irrevocably destroyed
by the war, and that an entirely new order had arisen in which Soviet
power dominated half of Europe, Anglo-American power the other half.
It was not seen that, this being the case, the only choice before the
United States was to decide what attitude to take in face of the situation
thus created in Eastern Europe.

Perhaps the United States might have accepted Soviet hegemony in
Eastern Europe as practiced in Finland, or in Czechoslovakia in the first
phase. But the brutality of Soviet policy in a place as sensitive as Poland,
and then elsewhere, did not make it easy for Americans to face these
facts—indeed, perhaps made it impossible. If so, then the grand design
for the postwar world was clearly inadaptable to the realities of Soviet
policy and could only be abandoned, as it was.

If, on the other hand, there *was* any chance of maintaining some kind
of postwar entente among the Big Three on the more realistic basis of
mutual acceptance of respective spheres of influence—and too little is
known about Soviet policy intentions for discussion of that question to be
other than conjectural—then the American effort during 1945 to induce
or coerce the USSR to loosen its hold over its own sphere had the effect

8. Ibid., p. 816.

of narrowing to one whatever options *might* have existed in Soviet policy for the tenor of postwar Russian-American relations. Since American interests in Poland were far less important than Soviet interests, U.S. options for response were perhaps more numerous. In this sense the Polish issue was the key to American postwar policy even more than it was to Soviet.

It may be that Roosevelt, for all his rooted dislike of spheres of influence, would in the end have given highest priority to maintaining the entente with the USSR, particularly after the advent of the atomic bomb. He would have had to swallow much bitter medicine to do so, not only in terms of his own postwar plans but also of the impact on American opinion of Soviet proceedings in Eastern Europe. But he might also have foreseen the risks of prolonged tension with the Soviet Union and the economic, psychological, and institutional costs for American society of such tension. He might then have chosen to try to deal with the Russians on the basis of their priorities in Eastern Europe and to have led American opinion in that direction, as he had led it, in part for the same reasons, to and through the war.

Whether or not Roosevelt might have done this, Truman and the political and diplomatic advisers to whom he turned did not. Considering the intellectual world in which the American leaders and people then lived, and—it should never be forgotten—the goals for which the war had been fought, we cannot be surprised that the administration made the choice it did, that is, to protest, though ineffectively, the imposed communization of Eastern Europe. Perhaps it was out of the question that the United States could have accepted Soviet policy in Eastern Europe as a precondition, from the Soviet point of view, to whatever pattern of relations was to be established between the United States and the USSR, cooperative or antagonistic. For, in addition to rooted American hostility to the old forms of the European power system, including the crudities of unvarnished domination of one people over another by armed force, the USSR was, for Americans, a peculiarly difficult prospective partner.

It is true that the image of the Soviet Union was good in the United States in 1945. The successes of the Red Army had raised Russian prestige high, and there was a widespread tendency, born of the wartime coalition, to pretend that both countries were on the same side of the ideological fence vis-à-vis the Axis opponents in the things that mattered. Indeed, this self-induced belief had been almost essential to America's prosecuting the war in alliance with the Russians.

Nevertheless, communism had been an evil word in the United States for over thirty years, and socialism long before that. Both were identified with state control of the economy, social egalitarianism, and political tyranny, not to mention atheism and free love. Many Americans, even during the war, found it hard to foresee a long-term partnership with Moscow, and many others quickly reverted to a hostile view as the quarrel over Eastern Europe developed. The diplomatic establishment, in particular, had always been deeply suspicious of the Soviet Union. Once Roosevelt's controlling hand was gone, it promptly led the way in taking a harder line toward Soviet behavior and intentions.

This does not mean that domestic opinion pushed the Truman administration to the policy it evolved or that its policy could not have gone another way. It does mean that some elements in opinion (not so much individuals as currents of thought) were congenial to the direction the administration chose, just as there were elements that—as during the war—could have been congenial to another kind of lead.

Some Americans tried to keep the alliance going by explaining away Soviet actions in Eastern Europe. Few were ready in 1945 to face those facts boldly and coldly and argue that a Soviet-American entente was indispensable to peace even at that price. Few, whether firm or friendly, hardline or soft, were able to draw realistic conclusions from the fact that the Soviet Union had won the war as much as the Western Allies, and that as a great power which had been invaded many times and had been excluded from affairs to a large extent after 1918 it would expect to reassert itself, particularly in contiguous areas which the Red Army occupied.

The American noncomprehension of this fact is amazingly conveyed in a statement of Truman's to Harriman and others a week after he took office. He agreed that there would have to be give-and-take negotiations with the Russians and "that we could not, of course, expect to get 100 percent of what we wanted but that on important matters he felt that we should be able to get 85 percent."[9] Obviously Truman took for granted both the moral rightness of U.S. policy preferences and its economic and military supremacy (even before he could have given weight to the atomic bomb). What he implied went far beyond the quid pro quo approach to dealing with the Russians that Harriman had called for since 1944. It is as if the United States moved within a few months from accommodating the Russians to asserting its will over them, bypassing in both cases the middle way of hard bargaining on a basis that reflected the facts of life in postwar Europe.

Of course, the United States did go part way to accepting the Soviet

9. *Foreign Relations of the United States, 1945* (Washington, D.C.: Department of State, 1967), vol. 5, p. 233.

sphere of influence. It acquiesced in Russian territorial annexations, as well as the concept that Russia's neighbors should have governments friendly to it. The United States also accepted the restoration of Russian interests in Manchuria, lost to Japan in 1905. It dealt with the Soviet Union in various three-, four-, and five-power councils. Even so, the American government could not, or at any rate did not, accept the full implications in this respect of Russian strength in the postwar world. It did not come to grips with the full implications of living in the world with the Soviet Union. It signally failed to prepare the public for this reality, particularly as it took shape in Eastern Europe. Therefore, the one chance, however great or small it might have been, for even the partial success of the American design for a great power condominium of the postwar world failed in the face of two facts: Soviet determination to secure Russia's frontiers and control of its European neighbors as the highest priority of Soviet policy, and American refusal to acquiesce in that Soviet priority.

The American failure to try to maintain entente with the Soviet Union on the terms which Soviet actions set as the condition was not taken at once but got well underway in the spring of 1945 in the wrangling about Eastern Europe. For the United States, it was but a step from treating that Soviet sphere as illegitimate to seeing all Soviet activities in world affairs—great power and co-victor though it was—as equally illegitimate, aggressive, and inherently hostile to American ideals, interests, and plans. After all, the Red Army was now only 100 miles from the Rhine—a long way beyond where it stood in 1939, that year of false reference. For the Russians, economically devastated, it was but a step from seeing the United States challenge the fruits of their hard-won victory in the area of greatest importance to their security to seeing—not unexpectedly—an American effort to encircle and perhaps extirpate the homeland of socialism.

The Soviet government, as I have suggested, was at least as ready as the American, and probably much more so, to see the other great power as inherently hostile ideologically. These old fears were exacerbated by the fact that one was using its local military superiority to impose police states wherever it could, while the other, though it soon withdrew most of its forces from Europe, was armed with the atomic bomb and the vast wealth it had developed during a war which had impoverished all the European participants. The competition between the superpowers, the ground for which was thus prepared with respect to issues which were already settled in practice, was readily accounted for by both parties in preexisting ideological terms. It then spread even more easily to other issues, including the disposition of Germany. In due course it attached

itself to or even created conflicts in every corner of the world, before the
two powers returned, after a nervous and disrupted quarter-century, to
a second effort to achieve at least some relaxation of systematic tension if
not, eventually, a new form of entente. Between these two attempts to
define American-Soviet relations in some way other than total hostile
competition lies the cold war.

CHAPTER 7

The Building of a New State System

One student of the cold war has concluded that "There is no comprehensive theory of the contemporary crisis."[1] Another, however, analyzes no less than six ostensibly comprehensive theories that have been suggested to explain the confrontation that has taken place between the United States and the Soviet Union since 1945, and ends with a seventh which probably comes as near to giving meaning to the facts as we are likely to get so soon after experiencing them.[2] From this point of view, the two superpowers, meeting each other seriously for the first time, and as the co-arbiters of Europe, might have worked out their mutual relations in any of several possible ways. For reasons stemming from history, ideological preconceptions, and the actual circumstances they faced in Europe, the meeting was hostile rather than collaborative. The working out of their relations took place in an atmosphere of acute tension and recurrent crises that several times seemed likely to lead to war. In the end they *did* establish the bases of a relationship in Europe within which they could live together without war, but almost without realizing, until late in the day, that they were doing so.

The meaning of the cold war has thus turned out to be a search by the two superpowers for a new system in Europe to replace the one finally swept away by the war—that is, a search for means to define their relations to each other in such a way as to assure the survival, physical and political, of both and the countries grouped around them. This search, as Paul Seabury has made clear, was integrative as well as divisive,

1. Gabriel Kolko, *The Roots of American Foreign Policy* (Boston: Beacon Press, 1969), p. 48. The author then goes on to provide such a theory, resurrecting the old notion of international relations as a struggle for markets and raw materials—in this case, an agressive American grab for them that was resisted by oppressed peoples everywhere. In this view only one great power, the United States, has had an active foreign policy since the war; the Soviet Union has played a passive and reactive part. Indeed, the cold war between the two shrinks to the sidelines in face of the alleged great American struggle with the third world.

2. Paul Seabury, *The Rise and Decline of the Cold War* (New York: Basic Books, 1967). My qualification arises from the obvious fact that new interpretations, developed in the perspectives of time to come, may take approaches to these familiar events quite different from any we can imagine now. In the long term the American-Soviet rivalry after 1945 may seem important only as the catalyst to the global ascendancy of some part of the third world. In the longest term, that rivalry may be a meaningless footnote to man's "conquest" of space.

sociative as well as alienative. The foundations for its positive outcome
were quietly developed but overlooked in the fracas of confrontation.
Only after many years was it noticed that amidst the smoke and noise of
the cold war there was coming into being in Europe a new system of
relations which *did* fulfill, for the member states, the essential functions
of a state system.

In the context of this study, the essential point about this development
is that the superpowers not only eventually managed to define their own
mutual relations in Europe but in the process, and as a by-product of it,
also established a system of relationships with and among the countries
of Europe, their own allies and dependents, and those of the other. They
thereby provided a solution, inadvertently, to the problem which the
countries of Europe had faced and failed to master since 1890: the place
of a too-powerful Germany in a European system which could not of
itself preserve the independence of its members in the face of German
strength.

Germany's victory in 1940 swept away forever the shadowy remnants
of the old European system; its defeat in 1945 opened the continent to
an American-Soviet occupation and rivalry; their competition, in turn,
resolved the German problem in an unintended way and at the same
time brought into existence a bipolar set of relationships which taken as a
whole constituted a state system encompassing not only the superpowers
whose actions created it but the European states as well. As Seabury put
it:

> What a comprehensive peace treaty did not do, after 1945, to
> establish new order in Europe was done by processes of conflict and
> hostile interaction.[3]

This system, it has turned out, is the first stable set of relationships
Europe has known since the rise of German power.

This stability, of course, is a relative thing. Structural stability does not
imply stasis; on the contrary, much has happened in Europe within the
bipolar structure. It is also true that for the European states the new
system is basically worldwide and therefore no longer theirs. For the
superpowers themselves, the creative stabilization of their competition in
Europe, important as that is in itself, is still imperfect in the absence of a
yet to be achieved worldwide stabilization—and in the world, unlike in
Europe, other forces at play may be too powerful to be stabilized by
anything the United States and the Soviet Union can do.

3. Ibid., p. 105.

Nevertheless, the new European system of order fully deserves that description. It has preserved the national independence of the member states, though severely circumscribed in the case of the Soviet Union's dependents. Indeed, it has done more than that minimum required of any state system. It has kept the peace too, in circumstances when war might well have meant the physical as well as political annihilation of the European participants. Since it has reflected the distribution of power in Europe, it has already maintained its distinctive form over a considerable period. It is clearly not a way station back to the earlier system. But neither is it necessarily a way station forward to some other system. For, unless the essential power facts change, why should the state system that expresses them?

The conflict between the superpowers in Europe that began in 1945 over Poland proceeded through two decades of tension not to war but to a balance of terror and a stalemate—perhaps an end?—in which each side held very nearly what it did at the beginning but with the stability of this outcome apparent to all. As was appropriate in a new age of ideological conflict, the participants quite naturally applied the seventeenth-century principle of *cujus regio, ejus religio* to the territories they occupied when hostilities ended, and then mutually recognized the validity of the results. The "rule" of the United States has been described, according to the analyst, as embodying Western, Christian, capitalist, or free principles, or simply as the U.S. bloc. The Soviet "rule" encompassed, from the Western view, Eastern, atheist, Communist, or slave principles, or simply the Soviet bloc.

But whatever the "religion" that was said to prevail here or there, the "rule" everywhere was that of one or the other of the two superpowers. The cold war in the end changed little or nothing in Europe as to "rule," and proved little or nothing as to "religion," but by prescription finally led the two great powers to see what they had done and to find it, if not good, at least tolerable to themselves. Meanwhile, the European states, large and small, responded and adapted as they could to the circumstances in which each found itself, as the smaller states of Europe had traditionally done throughout the long life of the European state system.

What follows, in this chapter and the next, is not a history of the postwar period in Europe but an outline of how a dynamic and creative process precipitated by Germany's defeat—the cold war—led in a seemingly roundabout way, without peace conference or treaty, to a solution or resolution of both an old problem (Germany) and of new ones (how to define the relations between the United States and the Soviet Union and between each and the countries of Europe). The outcome has been a wholly new system of state relationships which has lasted, notwithstanding many challenges, since it was perfected in 1955 by the rearming of West Germany.

The process got underway during the period between the Yalta and Potsdam conferences when the Russians quickly imposed control in Poland despite persistent Western attempts to prevent or mitigate it. The damage done in 1945 to Soviet-Western relations by developments in Poland was serious enough to start the cold war. But it was not until 1948 that Soviet control of Eastern Europe was finally consolidated (and, as it happened, was first challenged, by Yugoslavia). The very slowness of the Soviet Union's pace, for whatever reasons, provided continuous occasions for building up Western indignation at what was going on in Eastern Europe. The large number of troops Russia thought necessary for garrisoning these conquests fed Western fears that they might also be used for a further advance. As a result, the Soviet imposition of Communist regimes in countries which it had already occupied by May 1945 was seen in the West as a process of expansion of Russian power by aggression and as the harbinger of further aggression. The growth of this state of mind among Western peoples and leaders alike, stimulated by these developments and by others elsewhere tending to the same result, led straight on to those measures in the West which, in their turn, consolidated the division of the continent along the military line of May 1945.

Because of the cumulative impact of this process, particularly in the United States, it is worth recalling the steps—and the timing—by which the Soviet Union completed its control of Eastern Europe.

The game in Poland itself was not played out in 1945. Mikolajczyk and a few of his London associates entered the Communist-dominated Polish government in the summer and continued to press for the elections Stalin had promised at Yalta. But by the time they finally took place—in January 1947—the government was in such complete control of the situation that the widespread Polish opposition to the socialization as well as the Russian control represented by the new regime was in no position to show its strength. Mikolajczyk lingered on in Poland until as late as October 1947 but his eventual departure made no difference to the *fait accompli* of Communist control.

The same Russian motivations were probably at work, for the same reasons, in Rumania. The effort of the United States and Great Britain in the latter part of 1945 to do in Rumania what they had failed to do earlier in Poland led to the same result. At the three-power Moscow conference in December 1945 they settled for Soviet concessions in the makeup of the Communist-dominated Rumanian government, which in practice amounted to nothing. (The United States, as noted, scored its own points in the Moscow bargaining on other issues, notably confirmation of its dominant role in the occupation of Japan.) The Western powers then recognized the Rumanian government in February 1946, which was presumably what the Russians had aimed to get by making those concessions (not the first nor the last time that they seemed to think it important to secure official Western ratification of their dominant position in Eastern Europe). The November 1946 election produced results overwhelmingly favorable to the government, but the Western powers went ahead, in February 1947, to sign a peace treaty with Rumania. King Michael lingered on until December, but his ouster then and the establishment of a full-fledged people's democracy in the following April only advertised another *fait accompli*.

The Western powers tried to slow the analogous process in Bulgaria at the same time they tried in Rumania. But they got even more meager concessions from Stalin in December 1945 and the Communists and their associates took full power even more readily. The victors of the war, including the Western powers, signed a peace treaty with Communist Bulgaria in February 1947.

Soviet control of Hungary and Czechoslovakia was established more slowly. This may have reflected the greater strength of the local opposition or greater caution on Stalin's part in dealing with countries farther to the west, one of which at least—Czechoslovakia—was regarded very positively in the United States. It can be argued, however, that Stalin may not have aimed from the start at full satellization of these two countries, but, in the spirit of his 1944 deal with Churchill, may at first have thought it both possible and prudent to allow pluralistic regimes to survive provided that their foreign policies were acceptable to Moscow and local Communists played a large part in their governments.

With the Finnish exception to satellization in mind, this hypothesis cannot be dismissed out of hand, though it can hardly be proved either. What is certain is that reasonably free elections took place in Hungary and Czechoslovakia, in November 1945 and May 1946, respectively, and that governments were established which were not dominated by the Communist participants. The decline of both countries into satellization then took place parallel to, and perhaps in interrelationship with, the growing tension between East and West in Europe. This developing situation undoubtedly had some kind of impact of Stalin, just as it did on the Western powers, and, for all that can be said with certainty of his initial intentions toward Hungary and Czechoslovakia, may perhaps have influenced his policy toward these two countries, which were already in the Russian sphere but not yet part of a bloc in a rapidly polarizing Europe.

Once the Western powers had in effect written off Rumania and Bulgaria in December 1945, Stalin probably concluded that whatever he did in Hungary would not lead them to refuse to sign a peace treaty with it. In fact they negotiated such a treaty in 1946 and signed it in February 1947 along with treaties for the rest of Germany's ex-allies in Eastern Europe. Nevertheless, the Russians moved cautiously in Hungary. Having risked a relatively free election in 1945, they had to live with the fact that the strength of the local Communist party, which got about 22 percent of the votes, had been openly measured against other parties. Even in the presence of a Soviet occupying army the party apparently found it prudent to proceed slowly toward power. Stalin, who could readily have precipitated events, obviously found such restraint acceptable in Hungary, as he did not in countries more important to the Soviet Union.

By the time repression of the anti-Communist opposition in Hungary got underway in earnest in December 1946, the effort of the wartime Allies to find a common policy for Germany had clearly failed and the United States and Great Britain were moving toward a separate political organization of their own occupation zones. By the time Ferenc Nagy, leader of the majority Smallholders party, resigned as Hungarian premier in June 1947, the United States had moved to bolster Greece and Turkey and had proposed the Marshall Plan. In the August election in Hungary, the Communists imposed a common alliance on a broad enough spectrum of other political elements to win control of parliament and the government. They then moved, as they had elsewhere in Eastern Europe, to transform this supremacy into total control. The nature of the tie-in between initial Soviet intentions, the local situation, and the international context can only be conjectural in the present state of our knowledge, but it seems plausible that all three elements played a part in shaping the eventual outcome.

The same was no less true in Czechoslovakia. Unlike most other countries of Eastern Europe, Czechoslovakia saw the Soviet Union at first as a popular ally rather than a traditional foe or oppressor. In the election of May 1946 the Communist party won some 35 percent of the votes and its leader, Klement Gottwald, became prime minister of a coalition government. As late as July 1947 President Benes and Jan Masaryk, the foreign minister, still seemed to think they had sufficient freedom of action in foreign policy to take part in the talks that were to

lead to implementation of the Marshall Plan. They soon learned otherwise, and brusquely withdrew.

The international situation in which Czechoslovakia found itself in late
1947 was even more grave than that in which Hungary had been satel-
lized six months before. By then Europe was clearly divided between
those countries participating in the Marshall Plan, including the three
western zones of Germany, and those which would not—or could not.
The establishment of the Communist Information Bureau (Cominform)
in September 1947 and the outbreak of quasi-revolutionary strikes in
Western Europe at the end of the year carried the cold war a long step
forward. Even then, however, the Communists continued to have ups
and downs in their effort to extend their power in Czechoslovakia. As
the 1948 election approached the party seemed to be losing popular
support despite the divisions of the opposition. In February 1948, however, a cabinet dispute led the non-Communist ministers to resign.
Facing Communist control of the streets and fearing Soviet intervention,
Benes accepted a new cabinet made up entirely of Communists and
those allied to them, plus Masaryk. These events, climaxed and symbolized by Masaryk's death, marked the end of democracy in the first
and last country of Eastern Europe to have enjoyed it.

Was completion of Soviet control in this way preplanned and inevitable, delayed only until the Czechoslovak opposition was sufficiently
weakened? Was it related to Stalin's increasingly autocratic tightening of
controls in the Soviet Union itself as well as in the nations it occupied?
Was it precipitated by a Soviet decision to make sure of complete control
over Eastern Europe in face of the Marshall Plan and the impending
decision of the Western powers to reestablish a German state in their
occupation zones? The mix of these and other elements cannot be
determined without access to the records of Soviet decision-making.
There are no more certain grounds for ascribing total predestination to
Soviet policy than to represent it as reacting passively to a succession of
hostile Western moves in Europe.

Whatever the answers to these questions, the hopes or last vestiges of
Czechoslovakia's balancing act fell victim to the division of Europe precipitated by the Marshall proposal. The Prague coup, in turn, in the
most democratic country in Eastern Europe, following on the prior
developments in the area had the effect in the West, particularly in the
United States, of producing such shock and revulsion that the cold war
became not so much as an international political competition as a stark,
all-encompassing ideological and moral confrontation.

American public and official thinking had been moving for a long time, of course, toward hostile confrontation with the Soviet Union. Its policy was increasingly seen as ideologically motivated and aggressive. The Polish case focused tension as early as the spring of 1945 for Truman and others, followed by skirmishes with the Soviet Union over other Eastern European countries and counterproductive disputes with these countries—about nationalizations, trade, and aid—aimed forlornly at strengthening American influence. Many developments made their contributions, including the Iranian crisis in early 1946; Soviet pressure on Turkey for changes in the Montreux convention and the Turkish-Soviet frontier; the interminable pseudo-parliamentary wrangling in the United Nations and the conferences where the ex-satellite peace treaties were negotiated; the permanent dispute over German production levels, reparations, and political organization; and the Soviet rejection of the American plan for international control of atomic weapons.

The effects of the atomic problem on both official and public attitudes was particularly important because of the fears it aroused. Long before the bomb was tested scientists and others had pressed Roosevelt and Churchill to approach the Russians on the matter, but without success. From the summer of 1945 the Truman administration debated whether to try to establish some kind of international regime for the atomic bomb that included the Soviet Union. Were there secrets to be kept, and if so for how long? What would be the Soviet response to sharing or to exclusion? What role could the United Nations play? The upshot was an agreement reached in November 1945 among the United States, the United Kingdom, and Canada—without the Soviet Union—to propose that the United Nations establish a commission to plan the eventual elimination of atomic weapons. A month later the Soviet Union agreed to cosponsor the resolution and the commission was duly established in January.

But the substantive American proposal developed by Bernard Baruch with Truman's approval on the basis of an initial plan drafted by David Lilienthal and Dean Acheson could hardly have been expected to lay a basis for realistic negotiations with the Soviet Union. Baruch's appointment in itself reflected Truman's awareness of congressional nervousness about giving away secrets. The plan Baruch presented to the UN Atomic Energy Commission in June 1946 also reflected American concern that the actual prohibition of atomic weapons, if it could be achieved, would deprive the United States, in the face of its massive conventional disarmament, of its most effective balance against Soviet power in Europe. For these reasons, and because Baruch assumed a long American monopoly of atomic power, or at least a long lead in its application, he felt strong enough to call for the impossible: Soviet acceptance of international inspection of their territory to ensure Russian nondevelopment of nuclear weapons, and veto-proof sanctions against violations of that ban, in exchange for a phase-out of U.S. weapons at some future date, until which time production would continue. Nothing in this could persuade the Russians to slow their own drive for nuclear weapons.

We can wonder whether anything could have persuaded them even with serious U.S.–Soviet discussions of the problem at any time, which never took place. Probably it was unrealistic to attempt to transcend normal international politics by trying to remove one weapons system from the game just when relations between the most interested governments were worsening in every other way. Certainly the Soviet counterproposal, calling for prohibition of the production or use of atomic weapons, was if anything even more unrealistic than the American plan. The upshot of the debate was a public opinion victory at home, and generally in the West, for the United States. What was seen as a display of Soviet unreasonableness in face of the American offer dismayed even some of the scientists who had been the strongest proponents of negotiating with the Russians to stop the arms race. This drawn-out debate in 1946–47 further envenomed emerging cold war tension.

But neither American policy nor American opinion moved unswervingly toward confrontation with the Soviet Union. Many Americans feared that they were being dragged by Great Britain into its quarrels with the Soviet Union (as many during the war had feared both Anglo-Soviet rivalry and Anglo-Soviet deals). When Churchill made his "iron curtain" speech at Fulton, Missouri, in March 1946, Lord Halifax, the British ambassador, could not disguise the cool response:

> Although general comment is critical of some or all aspects of the speech it cannot, except in the case of the extreme left and Russophils, avoid recognizing some truth in the analysis of the situation, however unpalatable. Left-wing press and radio (ie, majority of broadcasters) denounce the speech as war-mongering, imperialistic, the call to a new anti-Comintern pact, justifying the worst Russian suspicions, etc. . . .[4]

Truman, who was on the platform and had known the contents in advance, found it politic to dissociate himself to some extent from Churchill's blunt attack on Soviet policy, and certainly from his call for

4. British Cabinet papers, quoted in *The Economist* 262 (January 1, 1977), 16.

an Anglo-American alliance. Opposition to the latter was one of the main themes of those, left and right, who argued during the first half of 1946 against approving the loan to Britain.

Yet just in that period the administration's approach to the Soviet Union was hardening again, this time—after the ebb and flow of firmness in 1945—more definitely. Byrnes was widely blamed for the Moscow bargain, and his critics included Truman. He regained his popularity by taking a tougher stand toward Soviet policy, under the name of "patience with firmness." There continued to be a spirited public debate in the United States through 1946 on the subject of relations with the Soviet Union. Between winter and summer anti-Sovietism clearly rose, as was reflected in the last phase of the acrid congressional debate on the British loan. But Henry Wallace, the leading critic of the Truman-Byrnes policies on Eastern Europe and atomic issues, did not leave the cabinet until September, and even then the debate in the United States was not finished.

The circumstances surrounding the American response in March 1947 to Britain's announced withdrawal from Greece—not unforeseen in itself—and the need felt by the administration to sharpen its rhetoric to get the support it wanted ("scare hell out of the country," as Senator Vanderberg put it) do not suggest confidence that the receptivity of either Congress or the public to what was then asked of them could be taken for granted.[5] Nor did the response of, for example, Walter Lippmann to Truman's policy and to George Kennan's rationalization of it suggest anything like an elite or public consensus on the problem and even less on the remedy. The debate on American foreign policy that took place in mid-1947 is instructive, both for what it says about American attitudes at that time and for the light it casts on fundamental issues that were not seriously examined again for almost twenty years.

When Truman went before Congress in March 1947 to urge that the United States pick up the burden that the British were dropping of sustaining Greece against internal subversion and assume its own burden of helping Turkey resist possible external aggression, he undertook not only to outline the specific situation as he saw it in those countries but to put the new American policy—and world role—in a broader context that would rally public as well as congressional support. His administration had, of course, been working to contain Soviet expansionism at least since the Iranian crisis in early 1946. But he had not yet found it necessary to promulgate a comprehensive doctrinal basis for specific

5. Eric Goldman, *The Crucial Decade—and After: America, 1945–1960* (New York: Knopf, 1966), p. 29.

policies. The scale of what Truman asked of Congress, and the state East-West relations had reached by early 1947, required, as Dean Acheson put it in another context, making points "clearer then truth." [6]

Passing from the particular to the general, Truman defined American policy in those broad terms which were cited for many years afterward as underlying every problem situation.[7] A primary objective of policy was said to be to create conditions under which the United States and others could live free from coercion—the same goal as that of World War II, now applied against the Soviet Union. To this end, the United States should help those resisting aggressive movements which sought to impose totalitarian regimes, for regimes thus imposed "undermine the foundations of international peace and hence the security of the United States."

Without naming Russia or Communism as the villain, Truman described a worldwide struggle between two ways of life, one based on the will of the majority and free institutions, the other forcibly imposed by a minority and based on oppression and terror. With the world thus cleanly divided between white and black, the president's operational conclusion was that "it must be the policy of the United States to support free peoples who are resisting attempted subjugation by armed minorities or by outside pressures."

In these words, which remained the almost unquestioned underpinning of American policy and thinking until the late 1960s, Truman tried to make the issue posed by the immediate crisis so clear to his fellow countrymen that they could constantly and readily reapply it to many other situations. Of course this distinction between free and unfree could not be applied rigorously. The administration itself soon wrote off Nationalist China—and found itself, to its great cost, hoist on the petard of its own rhetoric. But the distinction between those whom the United States chose to support and those whom it found to be threatening them and itself provided an easy, almost mechanical definition of national interest. American foreign policy thinking, official and public, became and remained dichotomous, however the dichotomy was defined and however qualified it was in practice by local circumstances. And, as the "great debate" stirred up by the Korean war was to show, it became even harder to limit the application of rhetoric which all too successfully took on a policy life of its own.

The importance of the Truman speech is that the United States not only assumed a specific obligation in the Eastern Mediterrean but

6. Dean Acheson, *Present at the Creation* (New York: Norton, 1969), p. 375.
7. *The Department of State Bulletin* 16 (March 16, 1947), 534–37.

framed that decision so as to enter on an ideological crusade—though a defensive one, as the administration made clear—against a hostile nation. Truman himself established continuity between the struggle of World War II and the new policy, and what was known in the United States by then of Stalin's behavior at home and abroad made it easy (however fallacious, on close analysis) to equate his policy and ambitions with Hitler's. In this way, the United States was able to define its exceptional mission in the postwar world in a manner that was consistent with the recent past. This mission was not what Roosevelt had hoped it would be, but it did meet the requirement of being something grander than merely joining the old system of international power politics.

The policy line expressed by Truman to Congress and the public in March 1947 was expounded to the foreign policy elite in a more sophisticated manner by George Kennan, in his renowned *Foreign Affairs* article, signed Mr. X, of July.[8] Kennan pictured the Soviet regime as inherently hostile to any possible community of aims with non-Communist states and committed to "unceasing constant pressure toward the desired goal," which presumably was the conquest or subversion of whatever territory it could seize until the whole world was communized. Yet the Soviets had no timetable for aggression and, more important, were capable of falling back without panic whenever their advance was firmly resisted. The Western response to this pressure, therefore, should be "firm and vigilant containment." If the United States was patient and persistent in this course, and displayed its "spiritual vitality," then in ten or fifteen years the Soviet internal system might mellow or decay. As a result of such internal change, and only then, the Soviet regime would abandon its outward pressure.

It is symptomatic of the time and place that Kennan's argument for a patient, long-haul response to Soviet pressure seemed to prudent people a reasonable answer to those impatient Americans who thought that war was inevitable and that we might solve our disputes with Moscow by dropping an atomic bomb on it. Nevertheless, it is a curious and unsettling experience today to read the article of Mr. X and reflect on its influence in shaping elite and popular thinking about the Soviet Union.

On the one hand, Kennan derived Soviet foreign policy entirely from the nature of the regime. If only the Bolshevik regime would mellow over time, Soviet foreign policy would lose its "expansive tendencies," as if these were specific to Bolshevism and not to the victorious Russian state. He conveyed no sense of the historic Russia, a state with well-defined national interests which are distinguishable from its ideology

8. X, "The Sources of Soviet Conduct," *Foreign Affairs* 25 (July 1947), 566–82.

and which any Russian government would have pursued after victory in World War II, when Germany's defeat provided the opportunity to assert Russia's old power and old ambitions in Eastern Europe.

On the other hand, was Kennan's extravagant geographic commitment to contain Soviet assertiveness everywhere different in practice from Truman's extravagant ideological commitment to help free peoples resist subversion or aggression? At first glance Kennan's universalism seemed more realistic than Truman's, but only if one overlooked his definition of the threat. Taking it as described by Kennan, it was as ideological as Truman's and as openended. Every manifestation of Soviet power or interest anywhere became a challenge to American interests that had to be resisted, for Truman to protect the free, for Kennan to show U.S. mettle and, eventually, dampen the aggressiveness inherent in the Soviet regime. Everything, in this eye upon the sparrow definition of national interest, became a test of American fixity of purpose. Only by demonstrating such fixity on every occasion could the United States hope to induce that eventual mellowing of the Soviet polity and policy which was the only way to bring the world out of the universal bipolar confrontation thus described.

Throughout, there is no suggestion of any Soviet state interests which the United States must countenance because it had not the means to do otherwise, nor of anything on which the two sides might negotiate to mutual advantage. Though Kennan counseled cool temper, prudence, and patience, he did not contemplate diplomatic bargaining with the Soviet Union at any stage. While the USSR was in its aggressive phase such bargaining would be a sign of Western weakness, not to say of moral complicity with evil, inviting rather than containing the Soviet outward thrust. And when the Soviet regime finally mellowed or decayed, negotiations would hardly be necessary, for it would then behave in such a way that the world would at last become what the United States wanted it to be—that is, what it naturally would be but for the malevolent ideology of the USSR.

Kennan has written since that he did not mean to convey that the Soviet threat was military or that it should be countered by military means, nor that it was communism rather than Soviet power that was to be contained. Nor did he like the ideological dichotomy in Truman's speech or its sweeping commitment to assist all who were threatened by aggression, whatever their capabilities or will and whatever were rational American interests or means of action. On the contrary, the memorandum on aid to Europe drafted for Secretary of State George Marshall by Kennan's State Department planning staff urged that steps be taken to counter the popular view

That the Truman Doctrine is a blank check to give economic and military aid to any area in the world where the Communists show signs of being successful. It must be made clear that the extension of American aid is essentially a question of political economy in the literal sense of that term and that such aid will be considered only in cases where the prospective results bear a satisfactory relationship to the expenditure of American resources and effort.[9]

None of these qualifications, however, can be found in Mr. X's article, and it owed its official patronage and its public vogue to their absence. The article was first written as a private paper for Secretary of the Navy James Forrestal, who had found in Kennan's earlier analyses of Soviet policy from the Moscow embassy—especially the influential "long telegram" of February 1946—just the framework for his own obsessive fear of the Soviet Union. The article was widely praised and distributed by Forrestal before publication and became the handbook for the "new realists" inside and outside the Truman administration even before it was published and the policies it explained became public policy. To Kennan's regret, its ideas were used for years and decades to justify cold war policies which he himself, then and later, found excessively militaristic, ideological, and universalistic. It remained the intellectual framework in practice for the policies even of those who, like the John Foster Dulles of 1952, denounced it in theory as "negative, futile, and immoral."

Buttressed by the success of containment in Greece (which in fact owed much to the Stalin-Tito split), the Kennan article became the gospel of American foreign policy. But it did not pass without challenge. The flaws in its ahistorical and apolitical argument were spotted at once, with extraordinary prescience, by Walter Lippmann.[10] Lippmann, it is important to note, supported aid to Greece and Turkey and the Marshall Plan, but he rejected much of the official thinking behind them. The geographical sweep of Kennan's doctrine, he wrote, not only failed to distinguish between those areas of the world which mattered to the United States—especially Western Europe—and those which did not, but committed it, in lieu of being able to man the trenches everywhere around the periphery of the Soviet Union, to arming "a heterogeneous array of satellites, clients, dependents and puppets." The openendedness of this commitment resulted from a misreading of the nature of the problem presented to the United States by Soviet policy. It was not Marx and his doctrines but the presence of the Red Army in

9. Joseph M. Jones, *The Fifteen Weeks* (New York: Viking, 1955), p. 252.
10. Walter Lippmann, *The Cold War* (New York: Harper & Brothers, 1947).

Central Europe that affected American interests, and it was *that* which
U.S. policy should try to change.

> It is to the Red Army in Europe, therefore, and not to ideologies,
> elections, forms of government, to socialism, to communism, to free
> enterprise, that a correctly conceived and soundly planned policy
> should be directed.[11]

There was only one way to get the Red Army out of Central Europe: by
negotiations—that is, by giving something in return for which the Soviet
Union would give what the United States wanted. The objective of
American policy should be to settle the war in Europe, if it could be
done, on these terms; the means was to bargain with the Soviet Union.
Diplomacy did not require a common outlook or common purposes but
only a common interest in seeking accommodation as preferable to
tension and war.

In the long term Lippmann's most acute insight was to foresee that the
Truman and Kennan formulations would become dangerously facile
and misleading guides when later applied to areas outside Europe without due examination in each case of the particularities of American
interests and the rational probability of applying American power—
great but finite—in local situations. It took twenty years to discover that
the sweeping generalities presented to the public as underpinnings of
policy in the 1940s had become not only shackles on policy but blinders
on the way the public and officials alike saw the world.

Lippmann was also right in believing that the only possible alternative
to the division of Germany was to negotiate its neutralization—that is, to
accept the withdrawal of both Western and Soviet forces from Germany
and its alignment with neither superpower. The notion of achieving
unification on Western terms ("in freedom") was a deception or a self-
deception. But Lippmann probably overestimated the possibility at that
date of negotiating with the Soviet Union the establishment of a united,
neutralized Germany in the midst of Europe, and also the benign
passivity of such a Germany—even if decentralized—could it have been
achieved. Above all, he underestimated the likelihood that a truncated
West Germany could be anchored to the West despite its longing for
unification—something on which the American government probably
agreed even as it took steps to consolidate the division.

Even by mid-1947, however, Lippmann cried in the wilderness. There
was opposition to much of the Truman policy from right and left, from

11. Ibid., p. 39.

Robert Taft and Henry Wallace. There was qualification even within the administration of the literal application of the new doctrine. There was considerable debate about the U.S. role in the world and U.S. policy, the need for and risks of increasing involvement abroad, the scope and costs of what Truman was asking. But out of this debate emerged a new consensus which, once established, limited further debate (though often sharp and partisan) essentially to questions of how, where, and with what means to implement containment.

The administration had presented its case effectively. After all that had happened in Eastern Europe and elsewhere since 1945, neither the American leaders nor people were ready to contemplate such negotiations as Lippmann wanted. They saw Soviet policy as motivated by aggressive ideology. They believed that negotiations with the USSR were wicked, or hopeless, or unnecessary, or should be deferred until the West was strong enough to impose its own will—scarcely Lippmann's idea of negotiation. This was particularly true with respect to the greatest problem of all, Germany. But if realistic negotiation was excluded, and also aggressive war, and if the kind of isolationism represented by Senator Taft now seemed dangerously passive to most people, then nothing remained but to strengthen and defend the Western side of the East-West division of Europe—and, as time passed, of areas outside Europe where the global rhetoric was all too available but where the policies it implied were to prove far less successfully applicable.

Lippmann and the administration agreed that this policy was not an end in itself but a means to an end. But they disagreed about that end. To Lippmann the policy should have been a prelude to serious negotiation with the Soviet Union. In the administration's view there would be no negotiation; rather, Soviet power, if resisted, would eventually mellow, wither, or fall back in the face of American resolve, and Germany and Europe would then be reunited "in freedom."

The irony of the actual outcome—whatever alternatives can be imagined—was that American policy brought about stability in Western Europe, and Europe as a whole, in a form which Kennan in 1947 would have rejected as immoral (because it left Eastern Europe under Soviet control) and Lippmann would have dismissed as impossible (because the Germans would not accept it). Both underestimated the degree to which the new structures established in the two halves of divided Europe as by-products of the cold war phase of U.S.–Soviet relations could, and would, take on lives and even validity of their own. It was neither a restoration of the old European system nor an American victory nor a negotiated compromise but something else.

Containment, it has been said, was the American grand design for the postwar world scaled down to reality.[12] That is, this reduced design was the positive aspect of containment. If the Soviet Union would not cooperate willingly, as some had expected, and if it could not be coerced into cooperation, as others had hoped, then there was nothing to do but go ahead without it and organize as much of the world as was available. Perhaps this element of continuity helps explain the official U.S. rhetoric of the cold war: just as the United Nations was thought to be an essential "something new" as compared to the unacceptable old power politics, so defense of freedom, after 1947, was seen as more likely to command public support than a mere effort to balance Soviet power. Even Kennan's approach, therefore, though much more analytical than Truman's, aimed in the long term to alter the nature, and not just contain the power, of the Soviet regime.

On the political side, both the means and the ends of policy had to be found, and they were. On the economic side, the former global goals were retained but new policies had to be developed to promote them in the unforeseen conditions of the late 1940s. It was clear to the administration that many countries faced, or would face, problems comparable to those of Greece and Turkey—weakness, in the face of Soviet pressure, based on economic distress and political malaise. At the heart of this general problem was the question, already very contentious among the occupying powers, of the productive capacity to be allowed the western zones of Germany. Decisions about that were obviously central to all decisions not only about the future role of Germany but about the economic recovery and political stabilization of Western Europe as a whole. Planning to provide a U.S. response to these problems began even before the Greek-Turkish problem was presented to Congress.

The United States, of course, had tried since before the end of the war to implement its economic design with the countries outside the emerging Soviet bloc. But it had met one disappointment after another. Britain's venture into partial convertibility in the summer of 1947, ill-advisedly required by the U.S.–British loan agreement, had been brief and disastrous. The tariff-cutting and preference-reducing achievements of the 1947 General Agreement on Tariffs and Trade could not but have only modest effects in the economic circumstances of the time. And the International Trade Organization, painfully negotiated in 1947–48 as the centerpiece of trade liberalization, was to be the victim of a three-year stall and eventual quiet interment by Congress.

These setbacks were linked to the production, export, balance of

12. Bruce Kuklick, *American Policy and the Division of Germany* (Ithaca, N.Y.: Cornell University Press, 1972), p. 235.

payments, and reserve difficulties that beset Britain and all of Western
Europe after the war. The United States had given considerable economic help to these ravaged, politically weak countries. But the measures of aid were always short of meeting the need, which was grossly
underestimated. Lend-lease, on which the British had counted for help
into the postwar period, had been abruptly terminated once the war with
Japan was over. The UN Relief and Rehabilitation Administration had
been debarred by Congress from promoting reconstruction and, besides, did not operate in countries that still had some foreign assets (that
is, most of Western Europe). The International Bank and the International Monetary Fund, though under American control, were not
equipped to take care of immediate postwar economic problems. (The
great days of the fund were to follow the restoration of prosperity in the
1950s.) The $3.75 billion loan exceptionally voted by Congress to Britain
and the Export-Import Bank credits granted to others were inadequate
to make the recipients economically self-sustaining.

These measures contributed to the surprisingly rapid political stabilization that took place in most of Western Europe in 1945–46. But a firm
economic base was not established capable of either maintaining that
stability or making possible the open door economic system the United
States wanted. Among the reasons for the economic crisis in Western
Europe were the disruption of traditional trade patterns between Western and Eastern Europe; Western Europe's enormous need for imports
from the United States and other dollar area countries—at rapidly rising
prices—for reconstruction but also for food, coal, and raw materials; its
inability to pay for these imports by exporting; and its loss of reserves
and of earnings from foreign investment and invisibles. Even production equal to 1938 and exports above that level would not allow Western
Europe to pay its way in these circumstances nor, obviously, take its place
in the new economic order. And even those levels were not likely to be
achieved while the western zones of Germany were required to produce
far below their capacity.

Postwar economic conditions were immeasurably more grave than the
wartime planners, preoccupied with the problems of the thirties, had
foreseen. Britain's strength and power, in particular, were constantly
overestimated by the American government and its basic problems were
seen as transitory. American leaders had made no wartime or postwar
commitment to provide reconstruction aid on the scale required. Having
oversold the merits of the Bretton Woods institutions and the British
loan, and used much of their credit with Congress to get these approved,
they were reluctant to ask for more or even to face the needs of reconstruction. It was not until the spring of 1947 that they were ready to

admit that what had been expected to be a transitional economic adjustment was turning into a permanent crisis that threatened both older economic goals and the emerging containment policy in Europe. None of the arrangements made during or after the war, whatever their virtues for immediate relief or long-term structural reform, met this problem.

The circumstances that led to the Truman Doctrine converged with a worsening of the European economic situation, and the administration planned at the same time to deal with both situations. When production in Western Europe fell from 83 percent to 78 percent of 1938 levels between the last quarter of 1946 and the first of 1947 it was believed on both sides of the Atlantic that economic distress would lead to social and political breakdown and that, in turn, to a situation which the Soviet Union would not fail to take advantage of, whether by internal subversion, diplomatic pressure, or outright aggression. Soviet policy and communism, in Washington's view, were not the cause of this situation but they would be the beneficiary.

Existing institutions and policies—including the ambiguous position of the West German economy—were obviously inadequate to meet this crisis. So was a repetition of ad hoc efforts like the one being made for Greece and Turkey. Beginning in March 1947, therefore, the Truman administration began to plan a new response, addressed to the immediate situation but also to the economic roots of the problem. The broad lines of its thinking were set out in a speech delivered by Undersecretary of State Dean Acheson in May. But public attention was drawn to the problem, and the U.S. response, in the speech delivered by Secretary of State George Marshall at Harvard on June 5.

Marshall admitted that earlier piecemeal efforts were not enough and proposed a *long-term* American undertaking to *grant* aid in support of a *cooperative* European *regional* effort to achieve economic self-sufficiency, "a cure rather than a mere palliative."[13] The words italicized signify the orginality and the historical significance of the offer.

The Marshall initiative and the policies that developed from it—for there was no plan at first—were at the same time continuous from the earlier American economic goals and a departure from them with respect to the means of implementation as expressed through lend-lease and the British loan. The United States now accepted a long delay in convertibility. It was now ready to tolerate special trading and payments arrangements which it had been trying to dismantle. Indeed, it undertook to foster European economic cooperation or integration—the terms

13. *The Department of State Bulletin* 16 (June 15, 1947), 1160.

were fluid, the details vague—as necessary both politically and economically for a comprehensive, effective, and cooperative European recovery program that could be presented to the American Congress and
people as something other than more-of-the-same bilateral handouts,
and to European opponents of the revival of the German economy,
which was necessary for reviving the European economy, as a guarantee
against renewed German preponderance.

The U.S. objective of a global trading system was thus refocused onto
a regional framework. The removal of barriers to intra-European trade
was seen as economically expedient for short-term goals but also as
contributing to the original goal in the long term, which, after all, could
not be achieved without a prosperous and stable Europe. The American
passion for European unity, which began to emerge in 1947 and
bloomed luxuriantly until the mid-1960s, owed much of its strength to
the conviction of its proponents, and their need to convince others, that
what looked like a step away from fundamental American goals was in
fact a step toward them. Thus, a European trading bloc was necessary if
Europe was to use its own resources and American aid efficiently to
recover its strength and stability. But such a bloc was not to be confused
with bad old imperial preference and the like. The difference lay in the
fact that the goals of West European recovery and unity were positive in
themselves and were the means by which other political and economic
goals could eventually be achieved.

In fact, the United States settled for little actual European economic
integration in implementing the Marshall Plan. Cutting off aid to any
country to force it along the path of unity would have been much too
heavy a sanction in terms of the other objectives of the program. But the
impulse at least lent a note of constructive novelty to the policy. Moreover, it provided the basis for powerful American support to the efforts
which the Europeans themselves would eventually develop—for their
own reasons—in the following years.

Some contemporaries wondered how a united Europe would fit into
the global system embodied in the International Monetary Fund (IMF)
and the General Agreement on Tariffs and Trade (GATT) and how the
United States could promote both levels with equal zeal.[14] But the subtle
problem of the long-term relationship between the kind of Europe
which the Marshall Plan aimed to call into being and the U.S.-led global
system of which the European states were a part lay in the future. The

14. Harry Bayard Price, *The Marshall Plan and Its Meaning* (Ithaca, N.Y.: Cornell University Press, 1955), pp. 287–88.

immediate political impact of the program created by the Marshall initiative was to confirm the already ongoing division of Europe.

The planners of the proposal tried to avoid giving the impression, which they believed was a fault of the Truman Doctrine, that it was crudely military and ideological and simply an instrument of anticommunism. Marshall had been careful to say that "Our policy is directed not against any country or doctrine but against hunger, poverty, desperation, and chaos."[15] Certainly there *was* more in the Marshall proposal than containment. The economic prosperity and political stability of Western Europe were important to the United States for more than one reason. But it was clear to the public on both sides of the Atlantic, from the context and the follow-up, that the new policy, like the Truman Doctrine, was part of the emerging response to what was perceived as a multiple Soviet and Communist threat. It is not likely that Congress would have approved the program on any other basis.

It was clear also that the regional cooperation promoted by Washington concerned Western Europe, not Europe as a whole. Though the American offer was nominally open to the Soviet Union as to other European countries, there could have been little expectation that it would join in the required cooperative response or, if it did, that the program would have received congressional and public support in the United States. As it turned out the Russians did refuse, and forced their satellites to do so, so that the onus for the division of Europe fell on them. The ensuing association in the Committee (later the Organization) for European Economic Cooperation (OEEC) and in the European Payments Union (EPU) of the sixteen Western Europe participants—including the West German zones—marked the first *positive* structural delineation of the postwar division of Europe along the military line drawn in 1945.

Here too support for European cooperation and unity proved to be a useful strand in American policy. It was not coincidental that the positive delineation of a two-bloc Europe—symbolized by the fate of Czechoslovakia—coincided with the first attempt to define a Western European entity within the emerging American-led Euratlantic bloc. The new American goal of a united Western Europe had, of course, several roots. An important one, as mentioned above, was economic efficiency. Another was the idea that such a Europe might help attenuate old European quarrels and, above all, provide an acceptable framework for the emerging West German state. This was to be important particu-

15. *The Department of State Bulletin* 16 (June 15, 1947), 1160.

larly for France, which had to accept that circumstances and American policy required creating such a state and that its economic power would be far greater than the French had thought tolerable in the first postwar years.

But for the United States, Western European unity was also a most convenient component of a policy which was contributing to, or at least advertising, the division of Europe as a whole. If the traditional unity of Europe (at least as contrasted with the sharp post-1945 division) could not be restored, and if the United States itself—not to say the West Europeans—was not ready, even when the Atlantic Alliance was signed in 1949, to conceive of a structured and enduring Euratlantic relationship, then the ultimate unification of Western Europe provided a rational and even emotional cause to work for beyond the exigencies of the moment. This was seen as being true for the West Germans, who had to accept the division of their country, and for the French and other neighbors of Germany, who had to accept its economic, political, and, very soon, military resurrection. As discussed in later chapters, the real framework for containing the new Germany was to be the Atlantic one, led by a United States immeasurably stronger than any of the European partners. But that was not seen as clearly in the late 1940s as it might have been. For that reason the dream of uniting Western Europe seemed an essential focus for the diverse hopes and fears of diverse Europeans.

The eventual result was the development from 1947 on of not one but two lasting sets of institutions that defined West as against East in Europe—the Atlantic-global, first in time and rank, and, within them, the European-regional. Both sets included political and security as well as economic components. The former, as the United States became more permanently engaged in Europe, proved stronger and more enduring than had been expected. The latter, partly for that reason, proved harder to build than had been expected. The relations between the two, subtle and ambivalent from the beginning in the Marshall Plan period to the present, are examined in chapter 10.

The structural response of the other half of Europe to the Marshall Plan and its offshoot was the formation of the Cominform in September 1947. This was seen in the West, and was presumably intended to be seen, as the successor of the interwar Comintern. There could have been no clearer declaration of ideological war between the two halves of Europe and their superpower leaders. The line of division expressed in Europe between those countries which took part in the Marshall Plan and those which joined the Cominform struck contemporaries as signifying a basic division and alignment going far beyond the actual programs of either. This was the more true in that it coincided with the breakdown in April 1947 of the long effort to reach a four-power agreement on Germany (discussed in the next chapter) and with the rupture in May between the French and Italian Communist parties and the governments in which they had taken part since the war.

Contemporaries were more right than wrong about this. Though one strength of the Marshall program was that it was economic rather than political or military, the economic ties it helped to revive and stimulate across the Atlantic clearly established powerful bonds of mutual interest that could not but have reinforcing political significance. In view of the powerful economic ties that bind the United States and Western Europe more than thirty years after the Marshall Plan was started, not only Marxists can see that this Atlantic economic system, developed within the framework of the cold war, is a major element in a broader system of state relations. Some, of course, have argued that the economic component was the main spring and motive of the system, perhaps even the system itself. More accurately, the Atlantic economic system that crystallized after 1947 was the American economic design for the post-war world scaled down to fit the part of the world then amenable to U.S. influence. But it was also more than this. The cold war gave political solidity, a broader dimension, to the economic system which it was not likely to have had in any other way.

Nevertheless, the division of Europe was not positively consummated in mid-1947, nor was the Western grouping (whatever may be said about the Eastern) which has emerged from that division. The division and the blocs became fixed by a series of political decisions which might conceivably have been made—despite the already strong impetus of the cold war—in some other way. These decisions concerned the mutual security ties between the United States and the West European countries, and, connected with those, the establishment and the arming of the West German state.

The United States in the first half of 1947 considered both Greece and Turkey, on the one hand, and the countries of Western Europe, on the other, to be in danger of being lost to the Soviet Union, but the American response differed according to the perception of the threat. The two Mediterranean countries, in the one case vulnerable to armed internal subversion and in the other to acute external pressure, were given military as well as economic assistance, though not a treaty of alliance. Western Europe was thought to be less exposed to outright attack than to internal breakdown which would lead to either Communist or outright Soviet rule (insofar as any such distinction was made at all). And, of course, the countries of Western Europe were major participants in whatever global economic system was going to emerge. The Truman Doctrine was directed to the first case, the Marshall Plan to the second.

It is an interesting comment on the evolution of the cold war that neither the United States nor the Europeans were ready in 1947 for a security alliance. Economic reconstruction was said to be the remedy for Europe's problems, as if Western Europe could be put back on its feet—politically and militarily—by large but finite doses of money. The sense of restoring rather than building new was still strong. Even then, however, some in Congress said that a military alliance with Western Europe was essential, and others concluded that such a degree of American concern was logically implicit in the Marshall Plan commitment itself. But there was no consensus on that in 1947, nor on the extent of the American interest—as defined by American commitment—in Europe, nor on the scope of the European problem itself.

Nevertheless, the evolving situation in Europe had already begun to give rise to the security system established two years later. The Anglo-French Treaty of Dunkirk (March 1947) is often seen as the first step in this process. In fact, the parties were thinking more about Germany than about the Soviet Union, more about politics than about defense. In theory, the treaty established the explicit mutual defense arrangement which Britain and France lacked between 1919 and 1939. In practice, it reflected the growing French conviction that de Gaulle's policy of Franco-Soviet collaboration on Germany was born dead and that France had to cover itself as best it could against a new German state whose emergence it could not prevent and whose partnership, in some form, it would have to seek. At Dunkirk in 1947, as at Brussels a year later, France entered into ostensibly anti-German arrangements to be able to accept German revival as part of an anti-Soviet policy.

The association of the Benelux countries with the Anglo-French alliance was a natural consequence of these considerations, but by the time it was achieved in the Treaty of Brussels (March 1948—a month after the Czech coup) there was no doubt but that the five countries were planning defense against the Soviet Union. More precisely, they were preparing the way for what their governments had by then come to see as essential to their security, and perhaps to their domestic tranquility too—an American guarantee.

By then the United States was ready for this step, as signaled by the Vandenberg resolution of the Senate. The Berlin blockade (see chapter 8) had clearly exposed Western military weakness in Europe, a weakness that would become even more dangerous when the American nuclear monopoly came to an end. There were three possible responses to the strategic and political problems of Europe as they appeared to the American and West European governments in 1948.

Senator Robert Taft, among others, suggested a unilateral American guarantee to Western Europe—an extension of the Monroe Doctrine. This was rejected by governments on both sides of the Atlantic because it was thought unconvincing—unreassuring to the Europeans and undeterring to the Russians. Besides, it seemed too much like a protectorate to be compatible with European dignity.

Both European and American military planners would have liked a buildup of Western military forces in Europe. This, however, was also rejected—or postponed—because of the weakness of the European economies, the political impossibility of arming the West Germans, and the unwillingness of Congress to pay for a major buildup of either American or European forces. The U.S. defense budget remained under tight control up to the Korean war. No coherent local military support in Europe was provided by the United States, even after the Berlin crisis, to back up its diplomacy.

The solution to the European security problem that was adopted provided for a commitment of American nuclear strength to Europe in treaty form. In July 1948—a month after the Berlin blockade began—the Brussels partners entered negotiations to establish a formal alliance with the United States. To encompass existing or planned American bases in a single security structure, and to round out its geographic scope, Canada, Norway, Denmark, Iceland, Italy, and Portugal were eventually included. The North Atlantic Treaty was signed by the twelve founding partners on April 4, 1949.

This choice, in contrast to the other two, had uniquely important strategic and political implications reaching far beyond the immediate circumstances. On the military side, an elaborate structure of committees was set up and an integrated defense concept was adopted—on paper. But the Truman administration denied any intention of sending more American troops to Europe or of arming Germans. It provided only a modest amount of military aid to the Europeans. The principal objective of the arrangement then was not to defeat or even deter an immediate conventional Soviet attack, for none was expected. Rather, the threat posed by Soviet power in Eastern Europe was to be equilibrated, psychologically as well as militarily, by formally linking American nuclear power to the protection of Western Europe—that is, by throwing a nuclear cloak over Europe. This was the first effort to use American nuclear power in a politically explicit way. Reassured that the U.S. nuclear arsenal stood behind them, the Europeans would have a secure basis for their recovery, their participation in the Marshall Plan's economic system, their social and political stabilization, and their resistance to Communist subversion.

The American nuclear guarantee has remained the keystone of the alliance. But the other military assumptions of 1949 proved shortlived, for the Korean war led to that conventional buildup in Europe, including a West German contribution, which the treaty-signers had turned aside.

In the long run the political implications of the alliance have been even more important than the military. For one thing, a peacetime alliance of this kind was, of course, a striking departure from American tradition. It reflected how far the intensity of cold war feelings had carried U.S. opinion even as compared to 1947. The American commitment has turned out, long after 1949, to be a fundamental choice, less in danger of being backed away from as circumstances change than of being taken as an example for other areas where different problems called for different kinds of solutions.

Second, it is notable that few Europeans of 1949 were distressed by the fact that beneath the formal egalitarianism of the alliance lay a fundamental asymmetry: the United States gave protection and the other allies accepted it. It was enough then that, behind this protection and the confidence it gave to Europe, the essential business of reviving Europe's economic strength, and eventually its political and military power, could proceed. When that did come about, the alliance's asymmetry was to prove a problem, but also a habit.

One of the most important implications of the choice made in 1949 for an Atlantic alliance rather than some other kind of security arrangement was that it provided a tangible expression of a much broader community of interests which the members already shared and which was to grow increasingly comprehensive in the years to come, partly because the alliance existed, partly for other reasons. These interests included but went beyond both the military and economic. They were handled by the Atlantic countries in many organizations, not only in NATO.[16] But because of the importance of its own functions as well as its symbolic visibility, NATO came to be seen as a state system in itself, so close and multiform were the ties among its members. More accurately, the community for which NATO stood has been a component or subsystem of a system which included also the Soviet Union and its allies—that is, a state

16. The alliance will henceforth generally be referred to here for convenience as NATO, notwithstanding the proper distinction among the treaty, the alliance it expresses, the organization through which the alliance has functioned, and the military aspect of that organization—all of which are sometimes referred to by the acronym.

system that included almost every European state but also included and was dependent on two states that were vastly stronger than any of these and were wholly or partially extra-European.

The emergence of two organized blocs in Europe—military alliances, but much more than that—was a long step beyond the East-West division produced by the war. But, though the blocs provided the structure of a new state system, they did not yet provide its stability. For that there had to be a tenable solution of the German problem which had caused the breakdown of the prior European system and led straight to the dual hegemony (even in antagonism) of the United States and the Soviet Union. Neither of these powers intended at first to bring about the German solution which, in fact, they did bring about. Yet almost everything they did with respect to each other led to it with as great a precision as if they had planned it. The completion of the division of Germany, the closing out of other options, is the most striking outcome of the cold war—except for the emergence of the two-bloc system whose stability first required and has since maintained that division.

CHAPTER 8

Consolidation of the Two-Bloc System:
The German Problem

During the war all the Allies considered what they should do after the victory to prevent renewed German aggression. The answer obviously lay in doing what was not done in 1919: somehow depriving the Germans of either the means or the will to commit aggression. But these two approaches covered a wide spectrum of possible policies, from partition of the country to reeducation of the people.

Of the four powers that would later occupy Germany, France's solution to the German problem was the most clearcut and most consistently pursued. It wanted separation and French occupation of the Rhineland, some form of international control over the Ruhr, or at least over its resources, and a decentralized regime for the rest of Germany. Great Britain, at the other extreme, can hardly be said to have had a comprehensive approach to the German problem. Of the two powers that counted most, little is certain about Soviet policy except that the Russians wanted as much reparation from Germany as could be obtained. We know a great deal more about American thinking than about Soviet—so much, in fact, that it is not easy to be sure, from the welter of ideas covering the ground from reeducation and reparations to partition and pastoralization, whether the U.S. government had a clear policy line, or several, or none. But here, as on other issues, the United States generally wanted to defer decision until the war was ended.

One obvious device all of them played with was the idea of partitioning Germany—inspired, no doubt, by the unsatisfactory results of the failure to do so in 1919. The Big Three governments seemed agreed in principle on partition in the autumn of 1943. A major step to that end was taken at Teheran in November, when it was agreed that Poland would lose its lands east of the Curzon line to the Soviet Union and would be compensated at Germany's expense by most of East Prussia and territory up to the Oder River. But this first step toward partition, which was taken as a by-product of Poland's territorial problem with the USSR rather than as part of a coherent policy for postwar Germany, was also the last in that direction. The problem was assigned for study to the European Advisory Commission but the United States, faithful to its policy of postponement, blocked any further work. By the time of the

Yalta meeting the American and particularly the British governments had second thoughts and agreed, despite Soviet pressure, only to refer the issue of partition to another committee for study. It too accomplished nothing.

When the war ended in May 1945, none of the Big Three was still thinking seriously of partition. The Americans had come to share the British concern about the economic costs of a fragmented Germany. The Russians had also reversed course, announcing publicly at the moment of surrender that they had no intention to dismember or destroy Germany. France still favored partition but, as the event showed, it lacked the means to implement this policy in face of the nonsupport of the others.

But while the Big Three had turned aside from partition as a policy goal, they had begun to implement it in the arrangements they made before the war ended for occupying defeated Germany. Unconditional surrender implied Allied occupation and government. Occupation in common was dismissed early on and with little discussion, as was also the idea of joint U.S.–U.K. occupation of the part of Germany outside the Soviet zone. The adopted plan therefore called for dividing Germany into three occupation zones (increased to four at Yalta when the British, who worked consistently to build up France as a postwar partner in Western Europe, persuaded Roosevelt and Stalin to give it a share in the German occupation). Each commander-in-chief was to be supreme in his own zone except as he was bound by the unanimous decisions of the control council for all Germany of which they were members. Berlin was to be similarly divided and similarly governed.

No one saw these arrangements as foreshadowing a partition of Germany on zonal lines. They were worked out as a practical framework for implementing common occupation policies during the interim period between Germany's defeat and a peace treaty. But the four occupants had not reached agreement before the war ended on such common policies. In particular there were no policies about reparations or management of the Germany economy during the occupation or afterward. The first postwar attempt to produce such policies, at the Potsdam conference, had mixed results. The most important long-term outcome was that the attempt to establish economic and reparations policies confirmed the division of the country. Partition was not considered at Potsdam in principle, but it was further implemented in practice.

At Potsdam—from which France was excluded, though it was by then a participant in the occupation and a member of the control council—the Big Three had little difficulty agreeing on a program to demilitarize and denazify Germany. They also managed to agree in principle to organize the machinery for devising a common economic policy for the four zones—a high priority for the Americans and British, whose zones needed food from the Soviet zone—and to establish the beginnings of a German administration to carry out, under Allied directives, whatever policy they would adopt. In two major respects, however, their disagreements proved more important than these agreements.

First, the Soviet Union made known that it had assigned to Polish administration the part of German territory in its zone up to the Oder and western Neisse rivers, which was thus subtracted from the area controlled by the four powers. The Western powers complained about the extent of the area (they had favored an Oder–eastern Neisse line, which would have left much of Silesia to Germany) and, above all, about the unilateral Soviet disposition of German territory. But they could not reverse the Russian decision. In the end they accepted it as part of a deal that also concerned reparations policy, while pretending to treat the line as only provisional—the beginning of a long and monotonous tale.

Second, and even more significant, the Big Three could not reach agreement on a unified policy of drawing reparations from Germany. This issue, of course, touched on the much broader question of the future role of Germany in the European and world economies, and on this too there was no three-power understanding.

Reparations then and later preoccupied the Russians much more, not unnaturally, than they did the Americans and British. The Russians wanted all they could get from all zones. But by July 1945 the Americans and British were unwilling either to let the standard of living in their zones be reduced to what they considered a dangerous level or to maintain it by providing aid to replace material shipped as reparations to the USSR. (Reparations in cash, which had been part of the Versailles model, were ruled out because of the post-Versailles experience.) This specific issue was meshed with a broader view of the future of the German economy. According to this, Germany should be deprived of its war-making potential but should remain an important industrial power, both because this was essential to the economic recovery of Europe as a whole and because a prosperous Germany was most likely eventually to become democratic and peaceful. The British came to this position even before Yalta despite the temptations of reducing German competition to their own trading position implicit in the Morgenthau plan or removing industrial equipment from Germany.

As for the American government, it came to see that neither partition, nor Henry Morgenthau's pastoralization ideas, nor Soviet demands for the massive removal of German equipment and goods were compatible with European and German recovery. After a period of fluctuation it rejected all of them. Whether or not all the American decision-makers were conscious of the fact at the time, these decisions implied that other ways would have to be found to handle the German problem over the long term and that the United States would have to remain involved in the direct management of European affairs for longer than it had expected during the war.

The Soviet Union and the United States had agreed at Yalta that the figure of $20 billion should be the "basis for discussion" of reparations (defined there as including both capital equipment and current production) and that around half the sum eventually set would go to the USSR. The British did not go along with this agreement even at Yalta, and the Americans in effect backed off from it when the time came, in June 1945, to discuss specifics. Led by a new administration, and confronting both the devastation of Germany and disquieting Soviet policies, the United States government shifted the emphasis from a total sum to percentages, and from priority for reparations to priority for the "first charge"—the cost of the imports needed to keep Germany alive and productive. It would be odd if at least some Americans did not also see a chance to use the Soviet preoccupation with getting reparations from the Western zones as leverage to induce the Russians to accept American ideas for German economic unity and strength. This aspect of American thinking was parallel to the U.S. attempt to use the Soviet loan application for policy leverage, and, as it turned out, was equally unsuccessful as policy.

The upshot at Potsdam was to leave the total reparations bill undecided—a heavy blow to the Russians—and to allow each occupying power to remove capital assets from its own zone, subject to later understandings as to overall production levels and economic policy for Germany as a whole. (The Russians undertook to provide reparations to Poland; the Western powers were to take care of other claimants.) This one centralizing element in a generally decentralizing plan was given some reality, at least potentially, and the Soviet Union was given limited access to the industrial wealth of the Ruhr, by the provision that 10 percent of the assets from the three Western zones "unnecessary for the German peace economy" (however that was to be defined) were to be given gratis to the Soviet Union and 15 percent were to be traded to the Russians for food and raw materials from their zone.

This clearcut falling back on the autonomy of the four zones might have been overcome if the central economic machinery envisaged at Potsdam had been implemented, though with what other consequences it is difficult to conceive. But at the one moment when the Big Three seemed ready to proceed on this road—in the autumn of 1945—the

French refused to concur unless the Rhineland and the Ruhr were removed from the area that was to be included under the proposed central administration.

It seems incredible that the Big Three, having given France an occupation zone and a veto in the control council, should first have excluded it from the Potsdam decision-making about Germany and then, despite early, explicit, and repeated French warnings, expected it to fall in with their plans without their paying any attention to its own. If France had been in possession of the Rhineland and Ruhr it might have followed the unilateral example set by the Soviet Union east of the Oder-Neisse; since it occupied only a part of the Rhineland and none of the Ruhr it used what leverage it had to prevent its policies from being blocked at the outset. The French veto was perhaps the first postwar example of France's capacity for surprising its allies by bold use of such power as it possessed to promote its distinctive policies.

More important in this case, however, is the question of what might have happened had the central economic administration envisaged at Potsdam been set up during 1945 or 1946, or if the Big Three had at least set up such a system in their own zones, as it seemed for a short time they might be ready to do. The question is perhaps the most fascinating might-have-been of postwar European history. Some have thought a single German government might have evolved, rather as was the case in Austria, and that a united—albeit probably neutralized—German state would eventually have emerged. Such speculation is tempting. Yet we can wonder whether either the Soviet Union or the Western powers, once the cold war competition emerged, would have risked letting their zones be swallowed up in a German state which would have been (despite the losses in the East) large, populous, rich, and, moreover, open because of neutralization to the influence of the other side. More likely is that the central administration, even had it been set up, would have been swept away by the forces that did in fact lead to Germany's division.

What would have become of a united but neutralized Germany if, somehow, it had emerged from the economic administration planned at Potsdam? The unity, once reestablished, could hardly have been called into question. But what of the neutrality? For all the trauma of war and defeat, would a rich, disarmed, and irredentist Germany have been content, in effect, to have no foreign policy? Possibly, if we can assume that the happy and widely unexpected evolution of postwar West Germany toward democracy and the sensible acceptance of partition and its diminished status can be traced in large part to the *tabula rasa* created by overwhelming defeat and unconditional surrender. But can we be sure that the restoration of a unitary state would have made no difference? If a united Germany *was* incluned to assert itself, would the Allies, for whom the division of Germany was a consequence and not a cause of their cold war competition, have been able to find enough agreement among themselves to keep it neutral and disarmed? Or would their continuing rivalry have led them to compete for German support by relaxing the limitations on its freedom of action? British and French policy toward Germany constantly diverged after 1919. Would the United States and the Soviet Union, engaged in a far more profound competition and hostility, have been likely to find and hold to a common line? Would the American hope of integrating Germany into the Western economic system have been pursued or realized? Since Germany could not possibly have lived in autarky, could such integration have been avoided whatever the United States or Germany or anyone else did? If so, what would have been the Soviet response?

There can be no definite answers about the fate of a neutralized and united Germany set up in, say, 1946–47, any more than there can be about what would have happened if such a Germany had come into being on some later occasion, for example, after 1952 or 1957. That these opportunities, whatever they amounted to, were lost seemed ominous or even tragic to some at the time, and since, because they assumed that a divided Germany would never be accepted by the German people and that German irredentism would be a threat to peace. This belief was held by both advocates and critics of the Western policies that led to the establishment of a West German state. The former proclaimed that the Federal Republic of Germany (FRG) would be only a temporary way station on the road to a Germany reunited "in freedom"; the latter feared that the temporary would become permanent, but dangerously so.

Both were wrong. The temporary has lasted and has defused the problem of German unity. Knowing what we know about that, and *not* knowing what course a united, neutralized Germany would have taken toward the competing superpowers, or they toward it, there is no compelling reason to believe now that establishing a three-zone administration in 1946 or a united and neutralized Germany later would have led to a more stable and peaceful Europe than the very stable and peaceful Europe that did, in fact, emerge as a by-product of the cold war rivalry that fixed Germany's division.

What was important in 1946 was that the Americans and British acquiesced in the French veto, after threats and blandishments, and that cold war competition then killed whatever chance there still was in late

1945 for development away from partition.[1] The idea of neutralizing a united Germany was taken up again periodically after 1945—by some, logically enough, before the Federal Republic was armed in 1955; by others, most illogically, soon *after* rearmament. But it was beyond realization.

So, however, was the absorption of the whole of Germany into either bloc. It is not clear when the United States (and Great Britain) on one hand, the Soviet Union on the other, decided to cement the part of Germany they occupied into their own systems rather than risk losing it in pursuit of the whole—or when they came to the conclusion that events left them no other choice. It has been suggested that the United States contrived—or at least accepted—this outcome as early as Potsdam and that the reparations agreement reached there signaled this policy. The detailed record of the following months and years does not seem to confirm this view. More likely, partition was viewed at first only as a fallback position, and a possibly dangerous one, if the inducement of reparations from the Western zones failed to lead the Russians to give up control of their own zone in favor of some all-German arrangement on lines favored by the United States. The hook baited at Potsdam failed to achieve this objective, but that does not prove that there was never such an objective.

Similarly, it can be argued that Soviet policy toward Germany as a whole in 1945–46, and in their own zone, reflected an early decision to secure possession of at least the part of Germany they occupied by any means and at whatever cost to their chances of extending their influence westward. But why would the Soviet Union have settled so early for so little? During 1946 the Russians seemed to be bidding for the support of

1. It is not clear why the United States, which had strong leverage on France, went to the brink of threatening to form a central administration in Germany without it and then drew back. Perhaps the American government—which was very divided on German issues—was bluffing, or feared to upset the French political scene to Communist advantage, or decided that the Russians, whatever they said at the time, would not after all cooperate in American plans for Germany and that a "trizonia" on any other terms would be more dangerous than helpful. See Bruce Kuklick, *American Policy and the Division of Germany* (Ithaca, N.Y.: Cornell University Press, 1972), pp. 195–97. The problem of France's activities in Germany preoccupied American policymakers very considerably in 1945–48. See John Gimbel, *The American Occupation of Germany* (Stanford, Calif.: Stanford University Press, 1968), pp. 167–69. This is not to say, however, that the Soviet problem could have been handled in a way satisfactory to the Americans and British even if they had used their full leverage on France. Perhaps their realization of this inhibited their leaning on France with their full weight. The Russians probably believed that the United States not only acquiesced in but sanctioned French behavior, which helped keep them out of the Ruhr.

German nationalists with calls for a centralized state and a higher level of industrial production. At the least they wanted reparations from the Western zones and some voice in control of the Ruhr. In either case, and even more so if their policy was openended and opportunistic, there would have to be bargaining with the Western powers and, therefore, some openness and fluidity in their own zone. The communization of the Eastern zone in fact proceeded slowly (as it did at the same time in Hungary and Czechoslovakia). Non-Communist parties had a meaningful though minority role in zonal political life through 1946. That communization of a fragment of Germany was the outcome does not in itself exclude the possibility of other options in Soviet policy to which other circumstances might have given life.

However that may be, the momentum of the cold war, well underway before the German problem began to crystallize, blocked *both* the absorption of all of Germany into either of the two emerging blocs *and* development toward unity in neutrality after 1945. But by bringing about a partition of Germany advocated by none of the Big Three in that year, it gave a stable institutional structure to the ad hoc military division of Europe created by Germany's defeat that could have been provided in no other way. In doing that it provided a solution of the German problem that had bedeviled Europe since the end of the nineteenth century. Thanks, ironically, to the cold war, the outcome of World War II was more sound, more lasting, and systemically more beneficent than that of World War I. Only the slow development and unsigned nature of the one settlement as compared to the other, and the persisting belief that the division of Germany was unstable and dangerous, despite the growing evidence to the contrary, have prevented this from being generally understood.

The four occupying powers addressed the German problem at periodic meetings of their foreign ministers, but to no positive effect. The important activity was elsewhere. American policy pursued a multiplicity of ends, some laid down before the war ended, others developed out of the exigencies of the occupation itself, the economic stagnation of the Western zones, and the widening competition with the Soviet Union.

> Besides wanting to denazify, demilitarize, decartelize, democratize, and reorient Germans and Germany, Americans were also interested in seeing to their own continued security, bringing about the economic rehabilitation of Germany and Europe, and guaranteeing the continuance of free enterprise. They wanted to frustrate socialism, to forestall Communism, to spare American taxpayers'

money, to counteract French plans to dismember Germany, and to
contain the Soviet Union in Central Europe.[2]

These goals were pursued by different officials with different degrees
of emphasis at different times. Not surprisingly, American policy, always
the work of many hands, appears ambiguous in its motives as well as in
its effects. Thus, the halt of reparations dismantling in the American
zone in May 1946 can be seen as a further attempt to get France and the
Soviet Union to implement the Potsdam policy of treating Germany as
an economic unit, or it can be seen as recognition that that policy was
hopeless and that it was time to move openly to implement the policy of
German economic revival already underway. Similarly, the decision to
merge the American and British zones at the end of 1946 can be seen
variously as promoting economic rationalization; inserting the United
States into the administration of the Ruhr; assuring that Western Germany
would be organized on the lines of American capitalism rather than British
socialism; pressuring France and the Soviet Union into accepting German
economic unity; or recognizing that there was no hope of such unity and
laying the groundwork for a West German state.

In any case there emerged in mid-1946, and to some degree even
earlier, the overall policy which Secretary of State Byrnes laid out in a
speech at Stuttgart on September 6. This was the first comprehensive
postwar statement of American policy toward Germany and a marked
departure from the harsh policy laid down in Joint Chiefs of Staff
Document 1067, which had nominally been the basis for American
occupation policy since April 1945. Publicly focusing into a coherent
whole the U.S. policy of promoting German economic and political
revival already being applied by then, Byrnes described with prescience
what would happen in Germany during the next three years. But the
speaker, of course, was not a prophet. He was a spokesman for American plans, and these plans—however mixed the motives behind them—
were leading to economic rehabilitation of the Western zones, German
economic unity minus the Soviet zone, and a federal political structure in
the Western zones that was, whatever qualifications were made, a new
state.

Negotiations on zonal fusion were already underway between the
United States and Great Britain when Byrnes spoke. Avowing frustration at their inability to implement the Potsdam decision providing for a
unified economic administration for all four zones, they agreed in December to establish a common economic administration at least for their
own zones. The agreement became effective on January 1, 1947.

2. Gimbel, *The American Occupation*, p. xiii.

If the Anglo-Saxon powers thought that their action might lead the USSR to "implement Potsdam" they were disappointed. France, which many Americans saw at the time as an even more important obstacle to a common administration than the USSR, also still held back from joining this bizone system, partly from unwillingness to align itself with what seemed to be (and was) an anti-Soviet policy, partly because it still hoped to bargain its cooperation in Germany against separating the Rhineland and the Ruhr, which Byrnes had ruled out. The French also continued to object to an increase in the level of industry to be permitted in "bizonia."

But events soon swept France, if not the Soviet Union, into the Anglo-Saxon system (and not only with respect to German affairs), just as they swept along (or over) the American and British critics of the economic revival of Germany, who were still numerous in 1947. There followed in quick succession the Truman Doctrine, the failure of a prolonged four-power ministerial meeting on Germany, initiation of the Marshall Plan and of American aid aimed to revive the flagging economies of Western Europe (including the German), and the practical and symbolic division of Europe that that policy precipitated and highlighted. The Communist ministers left the French and Italian cabinets in May. With emphasis in Western Europe now on economic recovery, seen as both an end in itself and as a means of strengthening the social and political fabric against Communist subversion or Soviet attack, it was obvious that Western Germany would be called on to play its part—a large part. A new American directive for the occupation of Germany, issued in July, expressed clearly what had until then been a major but somewhat muted and contested strand of American policy:

> An orderly and prosperous Europe requires the economic contributions of a stable and productive Germany. . . .[3]

The critics of German economic revival found it hard to resist in this framework, the more so as it promised to lift from the American and British governments the burden of subsidizing a West German economy producing far below its prewar level under existing policies.

It was not a long step to the conclusion that a reviving Germany with an important role in a reviving Europe could not remain forever under the direct military rule of the occupying powers. One motive for merging the American and British zones was a wish to counter Soviet appeals to German national sentiment and to show movement by the Western

3. *The Department of State Bulletin* 17 (July 27, 1947), 186.

powers. Byrnes at Stuttgart called for political as well as economic evolution in Germany.

The United States had begun to organize German administrations in its own zone at the *land* and zonal levels before the end of 1945, and some similar steps were also taken in the other zones. The pace of political evolution in 1947 was set on the Western side. In May, after the four-power conference failed to make any progress on a common economic policy, reparations, a peace treaty, or the future German political system, the Americans and British agreed to set up a bizone German Economic Council to be elected by the *land* parliaments—in effect a German protogovernment. In June the Russians established a coordinating economic commission among the five *länder* of their zone. Contact between the two parts of Germany, until then reasonably open, was now drastically curtailed by the Soviet Union. Zonal boundaries became a frontier.

In November and December the four foreign ministers met again and failed again.

> Mr. Molotov had failed to secure his reparations and had failed to prevent the creation of a western German state; General Marshall and Mr. Bevin had failed to secure the economic unification of Germany; M. Bidault had failed to secure even discussion of the Saar and was obliged to return to Paris without comfort concerning the Ruhr and the Rhineland. The alliance, holy or unholy, had at least reached Laibach, if not Verona.[4]

This multiple failure to achieve the goals which the powers had been seeking since Potsdam opened the way to new policies, already in gestation. The French problem dwindled as the last hopes for four-power agreement on Germany died and French dependence on the United States became confirmed. In February 1948, the same month as the coup in Czechoslovakia, the three Western powers (and the Benelux countries) held a conference in London looking to the formation of a West German state. The Russians responded in March by leaving the four-power control council on the ground that the West had alredy broken up the quadripartite government of Germany. If this was meant to slow down the pace of Western planning, the effect was the reverse. In June the six Western states announced their decision to establish a federal West German state. The French were satisfied (or not satisfied, as the

---

4. Peter Calvocoressi, *Survey of International Affairs 1947–1948* (New York: Oxford University Press, 1952), pp. 240–41.

difficult debate in the National Assembly showed) by arrangements which fell far short of the extreme decentralization they had favored for West Germany and the separation of the Ruhr and the Rhineland. What they got was de facto possession of the Saar (which they had long since begun to assimilate economically) and the setting up of a seven-power authority (including West Germany) to exercise some control over the reviving Ruhr industries, which, however, were to remain under private German ownership and management. A week later the three Western powers implemented a long-delayed currency reform in their German zones as a spur to economic revival.

The Soviet response to this reform, which they denounced as aimed to divide Germany, was to reform the currency of their zone and of all Berlin, which, they said, was located in the Soviet zone and economically formed a part of it. The Allies then introduced the new West German currency into West Berlin, though to supplement, not replace, the eastern currency. The Soviet answer was to blockade the western zones of the city. This action was obviously not only a reply to the currency issues or even an effort to end the Western presence in Berlin, though this was no doubt less tolerable to the Russians in a finally divided Germany than in the days of quadripartite control. The Russians aimed above all at blocking the formation of the West German state by discouraging the Germans, if not the three allies, from proceeding.

Once again, however, Soviet action if anything speeded up what it intended to prevent. The Western powers decided, almost reflexively, to hang on to their position in Berlin, realizing that abandoning it under pressure would have undermined the West German state before it was born and undercut the broader efforts to strengthen Western Europe. The willingness of the West German politicians to go ahead in these circumstances—despite their reservations about both the limitations on the authority they were being offered and the accentuation of the division of Germany that was explicit in setting up a three-zone state— pointed clearly to the future international role of that state. The Federal Republic, once formed, might possibly have tried to pursue unification by means of neutralization, or to organize Western Europe into a "third force"—neutral or mediating—between the superpowers, or at least followed later French efforts to that end. Many abroad feared that it might do one or another of these things and some at home argued, particularly in the early 1950s, that it should. But it has never done so. The Berlin blockade laid a strong prenatal basis for the Federal Republic's abiding reliance on the United States which has existed from that day to this. This was the easier for West Germany because the circumstances that led to the establishment of the Federal Republic also provided the Euratlantic framework—for security, economics, and more—in which it could find its place.

The Berlin crisis, which lasted for eleven months, was the first episode of the cold war seriously to threaten hot war. As such it powerfully strengthened public support in West Germany, Western Europe, and the United States for the new alliance against the Soviet Union. But the United States did not use its nuclear monopoly, nor did the Soviet Union use its local military superiority. Both sides acted with care. A few days after the West German constituent assembly completed its work in May 1949, the Russians ended their futile blockade in exchange for nothing but the termination of the Western counterblockade of the Soviet zone and yet another useless foreign ministers conference—the last East-West contact of that kind for more than six years. There was no restoration of four-power control of Germany or Berlin, even as they had existed early in 1948. The Berlin crisis, not as an outcome of Soviet planning, consummated the division of Germany.

The Federal Republic (FRG) was launched in September 1949. The basic law of the new state purposely described itself as provisional pending ultimate reunification. The three allies, moreover, while they terminated military government, reserved in the occupation statute important rights with respect to West Germany's policy and status. They could interfere in its domestic affairs, continued in principle to manage its foreign relations, and retained ultimate authority—along with their co-occupant, the Soviet Union—to dispose of Germany as a whole in an eventual peace settlement.

One month later, the German Democratic Republic (GDR) went into business with a parallel devolution of partial authority by the Soviet Union to a German government in its zone of occupation. This government was ostensibly multiparty but in fact was in the hands of the Communist-dominated Socialist Unity party, long since the only live party in the Soviet zone. The GDR, like the FRG, strongly committed itself to German unity.

When did the division of Germany in this form become inevitable or irreversible? With the zonal pattern of occupation? With an American decision, made at Potsdam or before, that all Germany should take part in the postwar economic system designed by American policy and that reparations from the Western zones would not go to the Soviet Union unless its zone took part? With a Russian decision to sovietize their zone at whatever cost? With the cold war developments which made it unlikely, perhaps impossible, whatever the original plans of the occupants, that they could agree on a common policy and peace treaty for Germany? With the establishment out of ongoing cold war tension—focused by the Berlin crisis—of two rival German states, each created by, and from its birth a member of, one or the other of the blocs into which Europe was by then already divided?

As late as 1957, George Kennan and others were still advocating what Walter Lippmann had called for in the very different world of 1947: a negotiated withdrawal of Western and Soviet forces from Germany and the establishment of a single, neutral German state—albeit to be built on the two states already in existence by 1957 rather than on four zones. But even if such a thing was conceivable as late as 1949, it certainly was not by 1957, nor has it been since.

If there were any difference in the availability of alternatives between 1947 and 1957, it lay in the decision by the allies and the West Germans in 1954 to arm the Federal Republic within the Western alliance. This decision, in turn, did not stand alone but capped a series of prior decisions, also by the allies and the West Germans, to integrate the FRG with the values and the economic and political institutions of Western Europe and the Atlantic world. Rearmament assured, if it was not already sure, the impossibility of disentangling the now sovereign West German state from the bloc within which it was born and to which it belonged by its own choice. Whether or not anyone might in other circumstances have been willing to risk turning loose in neutrality a united though unarmed Germany, once the FRG was armed neither its allies nor its neighbors in Western and Eastern Europe nor the super-powers themselves were likely to chance setting up a power in Central Europe with both the strength to play off the two blocs against each other to its own advantage and a motive—territorial and political—for doing so. Indeed, arming the Federal Republic even gave the Soviet Union an interest (not necessarily a preponderant one) in preserving the Atlantic alliance and the American military presence in Europe as bars to West German emancipation—just as the Western powers had an implicit interest in seeing the Soviets, if they would not give up the GDR to the FRG on Western terms, keep control of East Germany rather than use it to bait the hook of German unification on Soviet terms. The least unsatisfactory solution, then, whatever others there might or might not have been before 1955, was to leave the Federal Republic anchored in its alliance with the West. What was true of the West German state was no less true, if not by choice, of the German Democratic Republic. What was true in the mid-1950s has remained true since.

The James Byrnes policy forecast of 1946 runs out, achieved, in 1949, for he made no mention of what was to be the next phase, the arming of the Federal Republic. There was consideration of this in American

military circles and even some public discussion of it, stimulated by the
need felt after the Russians exploded their first nuclear device in August
1949 to strengthen defense on the ground in Europe. But there seemed
to be no urgency about the matter despite the Western assumption of
overwhelming Soviet conventional superiority in Europe. The political,
economic, and psychological obstacles to rearming Germany—or the
other European states for that matter—were too great to seem worth
tackling while American nuclear superiority was thought to remain
intact, particularly after the decision in January 1950 to proceed with the
development of a fusion weapon. American and French leaders were on
record in 1948–49 as opposing German rearmament.

Once American nuclear superiority faded in the 1950s and the deterrent credibility of an American atomic response to a Soviet invasion of
Western Europe declined, the United States would no doubt sooner or
later have pressed the Europeans to implement a forward strategy by
improving their conventional defense efforts, including a German contribution. The Joint Chiefs of Staff had already reached that position
before June 1950. The progressive emancipation of the Federal Republic from occupation controls would have pointed in the same direction.
But German rearmament would certainly not have come about when it
did, and possibly not at all, if there had been no Korean war. The war,
however, made the problem of German rearmament a predominant
theme in U.S. policy and, therefore, the dominant issue in Atlantic
affairs until a solution was found four years later.

That war had no particular roots in European affairs; indeed, its
origins remain obscure. Perhaps the Soviet Union wanted to curb
Japanese willingness to cooperate with the United States, or, after the
unexpected Communist victory in China, to buttress its own position on
China's flank, and Japan's, by spurring on its North Korean protégé in a
small war that promised to be victorious because of signs that the United
States had decided to write off South Korea. However that may be, the
American government, already battered by the trauma of losing China,
which severely curtailed any possibility of flexibility in dealing with the
Soviet Union, concluded that the Russians had changed their tactics in
pursuit of world domination from cold war to hot. The aggression in
Korea was seen as a harbinger of the same along the Elbe, the 38th
parallel of Europe; or an attempt to divert American attention from
Europe; or at least a testing of the viability and determination of the new
Atlantic alliance, and of American commitment to it.

The Korean war globalized containment and also militarized it in
Europe. We can ask now whether it was reasonable to suppose that the
Soviet government, which had not used force in Europe even to coerce

Tito's Yugoslavia, was likely to attack—or allow East Germany to attack—the Western zones, occupied (as South Korea was not) by the United States and her allies. But at the time Soviet willingness to use force in Asia was seen, at the least, as applying political pressure in Europe, thereby threatening to undo the American effort to stabilize the Western part of the continent. The conclusion drawn by the Americans—and others too—was that the local defense of Western Europe would have to be strengthened, to deter possible Soviet attack and to re-moralize the allies.

The Korean war, following as it did on the first Soviet nuclear explosion, not only impelled a massive overall buildup of American forces but melted the strong congressional opposition to a conventional buildup in Europe. A corollary policy was that in security, as already in the economic field, the Federal Republic would have to make its contribution. It would have to be rearmed as part of a general effort to give the alliance, for the first time, a meaningful local capacity to deter or resist a Soviet or Soviet-inspired attack on Western Europe.

The new American policy package thus included an integrated alliance force in Europe, an American supreme commander, financial aid for an allied military buildup, and sending more U.S. troops to Europe. All this was attractive in itself to the European allies. But the American government judged that it was not enough. Despite arguments to the contrary made even then by some in Washington, it concluded that a German contribution would be indispensable if the rest of the program were to make military and political sense.

The United States in September 1950 raised with Great Britain and France the question of German participation in the defense of Western Europe. Nor surprisingly, only five years after World War II, the Americans ran into sharp French resistance to arming the FRG in any form. As in the creation of the West German state, France was too weak simply to refuse, but strong enough to complicate and delay what Washington wanted. And the United States, for all its strength and all the urgency and fears generated by the Korean war, could not impose its will. The French government therefore proposed and the Americans eventually accepted the creation of a European Defense Community (EDC) that would include German forces but exclude national command of them or German admission directly to the alliance. Meanwhile the rest of the U.S. defense proposals would be implemented.

The American government was at first reserved about the practicality of this approach and the delays it would cause, and rightly so, for the French sought delay. But by mid-1951 it not only accepted the French approach because France—though standing alone in the alliance—could not be circumvented, but achieved a touching faith in both the feasibility and the benefits of the scheme. The Americans too, after all, believed that Germany was not ready for full rehabilitation or equality and that some constraint was necessary. In their initial planning they saw German integration in an alliance force under an American commander as providing sufficient control (and they were right). But they came to see the EDC, once the French invented it, as a spur to that united Europe of their dreams which, more than ever, was thought to offer the best framework for encompassing a Germany that had to be armed to help contain the Soviet Union and (as escalating German demands soon made clear) had to be released from occupation controls as the price for arming and setting aside the dream of reunification. What is more, European integration, then as later, seemed to provide the means which would let the United States make Europe prosperous, peaceful, and militarily strong, and thereby maintain its European interests at less direct cost to itself.[5]

American enthusiasm for the scheme soon far outran that of the French. The U.S. government, in fact, putting the European political problem ahead of the alliance military problem, and finding ever grander benefits in the EDC, almost lost sight of what were means and what were ends. Almost, but, in the end, not quite.

Under American spurring, the treaty establishing the EDC and the contractual agreement between the Federal Republic and the three occupying powers reestablishing German sovereignty were signed in May 1952. This energetic diplomatic phase was then followed, however, by a stagnant political phase. The treaty was not forwarded for ratification by the French parliament until January 1953. Whether or not the EDC might have been ratified in 1952, its chances waned and were lost in the maze of French politics, despite everything the outgoing Truman and the new Eisenhower administrations could do.

The long debate in France over the EDC is often treated mainly as a phase in the irregular development of European unity. The French cabinets, whose predecessors had constantly assured their parliament and people that there could be no question of rearming Germany, tried to make the project more palatable by presenting it as a sequel to the May 1950 proposal for a European coal-steel pool and a prelude to establishing a federated Europe (chapter 10 includes a discussion of

5. "[I]t was more a case of a particular policy objective (German rearmament) and a general policy goal (European unification) coming together in what was a policy means (EDC)." Or, more briefly, "the mushroom of European unification had sprung from the spawn of German rearmament." Robert McGeehan, *The German Rearmament Question* (Urbana: University of Illinois Press, 1971), pp. 145 and 171, respectively.

European integration). Some proponents of the coal-steel proposal had indeed hoped that it might in time lay the basis for a Franco-German relationship which would make eventual German rearmament and restoration to sovereignty tolerable to France. But this was very different from the French government's reluctant, hasty, and premature attempt to use the barely launched European vehicle to carry the heavy weight of German rearmament. The EDC, unlike the coal-steel pool, was an enterprise for which France was scarcely ready, the more so because the form in which its was acceptable to the Germans and finally took shape was very different from the initial French proposal.

Many in France, nevertheless, were prepared to accept the EDC at face value as useful as well as necessary in the circumstances, and to try to believe—or pretend to believe—that "the caterpillar of German rearmament" could be transformed "into the butterfly of supranational European integration."[6] But many others, for different reasons, either lacked the necessary imagination or did not like the butterfly any more than the caterpillar. Some opposed further integration if it meant German rearmament. More, as time passed, came to oppose German rearmament in the form proposed *because* it meant further integration—that is, loss of French sovereignty in the military sphere. To them, a merger of armies, far more than a merger of coal and steel industries (or, later, a common market), signaled the reduction of France from a presence in the world to "a cog in the wheel of Europe."[7] The junction of these groups with the Communists, plus the interweaving of the plan with the politics of the Indochina war and other matters, all in an atmosphere of reduced East-West tension in Europe after the death of Stalin and the end of the Korean war, delayed and finally defeated the project. The more intensely ideological the debate became, the more difficult it was to bring it to a conclusion one way or the other.

By mid-1954 there was more support in the French parliament for German soldiers *outside* a European framework (however distasteful that still was) than inside it. If the United States required that there be a German army, then at least the French should not be locked into a close military relationship (very different from a coal-steel community) which included Germany but not Great Britain.

By then there was also more support for this view in the French cabinet than in 1952. The Socialists, who had been strong advocates of European integration, had left the cabinet early in 1952 as the center of gravity in the new National Assembly began to move toward the right. In

6. Ibid., p. 33.
7. Daniel Lerner and Raymond Aron, eds., *France Defeats EDC* (New York: Praeger, 1957), p. 208.

opposition many Socialists turned against the EDC who in office might have remained faithful to it. The successive groups of Gaullists who then entered the majority and the cabinet were mostly opposed to the EDC. So no government dared bring it to a vote. Finally, the most prointe-grationist party of all, the Popular Republicans (MRP), long identified with the prosecution of the Indochina war as well as with the EDC, stayed out of the cabinet formed by Pierre Mendès-France in June 1954 to end the war after the disaster of Dien Bien Phu.

Mendès-France, who had been neutral toward the EDC, tried to find a compromise that would satisfy both its friends and enemies as well as the five other signatories. He failed, presented the treaty to the National Assembly, took no government position on it, and thus precipitated its defeat, which came in August on a procedural motion. Nothing he could have done would have saved the treaty at that late date. Nor did he need the alleged inducement of Soviet concessions in Indochina to act as he did on EDC—a myth some of his opponents, foreign and domestic, found it convenient to credit rather than face the real reasons, to which they had been singularly blind, for the failure of their EDC policy. Mendès-France had no interest in destroying his government in a futile attempt to ratify a treaty mainly supported by opponents whose latter-day zeal for it was in odd contrast with the fact that they had not chosen to bring it to a vote during the two years and more when they were in a position to do so.

Yet the long debate over the EDC in France had not been lost time. What mattered was not that the French had trifled with the cause of united Europe for four years but that it took them only four years, so soon after World War II, to accept the necessity (in the circumstances) of rearming the Germans. In retrospect the significance of the project is not that it was a setback for European unity, which was well on its way again in 1955, but that it was a four-year education of the French to accept without subterfuge the unpalatable reality pressed on them by the United States, the reality of an armed and sovereign Germany.

These four years were also a useful period of education for the Germans. It was not a matter of course that they would accept rearma-ment and the alliance with the West it entailed. Chancellor Adenauer had spoken positively of rearmament before June 1950 but even after that date many Germans rejected it for fear of what it might do to their infant democracy or to whatever chances there were for reunification. The Social Democrats waged a long fight against rearmament and the Western thrust of Adenauer's polity, favoring instead a serious effort to achieve a united, neutralized Germany. The Adenauer government, on the other hand, argued that rearmament was essential for German security (because it was the price for a continued American commitment to Europe), for the integration of the FRG into the European and Atlantic communities as a respected equal (because the remaining occupation controls would be terminated), and for reunification itself (because an Allied position of strength in Western Europe was the prerequisite for fruitful negotiations with the Soviet Union). The issue was debated with reasonable clarity in the 1953 Bundestag election and Adenauer won a large victory. His policy of anchoring the FRG to the West at whatever cost to unification prospects was thus confirmed. As it turned out, the anchoring helped to assure that rearmament, when it finally came, did not have the evil effects which many in and outside Germany had expected.

The West German commitment to rearmament in the Western framework, debated and definitely accepted while France hesitated, was maintained even when France's rejection of the EDC seemed to tear away its main pillar. The French assembly's defeat of the EDC by a substantial margin was, of course, a heavy blow not only to Adenauer but to the inflated dream of united Europe current in Washington. But the "agonizing reappraisal" of America's commitment to Europe, threatened by the secretary of state if the French failed to comply with his wishes, was not triggered. The French had been well educated. Most of them knew by then that their options were few and that rejecting German rearmament was not compatible with maintaining the American alliance—the loss of which most of the enemies of German rearmament (except the Communists) would not risk even to prevent it. In the face of continued American pressure for German rearmament—notwithstanding the changed international situation since 1950 and the "new look" American strategic concept, with its emphasis on massive retaliation—the French chose not to test whether the United States would arm Germany against their wish.

A quite satisfactory alternative was at hand to the catastrophe which the American government foresaw in the event that the EDC should fail. For it was again noticed, in Washington as well as in Paris, that the Atlantic alliance was available as an entirely suitable framework for containing as well as promoting German rearmament. What the French found unthinkable in 1950 had come to seem relatively beneficent by 1954 when compared to the EDC. Distaste for the latter had somehow softened distaste for the former. And if this particular solution, unlike the EDC, meant that the Americans would be less likely to be able after all to leave European defense to the Europeans, many in France did not share American disappointment.

No sooner was the EDC defeated than Foreign Secretary Anthony

Eden and Mendès-France developed the modalities for West Germany's direct entry into NATO. The FRG (along with Italy) was admitted to the furbished-up Brussels pact which, under the name of Western European Union (WEU), provided a fig leaf of continued control of German armament. (The real check on Germany, of course, then and since, was its security dependence on the United States, expressed formally in the Atlantic alliance and less formally in the very special relationship, already long underway, between Bonn and Washington.) The British and Americans made firmer commitments than before to keep troops in Europe. The FRG foreswore the manufacture of atomic, bacteriological, and chemical weapons on its soil without the concurrence of the supreme allied commander and two-thirds of the WEU members. All agreed that West Germany would not use force to achieve unification or change its boundaries.

This understanding was reached in October 1954, and was finally ratified by the French in April 1955. It was accompanied by the ending of the occupation and the almost complete establishment of the FRG's international sovereignty, claimed by Adenauer's government and conceded by the Western allies in exchange for German rearmament and the renunciation of whatever hope remained for early progress toward reunification. The Germany army was thus called into being at last, more than two years after the end of the Korean war which had given rise to it.

The Soviet government, which had used crisis to try to block the formation of the Federal Republic, used diplomacy to try to block the formation of a German army—with equal lack of success in both cases. More than once along the way to German rearmament the Soviet Union proposed negotiating the establishment of a reunited and demilitarized Germany on the basis of the equal representation of the two existing German states. This was aimed at those in France who opposed German rearmament altogether and at those in Germany who argued (rightly) that rearmament would cement the division of the country. But the Soviet proposal had no appeal to the United States, which wanted German rearmament in NATO, nor to the German government, which saw in the FRG's participation in the common defense the open road to recovering both sovereignty and respectability and, besides, would not tolerate parity with the Soviet zone. A prolonged conference of the four deputy foreign ministers in the spring of 1951 was entirely sterile and damped French hopes of somehow yet being able to elude the American push for German rearmament.

The Russians made a possibly more serious—at any rate more realistic—proposal in March 1952 (subsequently amplified) for establishing an all-German government through elections and permitting the rearming of the united German state, but outside any alliance. Whatever else was behind this proposal, it was timed to head off the EDC agreement which, by then, was nearly ready for signing. And, in fact, some of the EDC's opponents in France and Germany did argue, particularly after Stalin's death in March 1953, that ratification should be held off pending one last attempt to reach an agreement about Germany with the Soviet Union.

But whatever new the Russians might have had in mind, if anything, both the American and the Adenauer governments considered the FRG's rearmament in the EDC and alliance with the West as nonnegotiable, neutralization on any terms as unacceptable. Thus, Churchill got nowhere with his proposal in May 1953 that the Western powers meet "at the highest level" with the new Russian government as a step toward the solution of specific problems. The U.S. government insisted that if there was to be serious negotiation with the USSR on German unification it would follow, not precede, the establishment of a position of strength in Western Europe. As it happened, no such negotiation ever took place. Western power in Europe, notwithstanding German rearmament, declined with respect to Soviet power after 1955. Sufficient for defense, it was quite insufficient to force German "unification in freedom" on the USSR. But had this ever been more than a slogan?

It is difficult to imagine, therefore, what the Soviet Union might have offered that would have led the Western powers, including the Federal Republic, to renounce German armament and NATO membership. We know too much about Western policy goals and too little about Soviet to have much confidence in the notion that German affairs could have gone much differently once the Korean war put rearmament on the international agenda. Stories that Beria or others might have given up the East German regime in exchange for a neutralized Germany are extremely implausible. What Soviet regime, then or since, could contrive or tolerate the downfall of a socialist state over which it had military control?

In any case, the foreign ministers meeting held in Berlin in early 1954 was sterile with respect to the German problem. Stalin's heirs had nothing to say that interested the Western powers. In March 1954 the Soviet Union granted sovereignty to the GDR. And when the EDC was rejected by France, German rearmament was brought about without any further clear initiative from the Russians.

But then the Soviet Union, whose efforts to prevent what it feared so much had been so ineffective as to seem lacking in serious intent, adapted itself well to the accomplished fact. Though the Warsaw Pact, which nominally multilateralized Soviet military control of Eastern

Europe, was signed in May 1955, German rearmament, as it turned out, opened the way to an improvement of East-West relations in Europe. No sooner was this issue resolved in the spring of 1955 than the Big Four reached agreement, after ten years, on an Austrian peace treaty. In July they at last went to the summit, in Geneva, and agreed that Germany should be united by way of free elections—a decision, however, that led to nothing. In September the Russians and West Germans agreed to establish diplomatic relations—a clear signal (whatever Bonn might say) of the acceptance of a two-Germanies policy by both. The open creation in early 1956 of an East German army on the basis of a long-established so-called police force made little international stir.

The Soviet Union's quiet acceptance of a rearmed West German state in close alliance with the United States raises the question of the objectives of its German policy in the early 1950s as the FRG was constituted, armed, and integrated into the Western alliance system. Except, possibly, for their effort in March 1952 and later ineffective repetitions of it, the Russians did nothing which was conceivably likely to head off these developments. They took no step after the defeat of EDC—the optimum moment for a new attempt at East-West negotiations on Germany. Had the Russians too been educated to the inevitable by the four years of the EDC struggle? Did they accept this consummation of the status quo in the West in response, as it were, to the West's tacit acceptance of the status quo in the East that was revealed—to those who still needed the demonstration—by Western passivity in face of the GDR rising of June 1953? Or should we conclude that the Russians had become irrevocably committed long before to maintaining their own zone in Germany, not only for strategic reasons but because a Communist regime was established there whose disappearance, and the reflection that would cast on the system and the rulers in the USSR, could not be tolerated? If so, they must have seen, and accepted, that the inevitable counterpart of this commitment was the absorption of the Western zones into the new Western alliance system.

If Soviet policy was more complex than this between the Berlin blockade and late 1954, it was a failure. If not, it was very successful in its conservative goals. But so was American policy as it developed from Stuttgart on. Between them, the superpowers completed and fixed the new system of state relations in Europe. There was no peace treaty. There were not even serious negotiations between the Russians and Americans. On the contrary, there was virulent hostility. The outcome of this hostility, however, was not war but a resolution of Europe's old problem, the place of an overstrong Germany, which neither its near-victory in 1917 and 1940 nor its defeat in 1918 and 1945 had settled in a definite way. This resolution, which was achieved by the superpowers as a by-product of their conflict, was in turn a prerequisite to the emergence of any European system with a chance for survival. Once that was created, it provided in turn a powerful additional reason to those who welcomed such a solution—almost everyone in Europe outside Germany—to keep the system intact.

Had there been a U.S.–Soviet understanding on spheres of influence in 1945 or 1946 they might have looked geographically very much like those achieved in 1955. The permanent tension and recurrent crises of the period might then have been avoided. But such an understanding would probably not have established the structural firmness of the two subsystems of the new European bipolar system imposed by the cold war itself. The very tension that blocked a formal peace settlement led to a solution of the problem of German power in Europe that would have been inconceivable in 1945: a partition of the country that was accepted by the larger part because, though it had the freedom to make a different choice, it chose to put security ahead of the pursuit of unity. Would a system that had not been made rigid by dividing Germany into two states and arming each as part of a preexisting military-political bloc have proved as stable as the system thus created?

The German and European settlements reached in 1955, after a decade of cold war and because of it, have stood the test of more than twenty years. They have realistically reflected, and continue to reflect, the fundamental balance of power in Europe, and have served, and continue to serve, the interests of the European states with the capability to influence matters, including the interest to which the Federal Republic has given priority, security. It is not easy to make a convincing case that some other outcome *which could have been achieved* would have been more stable or even would have served the interests of those states better. This judgment does not overlook the most conspicuous victims of European stability in this form, the nations of Eastern Europe, left in forced dependence on the Soviet Union. It does not exalt stability as a value over self-determination. But analytically it is true that the European system came to be what it is because, to paraphrase Thiers, it divided least those with power to affect it.

CHAPTER 9

Challenges: East and West

By 1955 the military division of Europe brought about by World War II
had been structured and embellished by the cold war into a system of
state relationships with these characteristics:

—The United States and the Soviet Union, maintaining a rough but
stabilizing balance of military power between them with respect to
Europe, were both immeasurably more powerful than any European
state or potential combination of states. Their interaction, competitive or
cooperative, was the preponderant influence on the system.

—The states in each half of Europe were linked to their protecting or
hegemonic superpower by a thickening web of security, political, and
economic ties. In this way the division of 1945, long assumed in the West
to be unnatural, dangerous, and temporary, had come to look more
durable and less menacing ten years later. There was never a formal
postwar settlement, yet all the essentials were settled.

—The two subsystems thus defined were not, however, symmetrical.
The Western or Euratlantic subsystem was based on commitments that
were voluntary or at least acceptable to the governments of Western
Europe and most of their electorates. The most structured and visible of
these commitments, the Atlantic political-security alliance, was rooted in
fear of Soviet power. It was strongly reinforced, for all the differences
among the allies, by fundamental economic and close political ties. The
Eastern or Eurasian subsystem was based on the coercion of the lesser
members by the greater, which had overriding strategic and political
reasons for holding on to what it had gained as a result of the war. In
addition, the new Communist regimes were dependent for survival on
the maintenance of Soviet hegemony over their countries. The German
Democratic Republic, Poland, and Czechoslovakia also shared a concern
with the USSR about the officially revisionist aims of West German
policy and the implications for themselves of the fact that the Federal
Republic belonged to an alliance with means of action far greater than
those available to the FRG itself.

—Germany remained divided, as in 1945, but the four zones of occupation had become two states, each increasingly integrated into an alliance system headed by a superpower. The German Democratic Republic, a state but not a country, was perhaps the most anomalous

member of the Eastern bloc, its very existence dependent on the dominance of Soviet power in Eastern Europe. The West German people and government, living next to Soviet power, had accepted alliance with the West and rearmament rather than pursuit of whatever chances there might have been for achieving reunification through neutralization. The West German government of 1955 and its allies did not officially recognize the long-term implications of this choice—in fact, they specifically claimed that Western strength would lead to reunification—but the status quo was less and less challenged in face of the nation's security concerns and the other benefits it derived from its Western alignment.

Looking back over the last quarter-century it is obvious that much has changed in Europe. Yet, remarkably, the sketch of the system as it existed in 1955 has remained valid. There have been many changes but little change. There is still a bipolar state system dominated by two superpowers vastly stronger than their allies, still asymmetry between the Western and Eastern subsystems, still a divided Germany, the larger part anchored to the West by choice, the smaller tied to the East by coercion.

For all the flurrying international activity over Europe in the last quarter-century the system obviously has held. It is worth examining what this activity has been about and why it has had so little structural impact. There is, after all, something to be explained—about perceptions as well as events—when so much that has been written has dismissed the new state system as no system at all but an unstable transition to something else.

Many developments since 1955 in their time seemed likely, whether by intention or not, to bring about major changes in the system. They can all be thought of as challenges to the system, whether their consequences might have changed it for better or worse. To understand these challenges and their consequences there is no need to write the history of the last quarter-century in the same detail as I have given to 1945–55, the system-building years. The principal events are well known, have been amply narrated if not always soundly interpreted in a voluminous literature, and, above all, have had up to the present remarkably little net effect on the system except to maintain it. It is enough to examine the main kinds of challenging developments that have taken place (often simultaneously) and to consider why they turned out to be so ineffective—that is, why the elements of structural stability proved stronger than the elements of change.

One set of challenges, examined in this chapter, concerns the two problems which the system dealt with as it came into being, American-Soviet relations and Germany. These three states, after 1955 as before, had the most power to change the system—and did not. Another set, discussed in chapter 10, concerns problems particularly within the Western subsystem, where there have been greater freedom of choice, greater initiative, greater visible stress and challenge than within the Eastern—and, in the end, no greater effect on the system.

The Superpowers: Tension and Security

The two-bloc system consolidated in 1955 rested in the first instance on a balance of power established and maintained between the United States and the Soviet Union, the two nuclear superpowers of the world. Any serious upset of that balance would have changed the system. War would almost surely have done so, but so would a crisis which clearly showed preponderant strength on one side and weakness on the other, or a withdrawal of either superpower—whether voluntary or coerced—from the position it held in its bloc and in the system as a whole. But, after some twenty-five years of tension and détente, none of these things has happened.

During one period, between 1958 and 1962, a series of crises focused on Berlin and then Cuba raised fear of war. But there was no war. It may be that the Soviet government was determined never to let the challenges to the status quo that it stirred (particularly with respect to Berlin) reach the point of seriously risking conflict. If, more realistically, we postulate that it might have been willing to use force in Berlin or elsewhere if it thought it could do so profitably and at minimum risk, it follows that war has been averted because Western power has at all times succeeded in deterring Soviet attack, or armed probe, or aggression by proxy, or even a close risk of war.

Yet this fact of deterrence coincided with a practically permanent internal debate in the West since the mid-1950s about the right strategy, and the right numbers and equipment and deployment of forces, to deter the Soviet Union from using military means to promote whatever expansionist designs it might have had toward Western Europe (this debate is discussed in chapter 10). It would seem to follow that the more we are inclined to believe that Soviet policymakers had expansionist intentions and might have been willing to use force if the calculus of risk and advantage was ever right, the more we must credit them with cautious behavior in face of a deterrent which, in its various forms, the Western governments themselves over the years constantly—and publicly—undervalued.

At the same time, the United States and its allies were also effectively deterred from trying to change the status quo in Eastern Europe by force during the period of U.S. nuclear predominance and even more so afterward. Thus, for all the loose talk in the United States of "rollback" and "liberation," by which the Eisenhower administration claimed to differentiate its European policy from Truman's, there was little disagreement among the Western allies about how to respond—or not to respond—to the events of the autumn of 1956 in Hungary, any more than there had been three years earlier at the time of the rising in East Germany. If the West did not try to liberate Hungary even on this unique occasion, it was because the United States—for neither the first nor the last time—would not risk war with the Soviet Union to change the status quo in Europe.

It seems clear, therefore, that the balance of power between East and West in Europe has remained remarkably unchanged as measured by its applicable political effectiveness despite far-reaching changes in doctrine and weaponry on both sides since 1955. Qualitative strategic stability in the face of much visible change on this level goes far toward accounting for East-West political stability in Europe. The effect has been to preserve both peace and the new state system, the bipolar status quo.

While war or a signal defeat for either side in a crisis at the brink would surely have put an end to the European system, the withdrawal of either superpower from its role would have had a comparable structural effect. There have been recurrent expectations that either the Soviet Union or the United States might do that, with a resulting transformation of the European system, for better or worse. Yet neither has done so and there has been no such transformation.

A persistent thread of commentary over the last decades has pointed to an eventual loosening of the Soviet grip on Eastern Europe, perhaps eventually to the point that Germany, and the continent as a whole, could be reunited—an outcome which, however beneficent, would have produced a system very different from the one we have known. Russian rule in Eastern Europe has frequently been pronounced dangerous, bankrupt, anachronistic and unnatural. It has been argued at different times that the Russians would fall back from the strategic and political positions the war gave them because Western strength would somehow overawe them (the official Western doctrine in the early 1950s); or because their internal regime would mellow as they became more prosperous and secure; or because they would not want to pay the political price before world opinion of having to hold on to Eastern Europe by force (a belief brutally refuted by them in 1953 in Berlin, in 1956 in Hungary, and in 1968 in Czechoslovakia, yet of phoenixlike appeal); or because Western Europe would act as an irresistible magnet on Eastern Europe; or because they would more or less voluntarily redefine their subsystem in face of growing nationalism and restiveness in their ex-satellites, the more so to free their hands for dealing with China on their other flank (a view held by General de Gaulle during his détente phase of the mid-1960s); or because they understood that such loosening would be the necessary price or consequence of the pattern of relationships they sought to establish with the West after 1962—that is, that the expected benefits of détente vis-à-vis the West would have to be paid for by certain losses in the East. It was even argued, particularly during the heyday of détente, that increased Western economic and cultural contacts with the ex-satellites and/or with the USSR itself (the strategies varied) could help bring about the transformation of Eastern Europe, and thus of Europe as a whole, in a reasonably near future.

We can ask now how such patently wishful thinking could ever have been taken seriously. There has, of course, been a loosening of the Eastern bloc since Stalin's time. The Soviet quarrel with China, in fact, not only ended once and for all the fiction of a monolithic Communist bloc but opened the way, along with other things, to changes in the relations between Moscow and the Communist states of Eastern Europe. Soviet relations with them have become more a matter of state-to-state (and party-to-party) diplomacy. Innovations have been tolerated in foreign and intrabloc policy (Rumania) and domestic management (Poland and Hungary) which in Stalin's time would have been unimaginable.

Even so, the limits of change have been amply demonstrated. None of these developments has modified the fact that the Soviet Union continues to dominate Eastern Europe, by force when it must, by more flexible means when it can, just as the extensive relative mellowing of Soviet society since Stalin has not changed the fact that the Communist party, and a few leaders in it, continue to dominate all. The problem of how to maintain control in Eastern Europe has been persistent for the Soviet leaders and at times it has become acute (1953, 1956, and 1968). But successive Soviet leaders have made it abundantly clear that they take a basically rigid view of the strategic and political importance of the areas which their predecessors brought under Soviet hegemony in and after 1945. They have shown no intention of allowing these countries to slip into the orbit of the United States, or of a French-led or German-led "European Europe," as the Russians are convicted would be the case if *they* let go. Up to the present the Soviet government appears to have acted on the belief that it could preserve little influence in most of these countries should they recover policy independence, with or without the ending of socialism. So they have not been allowed to do so. The Brezhnev doctrine of 1968, asserting a Soviet right of intervention to prevent changes in any socialist country inimical to the socialist bloc as a whole, was new only in its expression, not in its summing up of longstanding Soviet policy.

In addition to the strategic and political considerations which motivated Soviet policy toward Eastern Europe in and after 1945, the way that policy was carried out has created still another reason for clinging to it. The Soviet leaders of the 1940s perhaps did not foresee the degree to which the stability and even the legitimacy of the Soviet regime itself would become bound up with the fate of the Communist regimes the USSR established in Eastern Europe after the war to maintain its position there. What may have seemed a political necessity or convenience then has since become at the best a limit on diplomatic flexibility, at the worst a mortgage on the credentials of the motherland of socialism. What Soviet leaders could lend themselves to a shrinkage of the socialist camp? How could they permit, not to say connive at, the downfall of another socialist regime? How could they even tolerate the development of such regimes in directions which cut across the grain of the institutions and policies by which Russia itself, in their view, must continue to be ruled?

In the 1870s Russian liberals asked why Czar Alexander gave a constitution to liberated Bulgaria but not to his own country. The czar's Communist successors feel the problem acutely but have chosen to handle it by avoiding his inconsistency. Some diversity has been permitted, but nothing (as in Hungary in 1956) which calls into question the international alignment of any Eastern country and nothing (as in Czechoslovakia in 1968) which calls into question the institutions of the Soviet Union itself. The pressures for change in Eastern Europe have not been removed—far from it—but the Soviet Union has shown itself firm, if not always prompt, in setting the permissible limits. And, of course, it has had ample means to enforce its will in this policy priority area once it has fixed its course.

But the Soviets have had to pay a high price for their enforced control of Eastern Europe. For all the assertiveness of their European diplomacy, their position in Eastern Europe has necessarily deprived it of the flexibility which might have allowed them to pursue their goal of weakening or breaking up the Western bloc with greater hope of success. De Gaulle, for example, thought that it was desirable and feasible to try to loosen and eventually even dissolve both blocs, but the Soviet action in Czechoslovakia in 1968 proved to any who doubted that there would be no dissolution of the Eastern subsystem. The Western subsystem was thus reconsolidated, if not by a renewed fear of Soviet attack, at least by something almost as strong: a renewed consciousness of the absence of alternatives to the structural status quo.

Even more serious for the Soviet Union was the immobilization of its policy in face of the fact that the West Germans, from 1949 to the present, *might* have been tempted to rethink their position in the Western alliance if they could ever have found reason to believe that the GDR's position in the Eastern bloc might also be open for reconsideration. That is, the West Germans might possibly have been willing at some point to reexamine their committment to the West if reunification of Germany could have been held out as a persuasive alternative. The Soviet leaders, one would have thought, had serious reasons to consider such a policy. They could not have welcomed the creation of the Federal Republic, its alliance with the United States, the prospect that it might in one way or another be given nuclear arms or some voice in the control of American nuclear arms. Further, the Russians had motives to divide and weaken the Western alliance.

But the Soviet Union has never been willing to do what would have been necessary to exploit the opportunities it found in the German situation. Its ties of mutual dependence on the socialist regime it created have prevented it from sacrificing East Germany to improve its own state position in Europe. The Russians have made a consistent choice since 1955 for stability—for ideological and domestic political reasons as well as others—which, one would think they must have seen, precluded an effective European policy on their part. In short, the Eastern bloc has proved too rigid to be tampered with, even by the Soviets who created it, and this has helped the Western bloc maintain itself in place. The Germans, among others, were too sensible to exchange something (security) for nothing (the mirage of reunification). Khrushchev's efforts to change the status quo in the 1960s foundered on essentially the same factors as de Gaulle's. The European system proved too rigid for either to change because it was too satisfactory for too many of its participants as compared to alternatives they considered feasible. In this, as in so many aspects of the postwar system, the absence of alternatives, to paraphrase Dr. Johnson, concentrated the mind wonderfully.

Bound to a policy in their own bloc of crude but effective coercion and ad hoc flexibility on nonessentials, Soviet diplomacy has been able to accomplish no more in practice than to obtain Western recognition of the Eastern status quo. In 1946–47 this effort took the form of writing peace treaties and obtaining Western recognition of the Eastern governments. Beginning in the late 1960s, it took the form of the long march to the Helsinki conference of 1975. One can wonder why this Western sanction has mattered so much to the Russians in view of their means of enforcement in Eastern Europe. How many divisions is the West likely to bring to bear, after all? Yet they have not only used their military power to enforce obedience but pursued patient diplomatic strategies to confirm it. They have even paid an embarrassing price (in the human rights provisions of the Helsinki agreement) to secure yet another Western sanction for a bloc which has long been established in fact and often reconfirmed, without challenge from outside, by the use of force. Presumably the Russians have thought that Western ratification of the status quo would discourage their dissidents, at home and in Eastern Europe. The Soviet success in this drawn-out but essentially marginal policy was a gain for them by their lights but not a loss for the West, except for the loss of illusions. It changed nothing in the European status quo except to reveal more clearly—to any who could not see— what the status quo has been and is.

The Russians have no doubt been uneasy in face of their bloc, and with reason, for enforced domination of 100 million people must impose a permanent sense of insecurity even on men who are willing if they think it necessary to use all the instruments of state power needed to maintain things as they are. But during this period they demonstrated the will and the means to keep the Eastern bloc fundamentally in line and to secure Western acquiescence in that. Western (including West German) recognition of this territorial and political status quo and closer trade and cultural relations with the countries of Eastern Europe have made no significant difference in these relatities. There has been no Soviet abdication in Eastern Europe nor, therefore, any structural weakening of that pillar of the European state system.

Although the Western countries have acquiesced in and recognized Soviet control in Eastern Europe they have never lost their sense of anxiety at the proximity of Soviet power which that control brought with it. That fact alone goes far toward accounting for the persistence of the Western subsystem alongside the Eastern, and therefore of the European system as a whole, in periods of low tension as well as high. Yet Western unity, and the American commitment to the system, have been challenged more than once by a relaxation of tension which some at the time hoped, or feared, might make the arrangements developed during the cold war seem anachronistic, and so undermine popular and even governmental support for them. Détente seemed to many people, for better or worse, the most probable solvent of a system built up by tension.

Almost as soon as the system had been completed by the arming of the Federal Republic, Stalin's successors set themselves to get rid of some of the liabilities bequeathed by his policies. In Europe, they acted as if they understood that the tensions created by Soviet policy had strengthened and united the Western countries rather than the reverse. They therefore tried to introduce more flexibility into what was already a rigidly stable situation and exploit divisive tendencies in the West by reviving the Soviet notion (dating to the 1920s) of peaceful coexistence. More confident than Stalin had been of Russia's growing strength, military and economic, they now defined peaceful coexistence to mean that competition would continue between socialism and capitalism but it would be more and more centered on economic growth and the ability of the two systems to meet the needs of the people. While they were confident of the victory of socialism, this might not require another war, as Stalin had taught, whether within the camp of imperialism or between it and the socialist camp. There could even be positive agreements between the two sides, both to limit directly the threat which nuclear war posed to all countries and to build up other forms of cooperation which would remove the causes or reduce the tensions that might lead to war.

The Geneva summit (July 1955) symbolized this new Soviet approach. The results were perhaps less sterile than they are remembered. Notwithstanding all the East-West tensions that have followed, the publicly perceived understanding at the time of the "spirit of Geneva"—that the superpowers, both armed with thermonuclear weapons, recognized the risks of war between them and the need to minimize those risks—has turned out to have had a certain lasting validity. Even the Americans, whose basic policy before and after Geneva was still to man the ramparts of containment, slowly accepted the fact that relations with the Soviet Union *might* consist of more than waiting in hostile confrontation for the Soviet Union to mellow. Geneva was an important moment in postwar relations because it signified that both superpowers were coming to understand that they might have certain interests in common, alongside many others that were conflictual, and that it might be worthwhile to search for ways to define and expand this area of commonality. This was not contradicted by the hope of both sides that relaxing tension would have minimal divisive effects on its own bloc and maximal ones on the other.

But this first essay in détente had no significant effect on the European system. The Geneva meeting was preceded by small changes in the European status quo that were marginally advantageous to the West (with respect to Austria and Finland), but no further changes followed. On the contrary, the Soviet Union in 1956 brutally demonstrated how narrow were the limits it placed on the evolution of Eastern Europe. The Western powers, for their part, made clear their acquiescence in these limits but also, despite strains and divisions of many kinds, their determination to maintain their own subsystem.

Notwithstanding the events of 1956 in Hungary, or perhaps because of them, there was a curious vogue in the West in 1957–58 for proposals looking to the neutralization of Germany or a wider area of Central Europe. These had the merit, in such sophisticated hands as George Kennan's, of suggesting that the West need not simply stand behind the barriers of containment and that negotiation with the Soviet Union might be possible and profitable. But such proposals had the flaw of being premised on the belief that neither Soviet control of Eastern Europe by force, nor West German acquiescence in partition, nor the situation of West Berlin could last for very long, and that the precariousness of these situations carried, in different ways, threats to security, stability, and peace. Yet all these situations have persisted to the present day and war, if not tension, has been avoided. No Western government then or since has been persuaded by these dangers to follow Kennan's advice and try to negotiate the withdrawal of Soviet forces from Eastern Europe at the price of a parallel American withdrawal at least from Western Germany. If a united, neutralized Germany might still have been feasible in 1947, when Walter Lippmann advocated it, it was not so in 1957, when two German states had become parts of two antagonistic blocs and, moreover, had been armed. A united Germany would also almost certainly have been armed, a fact that did not make unification any more attractive to Germany's neighbors.

Such proposals, not surprisingly, came to nothing, for it was Russian policy after the shocks of 1953 and 1956 not to dismantle the status quo in Eastern Europe but to get the West to confirm it. Nor did Eastern proposals to ban nuclear weapons from Central Europe (including the two German states) come to anything, for it was Western policy not to abandon the positions of strength built up since the 1940s. Change in Europe was not what the spirit of Geneva was about. Both superpowers acted in such a way as to preserve the status quo. The will of others to change it, and even more their capability, was slight.

These belated and sterile attempts to undo by diplomacy what the cold war had produced in Germany and Europe were followed by a more troubled period of East-West relations when the Soviet Union tried to play on the exposed position of Berlin—which *was* precarious—to go beyond the tacit understanding of Geneva and force Western recognition of the German Democratic Republic and the East European subsystem, and perhaps to impose permanent nuclear disarmament on the Federal Republic or some even wider understanding as well.

The placing into orbit of the first Soviet sputnik in October 1957 was followed by the most prolonged period of tension in Europe since the late 1940s. The seeming new strength of the USSR and what appeared at the time to be a weak U.S. and Western response to Khrushchev's assertive diplomacy provoked two crises over Berlin (1958–60 and 1961–62) which more than once seemed to threaten war. The first led to negotiations under the gun about Germany which proved sterile, then to a false springtime of better U.S.–Soviet relations ("the spirit of Camp David") and the aborted summit of May 1960. After a pause for the American election, the second crisis produced renewed tension between East and West and that ultimate symbol of the status quo, the Berlin Wall (August 1961). By then it was becoming clear that the Russians could not force concessions from the West by pressure on Berlin and, even worse from their point of view, that their supposed strategic preponderance was a myth.

The period of acute tension that began in 1958 ended abruptly when the Russians overreached themselves by placing missiles in Cuba, an act so rash as to suggest that they were after a global bargain of some kind with the United States, or at least something more comprehensive than a favorable settlement of the Berlin or German problems. The crisis of October 1962, the most dangerous of the postwar years, ended with a sharper setback to the Soviet Union than any sustained by either superpower since the war. It abruptly cleared the air of war clouds and ushered in a new phase of superpower relations.

In face of the perceived strategic ascendancy of the United States, Russian threats and pressure gave way to a prudent relaxation of tension and then to a more actice building of ties with the United States and the West in general. Soviet motives included a desire to avoid dangerous confrontations, exploit divisions in the Western camp, obtain Western capital and technology to spur the lagging Soviet economy, and block an American-Chinese alliance and otherwise cover themselves in the West against the risks of their now visible conflict with China in the East (a conflict which first France and later the United States tried to exploit in their own relations with the Soviet Union, but with little effect in either case on affairs in Europe). The limited nuclear test ban treaty of August 1963 among the United States, the Soviet Union, and the United Kingdom signified a new phase of the East-West relationship, a revival in more concrete form of the effort to reduce tension by a search for areas of agreement that had been vaguely begun at Geneva.

The Western powers had faced the Soviet Union with a fair degree of unity during the years of tension, at least with respect to the main issue, the freedom of Berlin and the allied presence there. Fear of war diminished sharply in Europe after the Cuban crisis and has never returned to the level reached then. Partly as a result, the centrifugal forces that surfaced within the two blocs as tension between them diminished seemed to foreshadow a new order of things in Europe. In the East there

were the strains caused by the Sino-Soviet quarrel, the open independence of Rumania's foreign policy, and the liberalizing developments in several countries that culminated in the Prague spring of 1968.
In Western Europe there were increasing prosperity, the first steps of
the Common Market along the road which was thought to lead to a
united Europe, American-German tension over several issues, and,
above all, General de Gaulle's attempt first to redistribute authority
within the Western bloc and then to end superpower hegemony altogether in Europe. His challenge, perhaps the most farreaching
mounted against the postwar European system from within the Western
alliance, paralleled and exploited both a debate about strategic questions within the West and a deepening monetary crisis. These trends
seemed to be reinforced by the dangerous tensions that arose in the
Middle East and Southeast Asia between West and East, or, more precisely, between the United States and the two Communist great
powers—tensions which revealed serious differences between the Western superpower and its European allies. All of this (discussed in chapter
10) suggested to many that changes were underway which, in an atmosphere of relaxation of tension, would have profound effects on the
European system.

Yet we can see now that the most important consequence of all these
events, nurtured by détente in Europe, was not to promote structural
change, as many had expected, but, once again, to confirm the status
quo. The signs of basic change that had risen up so bravely soon lamely
flickered out. De Gaulle's attempt to build a strong and independent
Western Europe actually divided it and weakened whatever chances for
that were implicit in its economic growth and the construction of the
European Community. Even more important, the Prague spring ended
in the invasion of Czechoslovakia by the Warsaw Pact, which reminded
those who needed the lesson—including de Gaulle—that Soviet hegemony over Eastern Europe was not about to wither away, nor the
postwar European system with it.

Before and after that event, the West European governments (except,
in a sense, for the French) never acted as if they held the view imputed to
them by many American commentators that there was no longer a Soviet
threat that required maintaining the U.S. guarantee to their security
embodied in the Atlantic alliance. Fear of invasion has been minimal
since 1962, but the West Europeans have shown—before 1968 as
after—that they understood what it meant to live next to a Soviet colos-
sus. Their consciousness of Soviet power, even without crisis, was far
more sensitive than that of observers at a distance who thought that the
Russian presence in Central Europe had ceased to have significance for

West Europeans. This knowledge had the same implications for West European policies in the 1960s and 1970s as in the two preceding decades. In this, the West Europeans had a better sense of their geographical situation and their real strengths and weaknesses than their American admirers, eager for the restoration of a European autonomy that most Europeans themselves well understood, however much they regretted the fact, was a thing of the past.

The most important trend in Europe since 1962 proved to be not European initiatives but the successful effort of the two superpowers to stabilize their relationship at a lower level of tension—that is, to define and extend the modus vivendi between them on the basis of the structural status quo. The reassertion of Russian power over Eastern Europe in August 1968 slowed the process only slightly. The new governments that assumed office in the United States and the Federal Republic in 1969 took up the effort not only with vigor but with a more concrete sense of the real possibilities. The former ratified the nonproliferation treaty and began strategic arms negotiations. The latter undertook a realistic effort to improve its relations with Eastern Europe by accepting the status quo in order to ameliorate and perhaps eventually transcend it. The highwater mark of these efforts was the German treaties with the Soviet Union (1970), Poland (1970), and the GDR (1972); the four-power agreement on Berlin (1971); and the American-Soviet treaty to limit antiballistic missiles and the interim agreement on strategic weapons (1972). These agreements taken together signified the reconsecration by the two blocs of the state system they constituted and of the continued ascendancy within it of the superpowers—de Gaulle, China, Rumania, Czechoslovakia, détente in Europe, and tension outside it all notwithstanding.

Since the climax of East-West negotiations in 1972 détente has remained the policy objective of most members of the European system but specific progress has been thin, particularly in reducing the major barriers between Western and Eastern Europe. There has been no return to tension in Europe but the atmosphere of constructive expectations has become more somber. In this context the 1975 Conference on Security and Cooperation in Europe was distinctly an anticlimax. For the Soviet government it was the fruition of diplomatic efforts it had pursued for years and decades to achieve Western recognition of the status quo in Europe. Yet the Helsinki meeting gave the Soviets little or nothing beyond what the West had already agreed to in the earlier negotiations respecting Berlin and the Federal Republic's relations with Eastern Europe, including above all Western recognition of the German Democratic Republic. Helsinki certainly did not, as many in the West had once feared, induce "détente fever" or the breakup of the Atlantic alliance. On the contrary, in confirming the European status quo the CSCE also ratified once again its two-bloc structure.

Looking back over the phases of tension and relaxation of tension since 1955, it is clear that the commitment of the United States to its own role in Europe and to the bipolar system has been as firm, in its way, as that of the Soviet Union. There has been no serious prospect at any time that the United States would withdraw from the Atlantic alliance, or cease to provide the strategic deterrent on which Western European security has depended, or the supreme commander of the integrated defense forces, or a substantial armed presence in Europe. It has remained the backbone and the impetus for the alliance. More, the web of political cooperation and economic ties among the allies has grown greatly since 1955. American investment in Europe, and trade and financial relations with it, have steadily increased American interest in the area—an interest which the Marxist leaders of the Soviet Union are not likely to have overlooked in calculating the strength of the U.S. commitment to Europe.

Yet there has been an American challenge to the system throughout its history. The steadiness of the U.S. commitment to Europe has often been questioned because it has been obscured, from 1955 to the present, by events whose importance proved to be transitory or were misunderstood by contemporary observers, both European and American. The U.S. role and the cohesion of the alliance itself have been least contested or doubted in periods when East-West tension was greatest, notwithstanding conflicts among the allies on priorities and tactics. In periods of relative relaxation, however, questions have been raised in the United States concerning whether the alliance was still necessary and whether its military dispositions (including the U.S. force presence) were worth the cost. These recurrent questions have been sharpened at times by U.S. balance of payments difficulties and by the American feeling that the European allies were either strong enough to do more for the common defense or too feeble and divided to do enough.

The Europeans, in turn, have sometimes felt—and exasperated the Americans by saying so—that the United States was expecting hegemonic advantages in nonsecurity matters in exchange for its security guarantee, or that it might sacrifice European interests to the broader exigencies of its global relationship with the Soviet Union. The allies have constantly disagreed about strategic doctrine and security dispositions, as well as economic issues and attitudes toward the extra-alliance involvements of various members (see chapter 10). At times these feelings and disagreements have become so intense as to raise questions on both sides of the Atlantic whether the primordial security tie should or could survive.

Questions about the continuing value of the system, and the U.S. commitment, have also been raised whenever there seemed reason to believe that the problems of European and German division which were left unnegotiated (and, as it was mistakenly thought, unresolved) between East and West in the 1940s might be taken up again and settled in some way other than that produced by the cold war. This was the case when schemes for the neutralization of Germany were bandied about in the late 1950s, and again when first de Gaulle and then the West Germans took initiatives of their own in European policy.

The U.S. commitment, nevertheless, has survived it all: fear and hope, tension and détente. These many challenges have been perturbing to the inner fabric of the Euratlantic relationship (and will be discussed more fully in that context) but they have had little effect on the broad structure of East-West relations.in Europe. If there has been no termination or significant dwindling of the American role in Europe, the reason appears to be that for the United States, as for the USSR as well, the system has continued to fill the purposes which it came into being, only partly by conscious design, to fill. Up to the present no more acceptable way has been found than that set in place in 1955. Neither the United States nor the Soviet Union has been prepared to build or allow others to build a new system that would diminish the preponderant role of both in Europe; nor, even less, have they been willing to tolerate a systemless state of confusion as an alternative to the status quo. They have had the means and the will to enforce their preferences.

Germany: Unity and Division

The most cogent argument made in the 1940s and 1950s against the probable stabilization of the bipolar European system was that anything built on the division of Germany was built on sand. Sooner or later, the case ran, the West Germans would be tempted to give up other ties, if need be, to secure reunification, and the Russians then would seize the opportunity to wreck the Western alliance by sanctioning German unity in neutrality. Some, like Walter Lippmann, argued from this that the United States itself should negotiate a neutralized, united Germany in preference to trying to integrate a part of the country into the West. Others argued from the same premise that a West German state should be created and bound to the West by every possible kind of tie. In the short term these ties would provide the Germans with a substitute for reunification and, in the case of European unity, something more positive. For the longer term, most of those who supported this policy, in and out of the Federal Republic, maintained that it did not cut across eventual reunification "in freedom" but would in fact help build up the Western position of strength which would eventually overawe the Soviet Union and somehow induce it to allow the reunion of its zone with a Western-oriented German state.

This thesis was challenged during the rearmament debate in the FRG. The decision of the electorate went to the Christian Democrats and their policy of integration with the West. Notwithstanding what was said then by the German government and its Western allies, few could have believed that the military integration of the FRG with the West was likely to encourage the Soviet Union to allow the strengthening of both the German state and the Western alliance by permitting the GDR to be absorbed by them. The choice made by the Germans and the Western powers in 1954–55 made sure, if the policies of the superpowers and the separate lives of the two German states over five years had not already done so, that the two halves of Germany would go their own ways, each linked to half of a divided Europe. Those West Germans who accepted rearmament in these circumstances clearly put present gains—in security and cooperation with the West—ahead of the already dwindling hope of future reunification. Most other West European governments, whatever their qualms about rearmament, understood at least as well as the Germans themselves, and accepted with even less hesitation, the negative implications of the emerging arrangements for German unity. One can wonder whether the U.S. government, zealous to strengthen Western defenses, thought or cared much about the solution it was providing for the German problem. Nothing the Americans did in practice made it less likely that the division of Germany would last at least as long as the bipolar division of Europe between blocs headed by the superpowers.

As I noted earlier, there was much discussion after 1955 of pursuing the policy choice which the decision made then had put beyond reach. George Kennan, the father of the theory if not the practice of containment, emerged as an advocate of a negotiated neutralization of an armed, united Germany. There were also both Eastern and Western proponents of schemes for excluding nuclear weapons from the two German states, and perhaps also from Poland and Czechoslovakia, or otherwise limiting armaments in that general area. The German and American governments stoutly resisted efforts which seemed to them designed to negate the benefits of FRG armament and, more broadly, to drive a political and security wedge between that country and its Western allies. On the contrary, the German government responded to the new U.S. emphasis on nuclear weapons by trying to enhance its role in alliance nuclear decisionmaking, and in 1958 the Americans agreed to arm the German forces (and those of other allies) with weapons capable of being fitted with nuclear warheads (which remained in American control).

The Russians presumably disliked any nuclear role for the FRG. But they did not dislike it enough to do anything to help the German opponents of this policy. Though the Soviet Union endorsed antinuclear weapons schemes, it never came anywhere close to offering the one thing which *might* have given the majority of West Germans second thoughts about their security policy: a realistic prospect of reunion with the Eastern zone.

Soviet policy toward Berlin after 1958 seemed on the surface to be trying to intimidate and isolate the Federal Republic to the end of accomplishing by threats what it had failed to achieve by diplomacy: avoidance of German access to nuclear weapons and Western confirmation of the status quo in Eastern Europe (or even some change to Soviet benefit). But these Soviet actions, which may have had even wider aims, seemed directed at least as much at the United States as at the FRG. In any case, the two Berlin crises (1958–60 and 1961–62) tested West Germany's profound commitment to the Western alliance, but in the end had no lasting negative effect on it.

Even so, these years were difficult for the U.S.–German relationship. The German government, wanting a larger role in nuclear decision-making, was most unhappy with the Kennedy administration's move away from such sharing and toward the new strategy of flexible response with its implied diminution of a credible nuclear deterrent and increased risk of a devastating conventional war in Europe. Further, the U.S. approach to the German problem also changed in this period. By 1962 it had become clear that the United States would not abandon Berlin or the FRG in the face of Soviet pressure. But it was also clear that Western strength would not be able to bring about German unification. The American efforts to find a more stable modus vivendi in Berlin, or at least to defuse the crises by negotiating with the Soviet Union, seemed to the Adenauer government to mean that the United States might be moving toward recognition of the division of Germany and the status quo in Eastern Europe—that is, renunciation of the lip service commitment to German unity underlying the U.S.–FRG alliance. The acquiescent response of the West to the Berlin Wall (August 1961) stimulated this concern. The American-Soviet-British limited test ban treaty of August 1963, which was reached over the heads of Europe, fed it further.

The official German response, in the last years of the Adenauer regime, was to establish a kind of cold war front with the France of de

Gaulle who, as I discuss in the next chapter, was quite willing in this phase to try to cement his own entente with the FRG by exploiting Adenauer's fears of U.S. policy. But this could only be a passing answer to the Germans' problem. It was not consistent with the FRG's unabated security dependence on the United States, nor could it be sustained in the circumstances of the 1960s, when U.S.–Soviet relations improved after the end of the Berlin and Cuban crises. The Erhard government, which succeeded Adenauer's in 1963, therefore chose to repair its relations with the United States at the expense of those with France and to follow—in its own way—the American lead thus tentatively given on relations with the East.

This shift reflected not only changes in the international landscape but also the evolution of German public opinion on Eastern policy in the postcrisis and post-Adenauer periods. De Gaulle, interestingly, saw where German opinion was going almost before the Germans themselves did. Partly for that reason, he switched almost overnight at the end of 1963 from being the last of the cold warriors to the role for which he is better remembered, the pathbreaker of détente. Soon he was out ahead of the German government in his advocacy of "détente, entente, and cooperation" with the East. For the new German government undertook to improve West German relations with the countries of Eastern Europe without accepting the postwar frontiers in central Europe, or recognizing the GDR, or renouncing the policy of seeking German unity on traditional Western terms—that is, by means of free elections and without excluding the later adherence of a united Germany to the Western alliance.

Even so, this policy of movement, for all its limitations, was important as the first effort *of German origin* to break openings in the cold war wall across Europe. The objective was to use economic power as a lever to increase German influence on the Eastern countries other than the Soviet Union and the GDR in order, over time, to somehow induce the Russians to permit meaningful change in East Germany's governance and its place in Europe. Unfortunately for the Germans this was not a realistic approach to the East, above all at a time when the pace of French–Soviet and American–Soviet rapprochement was picking up. The negotiations between the superpowers preceding the nuclear non-proliferation treaty of 1968 particularly irritated the Germans, the more so as they followed on the heels of the scheme for a multilateral nuclear force (MLF) which the American government had propagated with zeal and then aborted and the Erhard government in its Atlantic orthodoxy had supported not wisely but too well. The switch of American policy from offering the Germans a role in Western nuclear decision-making to negotiating a treaty with the enemy which appeared to deny them such a role strained American–FRG relations seriously, the more so as they knew that loyalty to the United States left them no choice but to sign the treaty. Here were the tensions of 1961–62 in magnified form. Some pessimists even thought that the United States was opting for détente over NATO.

Yet in these few years the Federal Republic had changed profoundly. The Germans not only put up with the American switch but creatively adapted their own foreign policy to the lessons of the disappointment. Détente began to offer more tangible international rewards than cold war. The failure of theMLF, it is true, contributed to Erhard's downfall in October 1966. But neither under his government nor under the more activist Kiesinger-Brandt grand coalition did the Germans dream of "going nuclear," or accepting French leadership, or pursuing a "Rapallo" with the Soviet Union, that misanalogized Western nightmare since the 1940s. Yet change was in the air.

Though the formation of the grand coalition coincided with—perhaps provoked—the sudden and ominous emergence of a substantial neo-Nazi movement in German politics, the important trend, as de Gaulle rightly judged, was the rise of the Social Democratic party with its call for continued Atlantic loyalty but a fresh approach to relations with the East consistent with the realities of the 1960s. The growing success of the Socialists, which carried them to the chancellorship in 1969, reflected many factors, domestic and foreign, but among them was an increasingly clear drift in German opinion toward a more dynamic and at the same time more accepting Eastern policy, however vague the connection between the feasible—and painful—early steps and the distant objective of unification. German pressure for a greater nuclear role was obviously not consistent with this new approach (nor with the state of U.S.–Soviet relations) and it dwindled as the latter picked up speed, the more readily as German security concerns about nuclear weapons were adequately satisfied by the consultative arrangement provided by the NATO Nuclear Planning Group in lieu of the abandoned MLF.

Unfortunately for the Germans, their policy of trying to work around the GDR and in despite of the USSR, albeit in so-called small steps, was destroyed by the Warsaw Pact invasion of Czechoslovakia in August 1968. The Russians made clear that they would not permit a marked growth of economic and other ties between their allies and the FRG, or at least would require in exchange a high political price in the form of German confirmation of the status quo including the frontiers of central Europe and the hitherto unthinkable concession, recognition of the other German state.

The government of Willy Brandt faced the dilemma of either pursuing an Eastern policy on these Soviet terms or writing off such a policy altogether, presumably for a return to a cold war rigidity which Germany's allies had abandoned—that is, to isloation East and West. With the support or acquiescence of the allies, but in face of the opposition of the ex-governing party, he chose the former and carried German opinion with him in this "redirection of national attention and consciousness."[1] A complicated diplomatic process lasting over two years and involving the Big Four and both German states eventuated in an interlinked group of agreements which provided for West German acceptance of the territorial status quo in Eastern Europe, balanced by an agreement among the Big Four establishing a less tense modus vivendi in Berlin. In this framework for German relations with Eastern Europe, the FRG negotiated treaties with the Soviet Union, Poland (recognizing the Oder-Neisse frontier), the GDR (recognizing it—as did the allies soon after—as a sovereign state), and Czechoslovakia.

There was much talk in the early 1970s that these arrangements were only the beginning of a process which might lead to a loosening of the Eastern bloc, or of both blocs, and the political coming together in some way of the two German states. Recognition of the status quo was to be, as it were, the preface to dissolving it. It is difficult to believe that such hopes were very seriously held. For the reasons discussed earlier in this chapter, the Soviet Union imposed severe limits on the changes permissible in Eastern Europe. Notwithstanding the strengthening of political and economic contacts between the FRG and Eastern Europe, there was no possibility of a relationship between the two German states which would change either their internal systems of government or their external orientation. Most Germans knew this. Despite fears expressed abroad that the Brandt *Ostpolitik* might be leading to a new Rapallo, there was no realistic prospect that any German government would even consider renouncing its Western security ties—still all-important even in a period of détente—for a mere mirage of reunification, or that the Soviet Union would do anything to make such a mirage less unreal.

East Germany was therefore not liberated by *Ostpolitik*, nor was West Germany "finlandized" (to use a grossly imprecise expression that has been popular with those who thought they foresaw this impossibility). The dramatic agreements of 1970–72 proved to be not the harbingers of more and better but the major steps of a policy which has since tended to become routinized, to revert again, as it were, to small steps. That may

1. Catherine McArdle Kelleher, *Germany & the Politics of Nuclear Weapons* (New York: Columbia University Press, 1975), p. 291.

not have been what the German proponents of *Ostpolitik* had hoped for, but then it is probable that their hopes were, and remain, much longer term. It was no small thing, after all, that the Federal Republic avoided isolation by this policy; lifted the weight of the German past as far as it was capable of doing so; and for the first time developed confidence for diplomatic initiatives. The FRG, it is true, has not been able to do a great deal with its new freedom. It could not in the nature of things become a political giant. But the days of dwarfdom were, though at a cost, over.

What is most striking in this brief review of twenty years of West German policy is the continual realistic adjustment of the German people to the world in which they lived. They have sometimes been described as pursuing policies not in line with German interests because of feelings of guilt and self-abnegation. Nothing could be less true. The Federal Republic has been aware of the historical sensitivities inherent in its relations with neighboring states, but its policies since 1949, while they of course took account of this as of other circumstances, have almost always been sound and sensible assertions of the state's interests.

The Federal Republic's initial postwar choice to pursue integration with the West—on the Atlantic and European levels—was realistic in the short term because it led to the early end of occupation controls and the restoration of self-government; in the middle term because it provided for security in an atmosphere of great international tension; and even in the longer term because it signified an understanding that a bid for reunification would be not only unsuccessful but disastrous for its security, political, and economic benefits derived from the postwar European system.

The same was true for the FRG approach to the important problem of nuclear weapons. On the whole it did not press beyond what its allies—and not only the United States—would tolerate. The illustrative climax of German nuclear assertiveness was Erhard's maladroit statement that the FRG would be willing to enter into a bilateral MLF arrangement with the United States if others would not join. This untenable position was quickly abandoned and nothing like it has been tried since.

Later, the Germans were again wise to realize that the time had come to give up the gossamer pretension that reunification was likely to emerge of itself from cold war confrontation. The slow development of a new Eastern policy, backed by the electorate at each step despite temptations to move in other directions, could be seen as a sensible acceptance of the irreversibilty of past events and at least a start toward removing some of the obstacles to a different sort of future. *Ostpolitik* in its time was as realistic as the earlier policy of alliance with the West, the more so as the old remained intact as the foundation of the new.

The fears held abroad about Germans and German policy have had more than emotional roots. It was not absurd for foreigners and many Germans alike to fear that the Federal Republic could not but pursue unification as soon as the most acute tensions of the cold war had ebbed. West Germany's neighbors had reason to be concerned that sooner or later it would try to use its great economic strength to assert some kind of local hegemony. There was no compelling reason to believe that the new democratic polity would prove stronger than that of Weimar, and some reason to think that the partition of the country would generate nationalist reactions which would reduce even more its chances for survival.

None of these fears was unreasonable, yet they have turned out to be baseless. Postwar Germany, like postwar Europe, has been different. It is as if the trauma of defeat in the circumstances in which—unlike those in 1918—it took place, and the ensuing division of Europe with the risks which that posed to the Federal Republic, produced a sea change in German perceptions of the world and the place of their nation in it. A most un-Faustian sense of limits seems as if by miracle to have followed on the mad hubris of what preceded. No doubt there was a causal link.

There have, of course, been many differences of goal and policy between the Germans and various of their neighbors and allies. Yet the Germans have accepted the division of their country, the inevitable uncertainties in the arrangements on which their security depends, a necessary degree of inequality in their international status, and a corresponding degree of inhibition in the use of their power. On this basis they have earned and won the cooperation of their allies. For these reasons, one of the strongest and most overlooked factors making for the emergence and survival of the postwar European state system has been its acceptance by the West Germans as being in their interest in both tension and détente and the steady adaptation of their policies— including their security and Eastern policies—to the exigencies of that choice.

CHAPTER 10

Challenges: Within the West

From 1955 to the present the three states most able to shake the European system have not done so: the United States and the Federal Republic of Germany by choice, the Soviet Union for some combination of reasons reflecting conservatism toward Eastern Europe and prudence toward Western. Much that they did, however, or were thought likely to do, strengthened the widely-held notion that the system was in permanent jeopardy. So did the tense stability of Eastern Europe. But the barrage of challenges from within the Western subsystem which threatened to destabilize both it and the European system as a whole have received even more attention in an abundant literature. The libraries are crowded with volumes diagnosing and prescribing for the Atlantic crisis.

The most important of these challenges have concerned the security dispositions of the Western alliance; the free world economic structure of which the Euratlantic countries (together with Japan) have been the dominant members; the cohesion and adequacy of the Euratlantic institutions; the attempt to restructure the subsystem by building up a stronger and more united Europe; and, a special case by itself, the French problem. Since, nevertheless, the structure of the European system is not very different now from what it was twenty-five years ago, it is superfluous to write here a detailed account of intra-Western relations during that period. Still, these challenges to the Western status quo have reflected significant changes in the relations among the members of that subsystem. It is useful, therefore, with an eye to the future as well as the past, to examine each of them and consider why they produced so little structural change.

Security

The Euratlantic subsystem came into being during the cold war with the objective, among others, to deter or win a hot war. During the years since there has been almost unquestioned agreement among the member governments on the continued relevance and validity of the fundamentals of the security system: the U.S. guarantee to Western Europe in treaty form, the strategic nuclear power which backed that guarantee, and (except for France) the integrated military force in

Europe headed by an American and including substantial U.S. forces. Yet at no time has there been a thorough meeting of minds among the allies about how to deter or fight. Since war *has* been deterred, however, it would seem (leaving aside the question of Soviet intentions) that the area of agreement among the allies has weighed more heavily on the East-West level than their disagreements over strategy, force levels, deployment, and so forth. The allies have usually understood this. Even so, these problems have been a major part of the day-to-day life of the subsystem over many years, strongly affecting its internal politics and the public view of it.

At the most basic level, these disagreements about how to deter war and defend Europe if war comes reflect the great differences among the geographical and power positions of a very disparate set of allies. Thus, there has been a vast and inevitable difference of perception between one superpower and fourteen other states. No alliance of unequals can be untroubled. In addition, there have also been inherent differences—affecting self-image and policy needs—between two, later three members with nuclear forces and those without; between four or five with significant military forces and the others; between those directly confronting the enemy and those not; between those on the northern or southeastern flanks and the others; between those facing the Atlantic or the Mediterranean; between those allies having quarrels with other allies and those not; between those with colonial or other extra-European political and military involvements and those without. This list of differences among nominally equal allies cooperating voluntarily because of perceived common interests is so long as to make it the more remarkable that the alliance has been able to achieve any kind of agreed security doctrine and practice at all.

The problem of diverse outlooks and interests among the allies has been compounded by the steady march of military technology over the years. NATO's internal strategic debate since the mid-1950s has reflected the intertwining of these differences among the allies on the one hand, the changing requirements of defense stimulated by the arms race between the superpowers on the other. As I noted earlier, the initial security arrangement suited all the allies well enough in that the U.S. guarantee, backed by anticipated nuclear preponderance, did not raise the problem of massive expenditures for defense by the European members, who were still economically weak. The Korean war changed that, leading to U.S. insistence on a considerable allied buildup, together with West German rearmament, to counter a feared Soviet conventional attack in Europe which the initial guarantee by the United States, now involved in war in the Far East, was thought insufficient to deter. This buildup, however, weighed heavily on both the United States and the allies, the more so as the United Kingdom and France were maintaining large and expensive forces to police restive or rebellious colonial territories, and the Federal Republic, of course, was unarmed until 1955.

The result was the unilateral development by the United States of what came to be called the "new look" or doctrine of massive retaliation. German rearmament was carried forward, but the basic concept was that U.S. nuclear power would be called into play if and when a Soviet or Soviet-backed conventional attack occurred in Western Europe (or—perhaps—elsewhere in the world). The clear benefit to all the allies was a deemphasis on costly conventional arms. A major disadvantage was that upgrading the role of nuclear weapons in alliance strategy meant downgrading the role of those allies—all but Britain—which had only conventional weapons, the more so as they faced the risk that the United States now planned to use tactical nuclear weapons in Europe to repel a Soviet attack. Both France and the FRG, in different ways, would challenge these implications of U.S. nuclear ascendancy in the alliance.

An even greater difficulty for the "new look" was that massive retaliation was enunciated just when the buildup of Soviet nuclear forces began to raise questions about the assumed American invulnerability to attack or retaliation on which such a doctrine was based. From the mid-1950s, discussion began to focus on whether the U.S. government would be willing to respond to a Soviet conventional attack in Europe with its own strategic nuclear forces, knowing that American territory was increasingly vulnerable to Soviet nuclear response. In crude form the question was whether the United States would risk New York for Berlin.

The problem was at first more agitated by American strategic pundits than by European governments, most of which lacked the expertise to engage in the increasingly subtle analysis of these issues and all of which shied away from too close inquiry into arrangements which suited their security needs and their budgets quite well. But this discussion, already underway, was powerfully reinforced by the first Soviet sputnik (October 1957), which showed the strides Russia had made in nuclear delivery systems, and by the ensuing debate in the United States about the so-called missile gap, which advertised the supposed inadequacy of Western defenses. The missile gap, as it turned out, was on the Soviet side, but the fact of Soviet strategic power rapidly undermined the rationale and credibility of NATO's doctrine and plans. Coinciding as it did with the tensions launched by Khrushchev's ultimatums on Germany and Berlin, this was perhaps the most serious period of internal doubt and division about security policy that the alliance has experienced.

At first the American government tried to meet the problem by de-

ploying intermediate-range ballistic missiles in European countries with
joint American–host country control of the nuclear warheads, and by
supplying nuclear-capable tactical missiles to the Germans and others.
But the Kennedy administration initiated a more radical revision of U.S.
and alliance doctrine, launching a six-year effort to move the alliance
from massive retaliation to what was called flexible response, a concept
for being able to meet Soviet attack at whatever level it occurred.

In addition to trying to meet the problem of the credibility of the U.S.
security guarantee, American policy in the 1960s gave rise to a wide-
ranging set of interrelated issues, including its parallel effort to secure in
effect monopoly control of nuclear decision-making within the alliance
by blocking development of a national French nuclear force and limiting
the further development or autonomy of the British force; the strains
created by the zeal and unilateralism with which the Americans acted;
the costs for all the allies of improving the capabilities of their conventional forces as called for by the new concept; the fears aroused in
Europe that flexible response implied some degree of American nuclear
decoupling from Europe—that is, a reduction of the deterrent provided
by U.S. strategic weapons and an increased likelihood of conventional war in Europe; the impetus these fears gave to European desires
for a greater nuclear role, in some cases for national or European
nuclear weapons; the U.S. efforts to counter both this impetus and the
fears behind it by bringing the allies—particularly the FRG—into closer
touch with nuclear policy- and decision-making without giving up
American control; the revival, to this end, of earlier schemes for a
so-called NATO nuclear force in the form of the ill-fated multilateral
force; and, intertwined with all this, the effort by General de Gaulle
(discussed more fully later in this chapter) to exploit the ambiguities of
American doctrine and the deficiencies of American diplomacy to the
benefit of French leadership in Europe.

This is not the place to write a detailed history of these complex issues
and their implications for the internal health of the alliance, and also for
East-West relations in Europe, because in the end this great debate on
fundamental issues, which at the time severely strained NATO, had so
little lasting impact on it or the Western subsystem. However, some
conclusions can be drawn from this long story which not only account for
the fact that such issues have been less acutely agitated in the last ten
years but which may even have relevance for the future if, as is likely, the
alliance will again be troubled, and for the same reasons, by questions of
how best to meet the persisting Soviet threat which is its security raison
d'être.

First, though the alliance has undergone a chronic and public internal debate on strategic doctrine and related issues, war has been deterred and security maintained. Successive doctrines may have lacked the rational precision that experts thought necessary, and force levels and capabilities have usually fallen short of those required by doctrine, but the Russians have shown themselves to be most prudent in probing the alliance's self-advertised military deficiencies. A quarter-century has passed since the alliance (at Lisbon, in February 1952) set itself a goal of 96 divisions (ready or available one month after D-day). This goal was never reached or approached, nor have the American and NATO military authorities ever been satisfied with the force levels and equipment the allies have been willing to provide over the years. Over twenty years have passed since the first sputnik, with all that it implied for Soviet long-range strategic delivery capability and American vulnerability. But there has been no war, nor, notwithstanding two Berlin crises, Soviet actions that came close to starting war in Europe. The alliance must have been doing some things well enough, if not well.

Second, the European allies on the whole have acted as if they understood this fact. Except for de Gaulle, who had his own reasons for trying to drive a wedge between the United States and Europe with respect to strategic doctrine (and many other things), allied concern for alliance deficiencies has been kept within tolerable bounds. Few in Europe, in or out of government, have understood the complexities of deterrence doctrine. Fewer have wanted to increase their defense budgets to provide for the conventional force levels required to make flexible response entirely convincing. Neither have they wanted to spend the money nor, even more serious, to face the political difficulties of trying to build national or European nuclear forces on a scale that could provide effective deterrence even as a supplement to an American guarantee of allegedly shrinking credibility.

In fact, a kind of "law" seems to have been at work by which, to put the matter starkly, most Europeans in times of crisis have clung to the protection offered by the United States whatever doubts they had about it, while in times of relaxation they have more or less forgotten about such deep issues. In no case have they (except for France) been inclined to make the financial and political efforts required to do other than continue to rely on the U.S. guarantee and acquiesce in its current doctrines whatever their ambiguities.

This was true above all for the West Germans who, as the most "forward" and exposed of the allies, were the most sensitive to shifts in American doctrines and plans but also the most eager to believe in the U.S. guarantees, most willing to follow American policy leads to maintain them, and least able to explore or threaten more independent nuclear or other options. There was, of course, a constant and sometimes tense U.S.–German dialogue, not blind German subservience. But from it the Germans got, if not always what they wanted, at least what they could live with tolerably—as compared to anything else they might do. It was true also of the British, who built a national nuclear force but as much or more for political reasons as because of strategic anxiety. It was even true to a certain extent of de Gaulle himself, who strongly challenged American doctrine and leadership but was probably less fearful of the risk of war in Europe even in his most cold war phase and less troubled by the in-credibilities of the American guarantee than he found it politic to concede.

Third, a very important source of intra-alliance tension with respect to these issues has been not so much doctrinal differences or inadequate force levels as American underestimation of the degree to which European dependence on the U.S. security guarantee was so deep-seated, for the reasons just stated, as to be proof against the alliance deficiencies which vexed the Americans so much, the irritations inevitably caused by the dependence itself, and even the French attempt to exploit these problems. No doctrine, after all, was likely to satisfy all the allies all the time in light of their disparate interests and resources. Massive retaliation, for example, kept down costs but increased the risk that the United States might not be able to deter a conventional Soviet attack in an era of mutual assured destruction. Flexible response provided a better means to meet such an attack but cost more and, besides, threatened to increase the chance of a devasting conventional war in Europe—a prospect some of the allies found less attractive than trying to deter war altogether by threatening quick nuclear escalation.

In light of all this (and much more), the doctrinal debate never ended to the satisfaction of all even when the United States secured ratification of its current views by the alliance. But the allies have had no viable alternative to going along with the U.S. guarantee in good logic and bad, in bad times and good. The European response to de Gaulle's effort to exploit the issue provides the clearest proof of this, but the history of strategic debate in the alliance points the same way. The United States government might have spared itself and the allies much anguish in pursuit of a consensus that could not be achieved and, even more important, did not need to be achieved for the alliance to do its essential job.

These American efforts gave rise to a number of mistakes that added further to alliance tension while trying to alleviate it. One was the inordinate concern expressed in the early 1960s that a national French

nuclear force, and even the United Kingdom's, might somehow destabilize centralized decision-making within the alliance, to the cost of
both its security and American leadership. De Gaulle, indeed, would
have liked to undermine the latter; the raison d'être of the French *force
de dissuasion* was more political than strategic. But it lacked the physical
means to fulfill its ostensible security function, and de Gaulle failed to
convince any other European government to risk loosening European
ties to the essential American strategic deterrent or to accept the French
force as a supplement to it.

Some Europeans may have doubted American credibility and even
been convinced intellectually of the need for independent strategic
power in Europe. But no government—above all the German—was
convinced that France could provide it or that *any* feasible effort to do so
would not cost more in alienation of the United States, among other
problems, than it could offer in enhanced security. And, as I noted, the
time was never right for such ideas to come to a head: when there was
tension, the allies had little choice but to rely on the United States; when
there was relaxation, few wanted the cost or bother of trying to devise
new arrangements for European security other than those which, after
all, had been shown to function well enough. The independent French
and British nuclear forces survived, their claims to deterrent efficacy
even acknowledged in the Ottawa declaration of June 1974 in language
that endorsed the arguments made earlier by de Gaulle and reversed
those made against him by the United States. But the American government has never had any serious reason to fear that life-and-death nuclear decisions for the West would be made by anyone but itself.

A related American mistake was to overrate European concern about
the implications for their security of U.S.–Soviet strategic parity and, as a
result, to try to reassure the Europeans without encouraging local nuclear forces, which were seen as both superfluous and divisive. These
efforts also reflected American misreading of German security intentions. Having believed erroneously that France would sit quietly in face
of American nuclear assistance to an independent British nuclear force,
the American government then made the opposite mistake of believing
that the West Germans would not sit quietly in face of an independent
French nuclear force. This misreading of both French and German
policy—that is, of motivations but also of feasible policy options available
to both—led not only to clumsy efforts to stop the French nuclear force
and to reinforce the links inhibiting the independence of the British
force, but also to an attempt to give the Germans a "finger on the
trigger" of a mock multilateral nuclear force while blocking what was
judged (wrongly) to be their inevitable desire to catch up with France

and achieve nuclear autonomy.[1] This project, aimed to satisfy the Germans' presumed needs for security and equality and, perhaps even more, to save them from the temptations of de Gaulle's "inward-looking" Europe, was the centerpeice of a zealous American diplomatic effort in 1963–64, reminiscent of the misdirected effort ten years before in support of the European Defense Community.

The Federal Republic, however, was too wise to pursue or even threaten a nuciear option, notwithstanding the supposed goad of the French example. Far from threatening to go nuclear in the mid-1960s, its genuine security concerns were quite readily satisfied at that time by the establishment of NATO's Nuclear Planning Group, the useful fallback device offered by the Americans when the more ambitious multilateral force capsized because of the divisiveness it created within the alliance and the American and German governments. By then the United States realized that its objectives could be achieved by far simpler means, and the West Germans realized that what they wanted was not a sterile drive for the shadow of nuclear "equality" but its antithesis, an effort to pursue détente with Eastern Europe.

For these reasons, debate about strategic doctrine and the quest for redefinition of nuclear roles in the alliance have never regained the intensity of the mid-1960s. Notions that there might one day be a European nuclear force, or at least a meaningful coordination of the British and French forces, have also faded away for lack of political motivation. Earlier talk that the United States might somehow devolve nuclear tasks to the European allies, or some of them, never became concrete. Since the misadventure of the MLF, few on either side of the Atlantic have wanted to delve again into the dark recesses of nuclear sharing.

Since its founding NATO has had to face the constant problem of adapting its force levels, deployments, and plans to ongoing military technology. American dependability has also remained a permanent problem for the Europeans and the alliance in that the dependence of one state on another for basic security can never be entirely happy. The United States, for its part, has been permanently discontented with the level of military effort provided by most of the allies and the shortfalls from theoretically desirable levels of manpower and equipment.

What the long record seems to show, however, is that years and decades of dispute and inadequacy have not provoked Soviet attack or

1. Harold Wilson put the case against the MLF pungently: "If you have a boy and wish to sublimate his sex appetite, it is unwise to take him to a strip-tease show." Quoted in Catherine McCardle Kelleher, *Germany & the Politics of Nuclear Weapons* (New York: Columbia University Press, 1975), p. 252.

the internal breakup of the alliance. The allies trust the effectiveness of the U.S. guarantee because it has worked over many years and through very diverse circumstances and because, whatever their doubts and discontents, they have no serious alternative that does not offer insuperable costs and difficulties. This may seem a less than rational or satisfactory basis for an enduring security alliance. Yet the turbulent history of the last two decades and more shows a consistently good performance by the debated alliance system with respect to its basic security purposes. Each year that has passed has, in fact, strengthened the common belief that the alliance would continue to work. That may seem complacent, but it reflects a fact that has been of great psychological and political value in stabilizing the alliance, the Western subsystem of which it is a part, and the European state system as a whole.

Economics

Economic relations were both policy means and policy goals for the United States in its wartime planning for the postwar world. After 1947 it remained attached to the objective of securing equal access for U.S. trade and investment in as wide an area of the world as possible. But circumstances required adaptation of specific policies. The devastation of postwar Western Europe and its need for security guarantees predisposed the governments of the area to cooperate with the United States, but the weakness which led the allies to such cooperation made it impossible for them to accept the economic system which the Americans wanted. The sharp reduction of tariffs and other barriers to trade and the introduction of convertible currencies, it was believed, would not only retard recovery but create conditions which would make internal political stabilization on Western institutional terms impossible.

The United States, for all its strength, found that it had no choice but to provide economic assistance to its allies for essentially political reasons in the short term, with the hope that when they were stronger they would . be able, and willing, to take the steps that could not safely be forced on them when U.S. bargaining power was at its height. The Americans therefore accepted not only continued high tariffs, colonial preferential trading arrangements, and monetary inconvertibility, but also the movement toward European unity that, whatever its hoped for economic and political benefits, provided in the near term for the progressive establishment of a large trading area—the European Economic Community or common market—which was discriminatory toward outsiders, including the United States.

The economic strand in the Euratlantic subsystem therefore did not take shape at the same time as the security and political components.

The international financial system designed at Bretton Woods came to life only when the European members were strong enough to accept currency convertibility, in late 1958. The most important effort in the postwar period to reduce trade barriers began only when the Kennedy administration obtained congressional enactment of the Trade Expansion Act of 1962, by which it meant to seize the opportunity offered by Great Britain's anticipated entry into the Common Market to break down the latter's particularism in a wide-ranging negotiation. Putting the trade relations of the United States and the Europeans on a new basis, important in itself, was also part of the broader Kennedy design for a "two-pillar" Atlantic partnership.

The political results of the Kennedy Round fell far short of American goals, for General de Gaulle vetoed British entry into the Common Market and blocked further progress toward greater unity of the hoped-for European pillar. But the economic achievements, though they too fell short of American hopes, were significant even in proportion to the time required to achieve them (1964–67). This negotiation, coming at a time of great strain between the United States and France and much questioning about the future of the Euratlantic subsystem, strengthened not only the economic ties across the Atlantic but, by doing that, the overall relationship as well.

For all the compromises of American economic goals, both before and after the recovery of Western Europe, and the two-edged thrust of the policies of those European countries which entered on the road to European unity, the real-life bonds of aid, trade, investment, and monetary cooperation grew very rapidly between the two sides of the Atlantic and beyond. The comprehensiveness of these ties and their structural institutionalization contrasted strongly with nineteenth-century and prewar arrangements. Involving the domestic as well as international interests of the dominant groups in the European countries, these structured bonds added a powerful dimension to the Euratlantic security-political subsystem.

It is useful to see the web of economic relationships developed in the Euratlantic subsystem as forming also an economic system in itself, defining the word system here, as earlier, to mean a group of states the major part of whose important foreign interactions are with each other over a considerable period of time. Since the European states were the metropoles for colonial or postcolonial economic relations with most of the world outside the Soviet sphere of control, this strand of the Euratlantic subsystem was truly a global economic system, supplementing the extra-European political involvements of the United States and many of the European members of the subsystem. The trade and monetary systems of the non-Communist states of the world have been managed mainly by countries which were security and political allies in the Euratlantic subsystem, plus one other U.S. ally, Japan, which was readily coopted into the existing system when its economic strength revived—a testimony to the ability of the system to adapt to new conditions.

What has been the balance sheet of the postwar economic system up to the present, the degree of its success with respect to issues on its own plane, and the degree to which the handling of those issues contributed to strengthening or weakening the Euratlantic subsystem of which its members were participants?

One touchstone for measuring any economic system is growth. On that score, the system has been an immense success for all its members. We have only to look at the growth of the principal members of the system to see how they have prospered (table 10.1).[2] An even more informative yardstick is the growth of per capita income (table 10.2).

These averages of course conceal serious problems of distribution and "justice." But it is obvious that there has been a marked increase in the standard of living of the large majority of the population in the postwar period as a whole. This has clearly contributed a great deal to the stability of democratic constitutional arrangements in postwar Europe and has helped promote that acceptance of diminished status after decades of fevered nationalism which has characterized most European countries since the war. The traumatic course of World War II had much to do with this, but postwar prosperity and its political consequences surely helped reduce the prospects for a revival of assertive nationalisms, among the defeated and the victors alike.

It is true, of course, that the accumulated perceptions and rancors of class and national outlooks have not been swept away, as some expected, by a plethora of television sets. It is true also that there were warning signals about the implications of the new prosperity even before it began to falter in recent years: the upheavals of 1968; the problems of distorted consumerism; the aesthetic, moral, and spiritual unease which it engendered, in different ways, in many people. Even so, the citizens of Western Europe since the late 1940s have enjoyed a life of greater material abundance, and connected with that in some way a greater civil freedom and political stability within national democratic frameworks, than did their parents and grandparents.

If the economic system has helped strengthen the domestic coherence and political stability of the members, it has also helped knit them

2. I am indebted for the statistical data in this chapter to Miss Lucie Kornei, senior specialist for economic statistics, Bureau of Intelligence and Research, Department of State.

Table 10.1   Gross National Product of Major Industrial Countries
(in billions of 1977 dollars at constant 1977 prices)

	United States	United Kingdom	France	Germany	Italy	Japan
1957	962	151	149	223	78	129
1967	1,424	204	245	352	134	336
1977	1,890	246	381	514	191	685

together. Their new wealth has been accompanied by the growing importance of foreign trade for all members (table 10.3) and the preponderant share of that trade that is carried on among them (defined
here as comprising the members of the Organization for Economic
Cooperation and Development and its predecessor). These patterns of
trade have been reinforced, as noted above, by the increasing inter-
penetration of investment among countries and, of course, their participation in an international monetary system based on the Bretton Woods
machinery.

This discussion so far has emphasized the integrative effects of the
developing economic relations among the Atlantic states. But they had
begun to face difficulties almost as soon as convertibility—and the common market—came into being. Though the United States had accepted
the creation of a preferential European Community, there was a series
of disputes from the first about such things as the "inward-looking" price
support and tariff system the Community maintained for its agricultural
produce. The chicken war of 1962–64 and many other specific trade
disagreements over the years sometimes seemed important enough to
jeopardize overall U.S.–European relations. But there have been no
such consequences. Neither the United States nor the Community could
dictate on these matters to the other; it was in the interest of both—
economic as well as political—to prevent trade wars and to keep the
issues in bounds. And they have done so. Negotiations on these problems have become part of the normal diplomacy of the Euratlantic
countries. The issues have had their importance, but not on a scale to

Table 10.2   Per Capita Income in Major Industrial Countries
(in 1977 dollars at constant 1977 prices)

	United States	United Kingdom	France	Germany	Italy	Japan
1957	5,593	2,931	3,365	4,151	1,592	1,423
1967	7,165	3,719	4,934	5,883	2,552	3,330
1977	8,715	4,410	7,177	8,371	3,376	6,017

Table 10.3   Trade of Major Industrial Countries

Exports as Percentage of GNP

	United States	Great Britain	France	Germany	Italy	Japan
1957	4.7	15.8	10.5	16.2	10.3	10.5
1967	4.0	13.1	10.5	18.4	13.0	9.0
1977	6.4	23.3	16.7	23.3	23.6	11.7

Percentage of Exports to Other OECD Members

	United States	Great Britain	France	Germany	Italy	Japan
1957	50.4	56.1	50.3	71.5	65.7	36.2
1967	66.1	67.1	70.3	77.2	72.8	49.4
1977	60.3	68.8	69.4	72.6	69.1	46.7

weaken the U.S. commitment to the European community and the alliance with Europe or the European commitment to the Atlantic subsystem. On the contrary, these very disputes have led them to create a new dimension of cooperative diplomacy.

There were much more serious difficulties besetting the Western economic system continuously from the late 1950s. They can be grouped under three headings: the monetary challenge; the third world challenge; and, related to both, the challenge in the 1970s of inflation, unemployment, and the dislocation of prosperity. The first of these issues will be reviewed in some detail because it was a major source of controversy among the Western countries over many years. The latter two will be looked at more briefly because they are still in the nature of current events and their implications for the stability of the Euratlantic subsystem are not yet very clearly in focus.

The Bretton Woods *monetary system*, finally implemented de facto with the establishment in late 1958 of convertibility among fixed-rate Western currencies, was based on the assumption that any country's balance of payments difficulties would be remedied by a combination of assistance from the International Monetary Fund to the country in deficit and domestic deflationary adjustments carried out by it in consultation with the fund. This system aimed to do by conscious management what the earlier systems were supposed to have done blindly—that is, provide international monetary discipline, but with greater flexibility and lower costs to trade, growth, and employment.

No sooner had the system gone into full operation, however, than the belief began to spread that the payments deficit which the United States had been running since 1950, at first overlooked or even welcomed as the counterpart of Europe's recovery, could not continue indefinitely. But it was also apparent that it would not be adjustable by the methods prescribed by the IMF system and imposed on other countries. The problem of reconciling American political strength and monetary (but not economic) weakness became a vexing issue for the United States and its allies.

During the Marshall Plan period and afterward the United States had encouraged the Europeans to maximize their exports, minimize their dollar imports and build up reserve surpluses, as a prelude to restoring convertibility, by holding on to some of the dollars they received in aid and otherwise. By the late 1950s, as European (and Japanese) growth and trade outran expectation, the supposedly chronic dollar gap had become a dollar glut—if not in relation to the actual needs of world trade for liquidity, at least in terms of the attitudes with which many Europeans viewed the matter.

But there was no obvious remedy. Deflation in the United States to a point that would end the deficits was a most unattractive prospect to the Americans because of the severe contraction required to produce a relatively small reduction of imports and to the Europeans because of the danger that such a recession would be exported abroad. But the Europeans also did not want the United State to save dollars by cutting back its overseas military presence or even, despite criticism in France and elsewhere, its private investment abroad. Nor did they want devaluation of the dollar. Not only was the United States already all too competitive an exporter but the dollar was so firmly entrenched as a major reserve and intervention currency and medium of international exchange that most countries had a clear economic interest in maintaining its position and exchange rate. The U.S. payments deficit in fact supplied the dollars with which international trade was increasingly financed, for gold came into the system relatively slowly and the pound sterling gradually lost its prewar role as the British economy faltered. Finally, most American allies felt they had a political interest in not allowing trade and monetary problems to become a source of serious tension with the superpower on whom their security depended. For all these reasons, the Bretton Woods rules, it appeared, could not be applied to the United States because its currency was not like the others.

The fact that the United States had a hegemonic role in international monetary as well as security-political affairs did not go unnoticed in Europe, particularly by the government of General de Gaulle, which was already challenging U.S. hegemony across the board (see the last section of this chapter). The U.S. government was aware of the strength of its special role but also of the costs and risks. Beginning with the Eisenhower administration, therefore, it sought answers along several lines. The United States on the whole resisted the temptation to turn to protectionism lest it invite retaliation, to the cost of all. A constant element of the U.S. response throughout the 1960s was to promote exports and maintain the domestic price level and the real value of the dollar. A second facet of American policy included measures enacted at various times to restrict spending by tourists abroad, reduce the side costs of assigning military and civilian personnel overseas, and require recipients of aid to "buy American." A third aspect of policy, from 1960 on, was to link security and economic policy by getting the richest European country, the Federal Republic, to provide offset for the foreign exchange costs of U.S. forces stationed there. In 1967 the FRG formally undertook not to convert its dollar holdings into gold and to buy agreed-on amounts of U.S. military equipment and medium-term bonds.

A fourth line of policy was the establishment from the early 1960s on of arrangements among major central banks and treasuries and in the IMF and the Bank for International Settlements to counter speculative movements in the gold and currency markets and provide short-term currency resources beyond the IMF's to countries in payments difficulties. The measures included a gold pool, a swap network among central banks, and the General Arrangements to Borrow. The practice of managing monetary crises cooperatively by these means paradoxically provided an important new bond among the Euratlantic countries.

American policymakers assumed through the 1960s that the chronic U.S. deficits would eventually be ended by their policies. Until about the middle of the decade they assumed also that this, together with the normal use of credit and IMF procedures to deal with payments problems, would steady and maintain the Bretton Woods system. The French, on the other hand, argued that the international reserve system should not depend mainly on the deficits of reserve currency countries for its resources. Their goal was to reduce the reserve role of the dollar and the special privileges they claimed that gave the United States, partly by a return to gold, partly by creating a collective reserve unit linked to gold and under the control of a few countries acting with unanimity.

As discussion of these issues advanced the American position shifted. Policymakers came more and more to the conclusion that the deeper problem which the deficits represented could not be resolved in the Bretton Woods system as it stood because, while they were a threat to long-term international monetary stability and economic growth, they were at the same time essential to financing world trade. The United States, having become a global "central bank," had reasons beyond domestic convenience or even hegemony not to dry up too quickly the main instrument for increasing world liquidity. But it also had reason to plan ahead for a time when the supply of dollars to the world would be reduced and the available quantity of dollars plus sterling plus gold would no longer suffice to finance expanding world trade. From 1965 on, as much or more official American attention was given to plans for meeting the liquidity and reserve problems which would have to be faced when deficits were reduced or ended as to dealing with the deficits themselves.

The American government rejected the two most radical solutions to the international monetary problem proposed in the mid-1960s: a return to a gold standard system (advocated by France) or floating exchange rates (advocated by some American academic economists). What the U.S. government proposed was that the IMF provide additional drawing rights to its members without additional payments. This amounted to the invention of a new form of liquidity to provide means to finance expanding trade in face of the anticipated decline in U.S. deficits and the continued shrinking of the role of sterling. Gold and floating both implied, though in different ways, a return to greater automaticity in the international monetary system; the U.S. proposal was consistent with the trend of postwar developments in looking to greater conscious management of the international monetary system by its members.

Long negotiations among the leading powers, and then including others too, led to the IMF's agreeing in principle (at Rio, in 1967) to establish Special Drawing Rights (SDRs). To bring along the French, who had cooled on their earlier proposal for a collective reserve unit as the United States had warmed to it, what was actually to be a new unit of reserves was called by a name suggesting credit. Also, stringent conditions were placed on the means by which the IMF could create and assign SDRs. The European Community members together, as well as the United States, had a veto on creation. Even so, this was a signal step toward the transformation of the IMF into a global bank of emission and the emergence of a new currency to supplement, perhaps eventually largely replace, gold, dollars, and pounds sterling in international transactions. Since monetary policy cannot be separated from economic policy, such a regime would be bound to lead to increased policymaking in common by the Euratlantic countries and Japan, who dominated the system.

This fundamental reform of the Bretton Woods system looked to the long term, presupposing the reestablishment of stability at fixed rates among the major currencies. It provided no answer to the growing instability of the monetary system which developed in the late 1960s. The cooperative machinery that existed or was improvised to deal with such problems worked well enough to provide a "solution" to each crisis but not well enough to prevent the next. Thus, the long-delayed devaluation of the pound (November 1967); the establishment of a two-tier gold market to insulate the reserve system from private speculation (March 1968); the feverish crisis of November 1968, triggered by the May upheaval in France, that ended with the refusal of the French to devalue and of the Germans—in the face of American and British as well as French pressure—to revalue; the eventual devaluation of the franc (August 1969) and revaluation of the mark (October 1969)—all these disturbances were patched up, but only by stopgaps and palliatives.

The fundamental assumption behind the measures taken on each of these occasions—that a regime of fixed exchange rates, and the particular rates of most currencies, should and could be maintained—was increasingly called into question by the continual failure to reestablish stability. Changes in exchange rates were not ruled out by IMF orthodoxy but they were supposed to be confined to cases of fundamental disequilibrium. There was great reluctance in all governments, particularly those of reserve currency countries, to recognize that their international economic situations, and the international monetary system as a whole, *were* in a state of fundamental disequilibrium because they themselves were less and less willing to subject their economies to the measures, whether of contraction or expansion, required to maintain exchange rates.

The economic price paid by the British in the years 1964–67 for trying—and failing—to maintain an untenable exchange rate and the cascade of monetary crises in 1968–69 convinced some that living by these rules might be more costly than changing or breaking them. But even those who became convinced that more frequent changes in exchange rates might be useful recognized the great political difficulties, involving both prestige and the interests of particular groups, that blocked the acceptance of such changes as a more or less normal phenomenon. In any case, it remained an article of faith for the American government up to 1971, and for others, too, that devaluing the dollar or breaking the gold-dollar link would be unspeakably dangerous to the world economy. Memories of the competitive devaluations and protectionism of the 1930s were cited, not to mention the prospective blow to U.S. prestige. The United States became more open to the idea of changes in exchange rates for others in difficulty, but not for itself. But other governments found it politically unattractive to accommodate the U.S. special position, as would have been required to keep the system going. International studies of how to move away from fixed exchange rates therefore came to nothing.

In the end the essential step toward replacing, or at least demolishing, the Bretton Woods system was taken unilaterally by the United States. In 1970 its balance of payments deficit was $9.8 billion. The following year promised to be far worse and another monetary crisis got underway in May, this time in the form of a flight from the dollar. The Germans floated the mark, which was helpful to the United States, but not helpful enough. Only the revaluation of all the major currencies would have sufficed and this was politically impossible to achieve. In the absence of this the Nixon administration acted alone, suddenly and drastically, to avoid the even worse fate (as it was thought) of devaluing the dollar. On August 15 the American government "temporarily" suspended the convertibility of dollars into gold, imposed a 10 percent surcharge on dutiable imports, and invoked a 90-day wage freeze. The president described these steps as emancipating the United States from the intrigues of international money traders and the effects of unfair exchange rates.

The form and substance of the American action produced the most severe crisis over economic issues that the United States and its major partners have ever experienced. It was, in fact, a major crisis of the Atlantic relationship, and of U.S.–Japanese relations as well. A relationship that survived that crisis had strong roots indeed.

In the months of negotiation that followed, the United States, represented mainly by Secretary of the Treasury John Connally, pursued ambitious goals. In return for giving up the import surcharge, it pressed for a $13 billion turnaround in its trade account, to be achieved by a restructuring of exchange rates (revaluation by others), trade liberalization (also by others), and a "fairer" sharing of defense burdens.

The United States had strong cards in this confrontation with its allies. But while it had political as well as economic reasons for wanting to end the dollar crisis on its terms, it also had political reasons not to push too hard. After much negotiation, the basis of a settlement was struck between Presidents Nixon and Pompidou. The details were filled in at a meeting of the finance ministers and central bank governors of the Group of Ten, held in December at the Smithsonian Institution in Washington. The package included suppression of the U.S. surcharge on imports, an increase in the price of gold from $35 to $38 per ounce, and a complicated reshuffling of exchange rates which had the effect of devaluing the dollar by some 6.5 percent to 7.75 percent against all currencies and about 10 percent against other Group of Ten currencies, to an estimated $8 billion advantage for U.S. trade.[3] There was a promise to pursue basic reform of the international monetary system and to negotiate trade problems. A "fairer" sharing of defense spending passed unmentioned. The most striking sign that the Smithsonian agreement marked the end of the Bretton Woods system was that the convertibility of the dollar into gold was not restored.

President Nixon hailed the Smithsonian deal as "the most significant monetary agreement in the history of the world." But it was shortlived. The United States had won an improvement in its trade position by the realignment of exchange rates, but the new rates proved as untenable as the old. Indeed, the quick return of monetary crisis demonstrated that a regime of fixed rates could not be maintained without stringent capital controls and rigorous manipulation of domestic economies, neither of which was tolerable to most countries. Yet one more sterling crisis, in June 1972, ended with the floating of the pound and a massive flight from the dollar. Yet another round of speculation, in February and March 1973, led, with much consultation but minimum difficulty— perhaps even with relief—to a second devaluation of the dollar and the addition of the Swiss franc, the yen, and the currencies of the European Community to the list of those floating.

This, it has turned out, is the post–Bretton Woods monetary system (except that floating is partly managed by the governments and the deutschmark and a few lesser European currencies float jointly in the so-called European snake—the vestige of a premature effort to establish a monetary union in the European Community). The drawn-out efforts to negotiate a new structure on the basis of stable but more flexible rates than under Bretton Woods produced an agreement on the main issues (at Jamaica, in January 1976), but there has been no decision actually to establish such a system. The temporary regime, in short, became not only tolerable but acceptable, even to the French. There were two main reasons for this.

First, the floating of most major currencies, including the dollar, had been thought of initially as a provisional arrangement suitable to counter speculative movements until something more permanent could be devised. But in the inflation that prevailed after 1972, and the recession that accompanied it after 1974, managed floating was soon found to be a workable means of balance of payments adjustment, more symmetrical

3. These figures, admittedly somewhat imprecise and depending on the method of calculation, are drawn (along with most of this discussion) from Robert Solomon, *The International Monetary System, 1945–1976* (New York: Harper & Row, 1977), pp. 207–08.

than the old system in placing some responsibility for adjustment on surplus as well as deficit countries and with fewer of the burdens of a fixed rate system which had come to seem unacceptable. As for the anticipated negative impact of floating rates on trade, they appear to have been much exaggerated. If traders had to deal with the uncertainties of floating rates, these have seemed scarcely more inhibiting than the problems presented by the allegedly "fixed" but really volatile rates of the preceding several years.

The second reason why the provisional has lasted in this case is that the quadrupling of the price of oil by the oil exporters in late 1973 radically changed the priorities of the advanced countries which until then had dominated discussions of a new monetary system. Those issues faded in importance compared to the urgent problem of finding ways to finance their oil purchases and counter the recessionary impact of the price increase. The temporary monetary arrangements of 1973 have turned out to be very useful in these unforeseen circumstances. The countries that dominated the Bretton Woods system have at least preserved its most important contribution to the postwar period: the understanding that it was in their common interest to avoid mutually wounding competitive monetary policies and, in fact, to continue their cooperation. With their currencies protected by floating from the kinds of crises so many of them experienced in the 1960s, they were able to devise means to recycle the wealth of the oil exporters to help those advanced countries whose balances of payments were hardest hit by the oil price rise. In the process the new financial superpowers have begun to be coopted into the global financial system, as Japan had been before. They will take their places in whatever new monetary system comes to be set up, the more easily because no such system was yet in existence in 1973.

In short, the failure of the advanced countries to build a post–Bretton Woods monetary system has been no unmixed curse. For all the quarrels which it created and the still uncertain shape of a new structure, it has had no negative impact on the existence of the Western economic system or of the overall Euratlantic system of which the latter is a part. The very breakdown of the Bretton Woods system and the efforts expended on trying to replace it or managing to live without a replacement imposed an unprecedented degree of practical cooperation among the leading countries.

The long challenge presented by monetary issues to the stability of the Euratlantic subsystem thus trailed off unsettled in face of a more urgent one, that raised by the *less developed countries* (LDCs), rich and poor, the outsiders in past international economic debate. The powerful eruption of the Organization of Petroleum Exporting Countries (OPEC) into the world's economic consciousness in late 1973 caused the main focus of international negotiation to shift from the monetary plane to what came to be called the North-South dialogue on problems of resource distribution. For the advanced countries—that is, those of the Euratlantic subsystem, Japan, and some others—the main issues were, first, how to finance their oil imports, and second, whether and how to concert their approach to the less developed to maintain their economic strength in light of changed circumstances (higher energy costs) and the threat of further change (redistribution of the world's wealth to the relative benefit of the poor).

In 1973 the OECD countries as a group had run a payments surplus of $11 billion. In 1974, with the rise of the oil price, this shifted to a deficit of $22 billion. In the first panic following the OPEC price increase it was widely thought either that production and trade in the advanced countries would be reduced catastrophically, for lack of energy or capital, or that the added billions needed now to buy the same amount of oil as before could be obtained only by selling off huge chunks of the Western economies to the newly rich oil producers. There was fear that each Western country would try to balance its increased deficit with OPEC by improving its trade and payments position with everyone else, a line of policy which, if implemented, could have led straight to the mutually ruinous beggar-thy-neighbor policies which the West had, on the whole, avoided so successfully since World War II. Finally, some foresaw a convergence of the energy-poor European and oil-rich Middle Eastern countries, economic but also political, at the expense of U.S.–European ties.

It was fortunate, as noted, that the advanced countries were operating at this point on a regime of floating exchange rates, which, among other things, made it easier for them to adapt without constant monetary crises to the potentially destabilizing fact that the burden of oil imports did not fall with equal effects on all of them. The United States, which imported much less of its energy needs than Japan and the countries of Western Europe, suddenly found itself in a far stronger economic position vis-à-vis them than had been the case for many years. Partly for this reason the United States was able to take the lead in devising schemes which allowed the advanced countries as a group to finance their deficits much more readily than had been expected at the beginning of 1974.

If the worst effects of the oil price rise that were foreseen did not take place, it is because the OPEC surplus countries have had to use their money somehow. The oil sellers have bought more goods and services from the West than had been expected; have invested some of their proceeds in the West; and have deposited their money with U.S. and European banks which, in turn, have lent it out or "recycled" it in such a way as to supply the means to all the advanced countries in deficit to pay their oil bills. This is clearly not a dependable, long-term arrangement, for money invested or deposited in one place today can be moved elsewhere tomorrow, and money borrowed has to be repaid or refinanced. Even so, and without overlooking the fact that the recession in the West reduced the relative demand for oil imports after 1973, the international monetary system up to the present has managed the consequences of the oil price increase with less disruption of the Western economies—and Western political relations—than had been expected. The same is less true, ironically, of the non-oil-producing developing countries. OPEC wealth has found its place, as it were, in the Western economic and monetary system, which has been adapted in the process, but it has been donated, invested, and recycled to the poorer LDCs only in relatively small amounts.

This brings us to the ambiguous subject of the North-South economic dialogue which has had a prominent place on the international agenda from 1974 on. This has gone on in many fora: the United Nations, the IMF, and the special Conference on International Economic Cooperation that was created at French initiative in February 1974 as a kind of overall directorate for discussing what the LDCs liked to call a "new international economic order." The subject matter everywhere was the broad question of how to distribute the world's riches and to whom. The specifics (with different emphases by different countries) included aid and investment transfers by rich countries (old and new) to poorer ones, trade policy, and the monetary machinery required to facilitate all this, including buying and selling oil at the new price levels.

The advanced countries entered into this dialogue to head off further increases in the oil price and to prevent formation of OPEC-like cartels by other producers of essential raw materials. The dialogue itself, with its implied promise of important changes in the international economic system to the advantage of the less developed countries, was a concession by the advanced to the power and alleged will of the oil producers to obtain a better economic deal both for themselves and for poorer LDCs who lacked their own leverage on the rich.

To date these efforts have produced results that are surprisingly meager considering the threatening atmosphere in which the dialogue began in 1974. The recession in the West, which reduced demand for oil, and the recycling efforts have reduced the pressure on the advanced countries to make large concessions. No new cartels have been formed. The ideological unity of the LDCs in demanding a new order has not been effectively translated into common policies for the obvious reason that the interests of rich and poor are increasingly divergent.

The divisions among the advanced countries which many foresaw in 1974 have not amounted to very much. The French have tried to cut an independent figure, and there has been competition among the advanced countries for OPEC markets and money. But the wealth of the oil-rich countries has been distributed with fair equity by the recycling machinery which has grown up. The advanced countries have not presented a common front in the North-South dialogue, but, looking over the record of the last several years, the tugging and hauling of their own internal dialogue have not significantly impaired their overall unity.

It is too soon to know what the international economic order will look like once the consequences of both the oil price rise and the inflation and recession with which it has been intertwined become more clear. But so far these extremely difficult and unprecedented developments, for all their serious effects, have neither broken the Western economies nor disrupted Western unity with respect to the most fundamental economic issues. To some extent these pressures have consolidated that unity.

The same judgment can be made—up to the present—with respect to the way the advanced countries have handled the third of the great challenges to their coherence, the double problems of *inflation and recession* in the last several years. There is no need here to examine the much debated question of why and how inflation soared in the advanced countries from 1972 on. For the OECD as a whole, prices, which had risen at the annual average rate of 3.7 percent between 1961 and 1971, rose 7.7 percent in 1973, 13.2 percent in 1974, and 9.3 percent in 1975 (in that year the United Kingdom was the worst hit, at 24.9 percent, the Federal Republic the least, at 5.4 percent). The increase in the price of oil contributed largely to speeding up an inflation already underway.

There had, of course, been bouts of serious inflation in the Western economies before. Most countries therefore applied the conventional deflationary measures to slow down price rises, and the effects of these were reinforced now by the shrinking demand for higher priced oil products. The result was a plunge into recession in 1974 which hit bottom in the first half of 1975, when GNP fell by 5.8 percent in the OECD countries and unemployment reached 15 million. What was unique about this situation was the stubborn resistance of inflation to the classic counterattack. For prices to rise by over 9 percent in a year in which GNP and employment fell off sharply was something the Western economic system had not had to face before.

Policymakers were in a quandary. Further deflationary measures threatened to produce intolerable unemployment, but any stimulus to employment threatened to heat up an already brightly burning flame of inflation. This dilemma has persisted, in various forms in various countries, to the present. The general trend since 1975 has been a slowing of inflation, though by no means to acceptable levels in many countries; a resumption of growth; and a continuous level of unemployment at rates that in previous years would have been thought unacceptable, at least in Europe. One other important outcome of these years should be noted: a widening gap between the relatively good economic health of the United States, the Federal Republic of Germany, and Japan and the malaise of most of the European OECD members. The revival of the United States and the diminution of the strength previously, perhaps prematurely, imputed to the European countries represent a striking reversal of what was thought to be the state of affairs in the early 1970s.

With a system of floating exchange rates, the diverse monetary ups and downs of the main actors have not required as much high-level policy attention as a fixed rate system would have. Much attention has been devoted to providing credits to those countries with most serious balance of payments problems. In this process the IMF, the main official channel for such operations, has strengthened its authority to impose deflationary policies on the recipients of its aid. It is striking that the most important institution of the postwar economic system, the IMF, has never been as active and important as since the breakdown of the Bretton Woods arrangements of which it was at first a part. The system, typified by the IMF, has proved stronger and more durable than the particular monetary arrangements which had been thought to embody it.

The main Western countries have also tried to deal with their common economic problems by means of a new consultative mechanism, the Western economic summit. Four such meetings have been held (at Rambouillet in November 1975; Puerto Rico in July 1976; London in May 1977; Bonn in July 1978). In a sense they were continuations at a higher level of the meetings of five or six finance ministers which had managed the many monetary crises of the late 1960s and early 1970s behind the formal mechanisms. That is, they included all those states, and only those, whose actions had a major impact on the economic system (leaving aside OPEC holders of vast monetary resources). The United States, Great Britain, France, the Federal Republic, Italy, and Japan were represented at all four meetings; Canada at all but the first. The presence of the president of the European Community's commission at the third and fourth summits was perhaps more a sop to the smaller members of the community, whom he represented symbolically, than a tribute to its own role as an economic actor.

In light of the state of the world economy since the first summit we can
wonder what they really achieved. If nothing more, however, the cooperation among the advanced countries that was symbolized—if not really
organized—by the summits *has* succeeded once again in warding off
policies that they might have been tempted to use in the circumstances
and that would have had a negative impact on all of them. The worst
recession since World War II, and one that coincided with the trauma of
the OPEC price rise, has not led to anything remotely resembling the
great depression. The habit of and belief in the importance of international cooperation, together with more sophisticated (if still insufficient)
understanding everywhere of how to manage the national economy,
goes far to account for the difference. If the major advanced countries
have all been baffled about how to restrain prices while reducing unemployment to politically and socially acceptable levels, they have at any
rate been baffled together and have acted on the whole as if they
understood that no one of them could solve its problems by itself. The
lessons of the 1930s, embodied in the postwar economic system, have not
been forgotten in the 1970s.

Looking back over all the economic challenges which the states of the
Euratlantic subsystem have faced over the last quarter-century, we find
on the one hand unprecedented growth and prosperity, on the other a
set of difficult structural problems that so far have rather been managed
than resolved. It is easy to focus our attention on the divisions among the
advanced countries at every point; the painfully worked out compromises; the spread of preferential arrangements; the backsliding into
protectionism in such forms as coerced "voluntary" limitation of exports;
and, of course, the two huge problems which remain open and
threatening: relations between the advanced and the less developed
countries, and the question marks that hang over prospects for growth
and near-full employment in their own economies, with all the possible
social and political implications. Western cooperation seems to have a
mixed record.

Yet, even leaving aside the fact that their policies have somehow given
most of the citizens of these countries higher standards of living than
they or almost anyone have ever known, it is worth considering again
some of the things that might well have happened in this sphere but did
not. If there have been numerous crises but no depression comparable
to that of the 1930s, it is impossible to believe that this could have been
achieved without conscious management of a considerable degree of
cooperation among the governments which made economic decisions
for the system. It is true, of course, that this cooperation did not follow
the Bretton Woods rulebook. It was often improvised and rarely tidy.

But the notion that economic divisions among the Western countries were overcome only because of the security ties among them, or because the United States exercised hegemonic authority based on those ties, is clearly not valid. On the contrary, there has been harder and more nearly equal bargaining among them on economic issues than on security or political ones. Weighing what the economic strand of the Euratlantic subsystem achieved and what it helped avoid, it appears up to now to have made a positive contribution on its own level to the overall cohesion of the subsystem.

Hanging Together and Hanging Separately

The degree of economic policy cooperation which the Western countries achieved has tended to be overlooked not only because of the real disagreements among them but also because of the institutional untidiness with which they conducted their economic relations. Far from working through a single institution, they made use of the IMF, OECD, GATT, and the United Nations, among others. The so-called Group of Ten emerged in the 1960s as the central focus of economic policymaking but it was supplemented by a smaller nameless group which managed the monetary crises of the period and eventually developed into an important but still not exclusive new institution, the summit of advanced countries.

It was not by chance that the Group of Ten included eight members of the Atlantic alliance, and that six of the seven participants of the most recent summits were alliance members. The fact that Western economic policy was made by practically the same countries as determined Western security policy helps account for the fact that the policies of these countries on the economic plane on the whole reinforced and were reinforced by their association in other ways. Yet there is a seeming paradox to be explained in the fact that none of the main instruments of economic cooperation was connected with the Atlantic alliance.

NATO communiques, almost from the start, called for closer economic cooperation among the members. This reflected the view that the members ought to coordinate their economic strategies as well as their other policies with respect to the Communist bloc and the third world. Later, the divergent trade and monetary policies which I have discussed gave added support to the feeling that states whose cooperation was essential in the security and political areas should also work to prevent disagreements from arising in other spheres that might weaken their collaboration.

From arguing that cooperation beyond the subject matter and the area of the treaty was useful and desirable, some took the next step to maintain that it was *essential* if the alliance was to fulfill its core functions, or even to survive at all. The premise was that if the allies could not work together with respect to economic problems and the world beyond Europe then they could not work together even in Europe itself. The conclusion was that *all* the major policy business of the members should be carried on under the alliance's aegis, that in effect they should face the world as one. In its most extreme form, it was argued, using Spenglerian metaphors, that the NATO plant must grow or wither, put out ever more roots and branches or die. In more measured language, the alliance was thought to face a challenge of institutional adequacy and adaptation.

The alliance, as we know, has conspicuously failed to meet this challenge and yet has survived. It is worth considering why it did not take on the functions and achieve the global policy unity called for and whether its primal tasks have been discharged the worse for that.

With respect to economic problems, the prophets of a greater alliance have been at least half right. The allies, for all their disagreements, did develop intimate economic collaboration, no doubt to the benefit of their relationship as a whole. What needs to be explained here is why this took place outside the alliance and whether that fact made any significant difference to the alliance's well-being.

One obvious reason is that Japan and a few other advanced countries were *not* members of the alliance. Their essential collaboration might have been coordinated with the alliance but it would have been awkward, perhaps even intolerable, for them to have to deal with the fifteen allies as a bloc.

A second reason is that some of the allies probably did not want to make even more explicit the tie which they were well aware existed among security, political, and economic problems and to make even stronger the advantage this tie gave the United States, dominant in the first field and in the alliance, with respect to American dealings with them on other matters. Everyone knew the tie was there; everyone knew that in economic negotiations, for example, the U.S. bargaining position was strengthened by powerful if intangible considerations of other sorts; but not everyone welcomed making this official by putting all their policy concerns in an institutional basket which the United States clearly dominated. This consideration became the more important as European economic strength grew more rapidly vis-à-vis the United States than did European military weight. For the French, therefore, and no doubt others too, it was more prudent and comfortable to discuss monetary and trade problems in places where the American defense quarantee was not quite so clearly on the table.

A third reason for the failure of the alliance to take off as a center for economic policymaking was simply that several other useful organizations were already operating when it came along. The IMF and World Bank, GATT, and the OEEC (later OECD) could, of course, have been downgraded, or used as frameworks for dealing with outside countries while the NATO members concerted their own economic policies within new alliance-related structures. But why should the allies have bothered to do this? The economic organizations did their work as well as the policies of the members permitted (it is doubtful that the problems of trade and money discussed earlier would have been more readily solved within NATO than elsewhere). GATT, the IMF, and the rest provided forums in which non-Atlantic countries could take part on a nondiscriminatory basis (useful with respect to Japan and a few other countries in the first instance and eventually to the less developed also). In short, the initial question can be turned around and the burden of proof shifted: why should new economic machinery have been developed in NATO when that which existed elsewhere was as effective as the participants' policies permitted it to be?

The only possible answer would be that economic issues may not have required such new machinery but NATO did. The notion has been widespread that the alliance had to take on new functions and new missions if it was not to lose public confidence in its ability to handle the old, particularly in periods of relative détente with the East, when it was feared that support for the Alliance would wither, or when the allies had been openly quarreling and, it was thought, needed to find new things to do together to remember the ties that bound them. Thus, every major crisis in the alliance has been followed by yet another study of or pronouncement about its role and functions and sometimes by the creation of machinery for dealing with issues quite outside its traditional domain.[4]

The fact is, however, that neither experience nor logic indicate that NATO can or must compensate for its defects in the security-military field by devising new institutions or taking on economic or other functions. Most of the Atlantic governments, whether they realize it or not,

---

4. Perhaps the most striking illustration of this was the creation in 1969 of the Committee for the Challenges of Modern Society (CCMS). This was to be the alliance's answer to détente and to the agitation by students and others for change in Western societies. The CCMS has no doubt done useful work in a number of fields but its contribution to the coherence of a "relevant" NATO or a stable Euratlantic subsystem, when measured against the other ties that bind, is appropriately reflected by this comment in a footnote. Even less need be said of the alliance's efforts to deal with those fashionable issues of the 1960s, the technology gap and the brain drain.

have been sensible enough to use Occam's razor with respect to institution-building—avoiding the multiplication of unnecessary entities and the assignment to existing entities of unnecessary functions. The alliance has always been judged by the member governments and their peoples in terms of their need for its essential functions and its ability to fulfill them. Most of them have never found it basically wanting in these respects. Less has been more, or at least enough, and the subsystem has not been the worse for that.

If the Atlantic countries did not manage their economic relationships within the alliance because there was no need for them to do so, they have not managed their relations there with respect to areas outside the treaty area because they have been too divided on the substance of policy to risk weighting down NATO with their divisions. More than one has tried over the years to interest the alliance as a whole in their own problems overseas: the French in Indochina and Algeria, the Portuguese in Africa, the United States in the Formosa Strait, Indochina, the Middle East, Africa. Time and again the NATO ministers have called for closer political consultation on the problems of relations with the third world, in language like the following:

> Our alliance cannot therefore be concerned only with the North Atlantic area or only with military defence. It must also organize its political and economic strength on the principle of interpendence, and must take account of developments outside its own area.[5]

The fact that these words might have come from the alliance's Ottawa Declaration of June 1974 but really come from the communique of December 1957 sadly reminds us that all efforts to widen the alliance's scope once and for all have largely failed. We can doubt that this situation has been fundamentally changed even by the most recent and perhaps most strenuous effort of the sort: the attempt by the United States in the ironically labeled "Year of Europe" (1973–74) to leave off policing the world and try, as it were, to police its allies. What the United States attempted was to bring the weight of its security and political preponderance to bear in order to bind the allies to accept, then and for the future, American economic desiderata and the American judgment of what constituted alliance interests in the Middle East and elsewhere beyond the treaty area. What the allies finally signed at Ottawa—after the sharp divisions among them created by the October 1973 Middle East war—was much the same as they had subscribed to in 1957, and before and since. Perhaps the Year of Europe helped educate them,

5. *The Department of State Bulletin* 38 (January 6, 1958), 12.

once again, on the facts of life in an interdependent world. In this case, however, as in so many others, the alliance was not seriously harmed even by overambitious and unnecessary efforts to improve it—another sign of its basic good health.

There should be no mystery about the difficulty of uniting the alliance to deal with problems outside the security-political sphere and the treaty area. All the allies have recognized that they faced a new dimension of Soviet power in the third world once Stalin's heirs rejected the idea that the newly emancipated ex-colonial states were puppets of the West and began to court their "bourgeois nationalist" rulers as potential solvents of Western power. But their response to this problem, and to the broader question of how to deal with the third world, has been marked by discord ever since the Soviet Union jumped the feeble barriers raised to it by the Baghdad Pact and provided arms to Egypt in 1955. This early case of allied disagreement was the model of others (usually less flagrant) to come. None of the allies liked Nasser's acceptance of Soviet arms, nor his nationalization of the Suez canal. But when the British and French attacked Egypt in 1956 to reverse the nationalization, the United States gave a very different response by taking the side of Egypt and, in a most embarrassing de facto entente with the USSR, forcing the halt of the Anglo-French attack. Eisenhower and Dulles thus showed that they would not repeat the mistake which Stalin's heirs had repudiated. For all their on-again–off-again approach to the third world and its neutralism, and at the cost of the most serious rupture the system has experienced among the main allies, they decided to compete with the Russians for the favors of countries whose policies, in another mood, they denounced as immoral.

But alignments on this new issue were not always the same as they were in 1956. Every ally has recognized the fact of interdependence— among the member states, between them and the rest of the world, among the security, political, and economic problems that are the objects of their policies. But there was no agreement as to whether or how they could deal coherently with problems outside the treaty area that one or another member found to be of compelling national and allegedly alliance-wide importance. They did not all agree with the Portuguese that the struggle against communism was to be carried on in Angola; or with the French (for a time) that it was in Algeria; or with the United States that resistance to Soviet expansionism in Europe required resistance to North Vietnamese expansionism in Indochina, or defense of Taiwan, or nonrecognition of Communist China, or support for Egypt in 1956, for Israel in 1967 and 1973. This was because the interests of the members, and their means of action, have been very diverse. Above all, the fact that the United States is a global power, engaged with the Soviet Union worldwide, while even the major European states are not has created a problem for the alliance which nothing could entirely obviate.

The difficulty which the alliance has experienced in trying to expand its scope into economic and extra-European matters is nicely counter-pointed by the relative ease with which it *has* developed a most important "second leg," the coordination of members' policies with respect to détente. When the pace of negotiations between the Soviet Union and its allies on the one hand and several Western countries on the other picked up in the mid-1960s, there was widespread concern not only that "dé-tente fever" would corrode NATO's defense base but that there would be a competitive "rush to Moscow" by the allies that would be det-rimental to the security of all of them. Yet that did not happen. At first defensively, so as not to seem to be lagging on détente, then more and more constructively, the allies individually and the alliance as a group learned to manage a complex set of negotiations with the Eastern countries.

France's withdrawal from military integration in 1966 provided the occasion—of course—for a review of the alliance's functioning. This, called after Belgian Foreign Minister Harmel, its principal author, not only reaffirmed the continued relevance of the alliance's security func-tions but gave much attention to the quest for a "just and stable order" in Europe. This was more than rhetoric. In light of de Gaulle's opening to the East (discussed in the last section of this chapter), the new Eastern policy of the German coalition government, and the U.S.–Soviet negoti-ations on a nonproliferation treaty, the alliance could not but develop some role in the diplomatic process underway. This was in the interest of the larger members, who needed to keep in step with each other, and also of the smaller, whose dealings with the East were minimal and who wanted to know what the others were doing and to be reassured that their interests would be protected. NATO thus acquired a new dimen-sion of real importance, particularly for the lesser members. They might complain that they were not taken sufficiently into the confidence of the others, but had there been no alliance consultations their input to U.S.–Soviet strategic arms limitation talks (SALT) or *Ostpolitik*, for example, would have been even less than it was. In this case, as in others, consulta-tion usefully mitigated the obvious asymmetry of the alliance.

NATO therefore increased its consultation with respect to the mem-bers' bilateral dealings with the East and gradually defined common if not identical positions on the major multilateral issues—the Conference on Security and Cooperation in Europe (CSCE), initiated by the Soviet

Union, and the negotiations on Mutual and Balanced Force Reductions (MBFR), the Western response. Without reviewing the tortuous history of these negotiations, the main point that needs to be made about them here is that the allies, working through the alliance itself as well as in other ways, managed to coordinate their policies reasonably well with respect to the major East-West issues: *Ostpolitik*, SALT, CSCE, and (with the exception of France) MBFR.

It is not surprising that the allies coordinated their policies in Europe with much more success than they did outside it. For one thing, the *Ostpolitik* negotiations, keystone of the détente arch, were necessarily multilateral, for they were linked early to negotiations for an improvement in the status of Berlin which had to be conducted by the United States, the United Kingdom, France, and the Soviet Union, and unofficially the Federal Republic as well. Second, those countries which were pursuing bilateral dealings with the East (particularly the United States and the Federal Republic) had important reasons to reassure the others that their policies would not jeopardize the security arrangements which underpinned their own negotiations. Third, Soviet insistence on a stage of multilateral diplomacy—the CSCE—as a linked part of the détente picture required the allies to develop their own formal and substantive role in such diplomacy. Since one part of their response was to insist on negotiations for force reductions in Europe, they then also had to define their thinking about how and what to negotiate with the Warsaw Pact in this respect. In this way defense planning for the future had to be placed in a political context other than, as hitherto, simple confrontation.

The record of the last ten years is not without suspicions and divisions among the allies but on the whole it shows that the alliance adapted itself very effectively to the technical needs of multilateral diplomacy and to the political needs of pursuing détente in a way that was consistent with continued defense requirements (no détente fever) and with alliance cohesion (no competitive rush to Moscow). The allies had little choice but to succeed. Not to do so *in this case* would have left the alliance in such serious political disarray as to raise fundamental questions about its ability to discharge its security functions. Since that was not in the interest of anyone, even France, the right conclusions were drawn and the right policies on the whole followed.

This record illustrates not only the ability of the allies and alliance to adapt creatively to changing circumstances but the fundamental convergence of interests in Europe which they have had even in such circumstances. All had an interest in reducing tension with the East, but also in negotiating the specifics of such reduction while maintaining the security and position of strength which the alliance provided. Neither the United States nor the Federal Republic nor any of the others except France had an interest in weakening the alliance in the process. French policy, as will be discussed later, *did* have such an interest but was in no position to turn developments in the direction it might have preferred.

This discussion suggests that the much-debated question of how to make the Atlantic alliance into a community has been sterile. We have been speaking prose and did not know it. By any meaningful definition the Euratlantic countries already constitute a community. It has not had to develop into anything beyond itself to survive and, by any realistic measure, to prosper. The multiple ties among these countries—historic, security, political, economic, cultural, familial, sentimental—have been, with only a few exceptions, far more intimate and important to them than those they have with any other countries. Both the United States and its European allies have felt that their ultimate security and well-being were more bound up with each other than with any others—a fact that has sometimes been lost from sight because it is so true that it is taken for granted. The absence of a single Atlantic institutional structure within which the member countries would carry on all or most of their business with each other has been quite irrelevant. The multiple Atlantic institutions have served their multiple purposes reasonably well. Unless the word community is code for federal state (in which case the goal is nonsense) or unless structural tidiness is a required element in a community, it is entirely proper to say that an Atlantic community is already in existence and has long been. It is, in fact, the Euratlantic subsystem which has been under discussion throughout this book.

The Uniting of Europe

The United States government has supported the movement for European unity throughout the postwar period. Much American academic analysis of the subject has been favorable to a united Europe and optimistic about its prospects. It may seem surprising, therefore, for this movement to be described as a challenge to the postwar European system. Yet it is not so surprising after all if we remember that the word challenge is used in this book to describe any development, whether for better or worse according to our ideas, with the potential to make a major structural change in the system as it has been described—that is, an essentially bipolar system dominated by two superpowers. From this point of view, it is obvious that a united Western Europe, should it come into existence, would have a profound, perhaps a fundamental impact on that system. Whether such a Europe became a more or less equal ally of the United States, as was the hope of many, or something closer to a third force between the superpowers, as was the dream of others, the resulting state system would have been very different from that with which we are familiar.

In fact, no such united Western Europe has emerged and the European state system has not been transformed in that way. If we were concerned only with structural outcomes, the topic would be adequately covered in a page. But we are also concerned with might-have-beens for the light they can shed on the things that *have* been, and sometimes on the future too. Further, the effort to create a united Europe occupied much of the policy attention of the principal Euratlantic states for many years and colored, even if it failed to transform, their relationships. The story therefore deserves more attention than its consequences for the system merit by themselves.

There had been a pan-Europe movement even before the war, as well as the vague proposals of Aristide Briand for allegedly uniting Europe. It was natural after 1945 that these general ideas would recur to Europeans of all countries and political views who turned their attention to the problem of doing away with the nationalisms that had led to such a catastrophe for all of them. Before it became clear that Western Europe would be caught up in a half-continental system led by the United States and that, in any case, there was no possibility in the cold war for a revival of intra-European conflict, the idea of a united Europe presented itself as the logical way to avoid repeating the bloody divisions of the past, as well as to enhance Europe's sadly diminished status. Churchill and de Gaulle, among others, called for something of the sort during and after the war. The ground was fertile for new initiatives as public opinion everywhere turned away from the old quarrels among nations. The idea of uniting Western Europe was therefore very much in the air in the late 1940s.

It might have remained there, notwithstanding all the support the United States gave it, but for a remarkable initiative of French policy— probably the most original and creative step taken by any European government since the war. It was clear by 1950 that a grouping as large and loose as the Council of Europe (the first fruit of the European movement) could not do much even to harmonize the policies of the members. The Organization of European Economic Cooperation (OEEC), which grouped the European Marshall aid recipients, and the European Payments Union (EPU) both failed to lead even to first steps toward economic unity, and certainly not to political. The deadlock of the attempt to move toward greater European unity along these lines was broken only—but definitively—by the bold and imaginative proposal made by French Foreign Minister Robert Schuman on May 9, 1950, to place the French and West German coal and steel industries under a joint authority with supranational powers, that is, powers in this defined field superseding those of the member governments.

This initiative met several immediate problems of French policy, and some farther removed. By that date it was clear that there would be a strong German state and that postwar limitations on its economic power could not be maintained for long in light of the need to increase European production. Having tried to block the creation of a German state, the French now had to live with it. In these circumstances, defined cooperation seemed more promising than hopeless resistance to the inevitable. The boldness of the Schuman plan as a solution to the most deep-seated problem of French foreign policy consisted in this: if the German economy could not be contained on a discriminatory basis, then France would propose to place what were thought to be its core elements, and those of *its own economy too*, under a system of control external to both.

The imaginativeness of what was in the first instance a defensive policy lay in the fact that it could be presented as something far more constructive and, in fact, *was* so. The constructive elements included the concept of delegating specific functional powers in an important but defined field to an authority above both states; the vision of Franco-German reconciliation as providing the political basis for the eventual unification of Western Europe; and the insight that giving the West Germans an honored (if not quite equal) founder's role in the great enterprise of uniting Europe would provide them with something to which they could commit their energies other then security, unification, or *revanche*.

The Schuman proposal had several other virtues in the eyes of its drafters. On the economic side, they hoped that opening up the protected French economy to German competition would force French industry to modernize. It was not by chance that the father of postwar French economic planning, Jean Monnet, was also the father of the Schuman proposal. On the side of domestic politics, a concrete plan for promoting European unity offered a common policy or ideological platform to the "third force" parties—from socialists to conservatives—which were then governing France with little in common but an attachment to parliamentary democracy and hostility to both communism and Gaullism.

Finally, on the international plane, the Schuman proposal promised not only to strengthen Western Europe in face of the Russian threat but also—though this was less talked about—to strengthen it vis-à-vis its indispensable but overpowering American ally. These Frenchmen, like many West Europeans, did not doubt that they had to rely on American strength for their security. But they did not want to rely entirely on the Americans to manage relations with the East which involved no less than war and peace, that is, the lives of the European nations. At the least a more united Europe could better influence American decisions affecting its vital interests; at the best it could break through the rigidity and risks of bipolar Europe by becoming strong enough to cease to be a stake of the superpowers in cold or hot war.

The Germans, for their part, readily accepted the French proposal. They knew by 1950 that they would eventually recover full control over their own economy, and sovereignty as well, because the logic of the cold war and of American policy so required. But the Adenauer government was wise enough to realize that it would do better to achieve these things with the agreement of its neighbors, and especially of France, rather than against them. Besides, the German chancellor may have shared some of the French ambivalences about the American alliance and some of their dreams about the role a more united Europe should and could play in the world. Joining the coal-steel community allowed the Federal Republic at the least to end the postwar economic restraints placed on it sooner than otherwise. If, beyond that, it offered the Germans, as noted, a respectable place in a reconciled Western Europe and something to think about besides security and reunification, all the better.

Italy was glad to join the community as a sign of its reemergence to respectability. The Benelux countries did not want to be left out of a union including their two most important neighbors. The British, still considered by themselves and others as a global power, were not a likely candidate for united Europe until those illusions had been dissipated—a development that was to take another two decades. Neither the Labour nor Conservative party was ready to place British industry under supranational control or diminish Britain's status by doing so. The United States did not particularly urge the British to join. So they stayed out and the Europe of Six was born. If France was at first clearly the most important of the members, there were important present benefits to the others, and beyond those there was the common bond of a dream—however diversely interpreted—of what Western Europe might yet become.

This combination of practical realities and less tangible hopes has characterized the European movement from that day to this. The policy of moving progressively toward greater Western European unity by means of delegating specific functional powers to a supranational authority—a precise process to which (and only to which) the name integration should be applied—rapidly became an ideology, a cause, in a way which the Atlantic arrangements, for all their great importance, have never become. To be for or against united Europe (so defined as to both ends and means) became an emotionally charged political dividing line in most countries. The strength of united Europe as a cause was amply proved by the way in which it rebounded from the shattering setback of the European Defense Community. The EDC, as discussed in chapter 8, was a premature attempt to make the popular cause of uniting Europe bear the weight of German rearmament. The French, repelled by the latter but unable to block it, turned against the former. Yet no sooner was the European army dead, and the Federal Republic on the way to being armed in NATO, than the Action Committee for the United States of Europe and the six governments (including the French) proposed two new communities: a common market and an atomic energy pool. It was as if the very strengthening of the FRG lent urgency to a new attempt to channel and circumscribe its freedom of action by erecting new European structures.

The Suez debacle provided another spur toward this relaunching. The British, sadly diminished in their power pretensions, nevertheless decided to hold back from Europe even then and put their cards on a renewal of their special relationship with the United States. The French, however, and the other five drew the conclusion from the Middle East crisis that greater unity might help them avoid another such catastrophe. In particular, they believed that a European effort to develop nuclear energy for power would help reduce their painful dependence on Middle East petroleum and the strategic and political vulnerability to both the Soviet Union and the United States which that, among other things, entailed for them.

By two treaties signed at Rome in March 1957, the six established the European Economic Community (EEC) or common market and the European Atomic Energy Community (Euratom). For a variety of reasons, including French national nuclear policy as it developed under de Gaulle, Euratom, which seemed to have a strong impetus in 1957, never achieved its potential or real importance. European energy vulnerability was as great in 1973 as it had been in 1956, and with the same consequences or worse. But the EEC established itself beyond what many in 1957 would have thought possible. If it has failed to achieve the long-term goals of its founders and if no politically united Europe has emerged, the EEC nevertheless has added an important new dimension to intra-European and intra-Western relations. Measured realistically against the European past rather than against dreams of the future, its accomplishments have been the more striking. The European glass may be half empty, but it is also half full—no small achievement.

General de Gaulle had opposed the treaties of Rome, but when he returned to power in 1958, before they had begun to be implemented, he decided to accept them as the framework for his own policy of creating a French-led bloc in Western Europe (see the last section of this chapter). It may be that the EEC could not have managed even to come to life if de Gaulle had not devalued the franc at the end of 1958 and taken measures that enabled France to begin dismantling its high tariff barriers. In any case, France's industry prospered rather than succumbed as tariffs fell; its exports as well as imports increased; it became an attractive recipient of foreign investment; and it successfully carried through the creation of the common agricultural policy which was called for but not spelled out by the treaty—the essential counterpart, in the "grand bargain" that underlay the treaty, to opening its frontiers to more competitive German industry. The customs union was actually implemented ahead of schedule, and France had little need to invoke the various escape hatches that it had built into the treaty to protect its anticipated economic weaknesses.

The negative side of this coin was that de Gaulle's attempt to lead the European bloc was less subtle, and less effective, than that of his integrationist predecessors. The other members would not accept the *overt* leadership of France, notwithstanding its nuclear bombs, and even less would they accept his effort to estrange them from the United States. He, for his part, openly scorned the integrationist ideology which had hitherto been the sacred underpinning of the movement, however realistic the actual parceling out of benefits and costs among the members. Worse, in 1965 he blocked the evolution of the community to the phase prescribed by the treaty when certain decisions might be taken by less than unanimous vote of the six members. At the same time he undermined the hope that the executive commission might be able to strengthen its independent authority vis-à-vis the six governments.

The community survived de Gaulle but it has never returned to the path from which he diverted it. For all we know for certain, less than unanimous decision-making might have grown slowly into a federal-like system. The commission, if led for long periods by strong leaders like Walter Hallstein, might have become a quasi-independent executive. Direct election of the European parliament, scorned by de Gaulle as a downgrading of the national state, might have provided a democratic base for the otherwise detached and bureaucratic machinery created in Brussels.

All of this might have happened without de Gaulle. None of it, however, has so far happened since he gave up power in 1969. One reason for that, of course, is that his political heirs have continued to prevent the French government from altering its basic course (except with respect to the election of the parliament). Another reason, most ironically, is that the British, whom he kept out, have proved to be his heirs in their opposition to integration, a sad and surprising development for those Americans who in the early 1960s mistakenly fancied that U.K. admission was bound to advance their dream of European federalism and a "two-pillar" alliance because de Gaulle opposed both. That both France and Britain have continued to oppose Monnet-style integration is a wry tribute to their confidence that there is no need to strengthen the community to contain the growing power of the Federal Republic because the Atlantic arrangement does the job so effectively, in economic as in security matters. But of course the limitations on the community in this respect further strengthened the importance of the Atlantic arrangements which contain the Federal Republic—not what de Gaulle wanted. American policymakers were slow to grasp that the real alternative to the integrated Europe of their dreams, which de Gaulle blocked, was not his European Europe but the Atlantic Europe which they themselves had created.

But there are also other, more basic considerations which suggest that the community would not have marched forward inevitably to federal union even without de Gaulle. It was not so difficult to establish a customs union and a common agricultural policy because these were to the economic advantage of the six countries as a whole, if not in every point to each of them. The community also had a natural common interest, once formed, in negotiating trade policy with outside countries as a unity and establishing special links to the former colonies of the members and various states around the Mediterranean with which they had close economic and other ties. The next steps, however, would have proved much more difficult in any circumstances. The effort undertaken in the early 1970s to establish monetary union failed because the management of a nation's finances is integral to the management of its economy as a whole. The former cannot be shared unless the latter is. But common economic policy has proved impossible to achieve. The national economies were usually somewhat out of phase with each other at any given time. National attitudes toward the priorities of economic policy traditionally differed. For these and other reasons, the larger members, at least, have refused to give up national control of growth rates, price and wage levels, or employment.

The members of the community have been even less successful in developing a coordinated and autonomous foreign policy, and least successful in the realm of defense arrangements. The European allies have had their problems with NATO but never to the point that they were impelled to organize a European defense effort either to increase

their influence within the alliance or to replace it. They lacked the sense
of need and capability required to motivate them. They might conceivably have done so had there been no American security guarantee and
American-led security system (though they might equally have resigned
themselves to dependence on the Soviet Union). But this would have
presupposed a political unity which they never achieved and, besides
that, cost and effort which it is difficult to imagine their accepting. Even
then one can ask whether Western Europe, crowded, narrow and highly
vulnerable, could ever have a credible defense strategy *of its own* whatever effort of armament was made. Can such an area be a great power,
or convince others or itself that it is? The Europeans have acted as if they
thought not. There were, of course, two national nuclear forces in
Europe, but they served political interests more than military.

It is striking that foreign and particularly defense policy has been well
coordinated by the members of the community—not among themselves,
however, but between them and the United States. Economic policy, the
first business of the community, has been less thoroughly coordinated
there than foreign and defense policy, the traditional core of sovereignty, has been coordinated in the alliance. European nationalism,
weakened though it has been, has proved to be more persistent on the
European level than on the Euratlantic, perhaps because the latter
required no renunciation of the forms of sovereignty. In addition, we
come again to the political use of Occam's razor. Why should the Europeans have been expected to evolve independent security of foreign or
even economic policies as a group when, in the real world they lived in,
practically every decision would then have to be coordinated with the
United States? Why not carry out the coordination, so to speak, all at
once, in whatever forum was appropriate to the subject matter: NATO
itself for security and multilateral East-West issues, a four-power group
with respect to German affairs, the IMF and Group of Ten and Western
summit for economic affairs, and other groups and bilateral contacts
with respect to other things? If there was to be an effort to coordinate or
concert policy, the process might most practically and easily have been
carried out—and in its essentials it has been—on the Atlantic rather than
the European level (not always with success, of course).

Since the degree of integration achieved by the EEC did not automatically engender an ever greater degree—as theorists of "spillover" had
fancied—the only real alternative to the ambiguous outcome we have
seen would have been for the Europeans, in an act of conscious choice, to
have delegated substantial further powers to a central authority—that is,
to have established a federal state to conduct foreign and defense policy.
But this they have not been willing to do. Perhaps they eventually would

have but for de Gaulle. Perhaps they would have had there been no Euratlantic subsystem, *preexisting* the European effort, which was for long and is still considered essential by most of the members to their security, political, and economic well-being. If so, it may be that the attempt to unite Europe came too late, that the community remained a unit whose prescribed competences would neither spill over nor be enlarged by conscious decision because the Europeans felt no need to do so.

This waning of impetus for further progress also reflected the decline of one of the initial impulses for European unity: a sense that Europe's security as well as its internal peace and international status required movement away from the national states of the past toward a wider union among them. Many circumstances contributed to this, but here de Gaulle *may* have had an effect which he would not have liked. For, far from converting the Europeans to his belief that Europe should and could play an autonomous role vis-à-vis the United States and an independent role in the world, he alienated them from it, lowered their European consciousness, made them more aware of how important the Atlantic tie was to them. Some of the integrationists had been moved by the same dream but they did not like the way de Gaulle tried to create this option for them. By then, it seems, many did not much like the option itself.

This can be laid to their overlong dependence on the United States but also to their realistic perception of their limits in the postwar world and the benefits to themselves of the Euratlantic subsystem. After all, Franco-German conflict was no longer a possibility, and the fading threat of war, far from ending West European dependence on the United States, actually removed one motive for tempering that dependence—namely, the fear that European division and weakness made Europe a stake of conflict.

Whatever the causes for the waning of the European impulse, the fact is plain and the implications to date seem obvious. As the Germans turned aside from the dream of reunification to pursue more attainable goals, so the Europeans have seemed satisfied, in the years since de Gaulle departed, to use the community machinery for their common good but to do so, and to pursue their other interests, in the Atlantic framework.

This attitude exasperates some Europeans and disappoints some Americans. Like so much in the postwar period they find this unnatural when compared to the great days of European global hegemony and speak of Europe's abdication, as if that which has been lost was within its power to retain. But more has been lost than political greatness and global reach.

> Something was lost to Europe in the first half of this century that can never be put back again. . . .
>
> What was lost to Europe between 1900 and 1950, and above all between 1939 and 1945, was the sense of predestined leadership which had been taken for granted since the days of Plato and Virgil, Charlemagne and the builders of Chartres Cathedral.[6]

It does not seem unnatural, in light of the history of this century, that Europe should have suffered this loss, or that that should have had the political and other consequences which have followed. We may regret the fact but that provides no valid reason to overlook it. In this case reflection on European history and the actual behavior of Europeans provides the best basis for judgment. My own conclusion from that evidence is that the Europeans have adapted with much intelligence to the postwar world in which they found themselves. The conflict between adaptation to a sadly imperfect world and pursuit of possibly nobler but elusive goals has been a staple of Western literature from Antigone to Hamlet and the Misanthrope and beyond. Our hearts go out to the heroes of quest but our heads, on reflection, may sometimes give the palm to their brothers who learn how to survive.

The French Challenge

It is fitting to conclude this review of the failed challenges to the postwar European system by examining the policies of France and of Charles de Gaulle, the Western nation and leader that were least accepting of Europe's "fall," least reconciled to the new order of things, and most persistent in their efforts to bring about change. It is clear from the preceding section that a common thread running through the history of the movement for European union was the effort of French governments, of both the Fourth and Fifth Republics, to use the Europe of Six as the vehicle for asserting their own leadership in Europe and France's status in the world. This goal underlay all French foreign policy since the war.

The defeat of 1940 removed France from the ranks of the great powers—those which had to be taken into account in the making of major international decisions. But General de Gaulle, refusing to accept

6. John Russell, *A Lost Leadership* (New York: The Museum of Modern Art, 1975), p. 3 (volume 9 of a 12-volume series, *The Meanings of Modern Art*).

this disaster as anything but temporary, managed by extraordinary stubbornness and brilliant diplomacy to recover for France at least the outward trappings of great power status: a permanent seat on the United Nations Security Council and a zone of occupation in Germany. His achievement provided the starting point and model for future French policy. Its limitations provided the agenda for de Gaulle's successors.

For, notwithstanding de Gaulle's efforts, the Big Three met without France at Yalta, Potsdam, and Moscow and took major decisions affecting its interests. The United States and Great Britain carried their wartime special relationship into peacetime and continued to exclude France from it. In light of this, and of France's weakness, the leaders of the hard-pressed Fourth Republic might have given up de Gaulle's attempt to recover a rank which, in the new age of the superpowers, far outran their resources. But since Great Britain, though weaker than it or anyone realized, did not think of doing so, the French set themselves the goal of recovering rank equal to its. France was, after all, the strongest power on the continent west of the Soviet Union; it still possessed a colonial empire; and, above all, it had the status and the leverage in the United Nations and in German affairs which de Gaulle had obtained. With these assets, it is unlikely that any country, and certainly not one with France's long history of intermittent disasters and recovery, would give up the attempt to protect its interests where decisions affecting them would be made—that is, in the councils of the great powers.

France had little choice after 1946 but to take its place in the economic and security system initiated step by step by the United States. It accepted Marshall aid in 1947; joined the Atlantic alliance in 1949; and agreed, with pain, to the creation and arming of the Federal Republic. But from the start France was the most reluctant member of the Euratlantic system as it stood, a country whose attempts to change the status quo of the postwar power distribution were far more insistent and persistent than those of West Germany, whose revival and revisionism it and others feared so much. On the positive side, the basic foreign policy goal of regaining rank may have contributed something to the policies which in the 1940s and early 1950s successfully laid the basis for France's remarkable economic growth and modernization. Certainly it was an important motive for the policy of European integration which, from one point of view, represented an effort by France, the one nominal great power in the integrating Europe of Six, to magnify its diminished voice in world councils by speaking for its five partners.

France was able to obtain a leading role in the Atlantic alliance, symbolized by its participation with the United States and the United

Kingdom in the military standing group, but it was conspicuously not able to establish a three-power political standing group because the Americans and British would not admit France in this or any other form to their exclusive inner group. (This French effort was an obvious harbinger of de Gaulle's similar attempt in 1958, which met a similar fate.) France's frustration in this respect from 1945 on led it to attempt to play an independent or mediating role in Europe long after the cold war division of the continent, and its own security and economic dependence on the United States, made that impossible. Thus, France defended positions in Germany from which it was driven step by step. It also tried to magnify its voice in Europe by clinging at great cost to colonial possessions which it could not hold. The climax of this rearguard action was the Suez debacle in 1956, its finale was the stubborn escalation of the effort to repress the Algerian revolution to a point which led in 1958 to the downfall of the Fourth Republic and the return of General de Gaulle to power.

The most important foreign policy initiative of the Fourth Republic, its European policy, was taken up by de Gaulle after his fashion. But this was only one facet of a policy which over eleven years used every asset of skill and national power and seized every opportunity presented by changing international circumstances to establish once and for all France's clear right to participate in the management of all world problems, and particularly of all European problems—that is, to reestablish its place as a great power which had been forfeited temporarily by the defeat of 1940. These goals were not so different from the Fourth Republic's; what was different was the boldness with which de Gaulle pursued his policies.

De Gaulle worked also, of course, to remove all serious limitations on France's freedom of action in international affairs, whether imposed by colonial encumbrances, economic weakness, or dependence on foreign states. Above all, he reversed the integration of France in Atlantic and European organizations which might deprive it of its ability to make decisions based on its own interests. He himself, it is true, did not appear to be very inhibited by the constraints which he claimed weighed on France. Presumably he feared that his successors might be less resolute in defending France's interests if he did not disencumber them in advance of dangerous ties. More important, he had in mind to convince the French people—by deeds, rhetoric, and symbolism—that despite the defeat of 1940 and the rise of the superpowers they were still the masters of their own fate.

But too much weight can be given to de Gaulle's constant talk of national independence—talk which was alarming to many outside

France because they feared it would reignite similar nationalisms elsewhere, and particularly in West Germany. De Gaulle did not seek freedom for its own sake. If he derided and resisted Atlantic and European
integration, he did so as part of his campaign to take part in Atlantic and
European organizations on his own terms. The independence he sought
was not splendid isolation but a recognized hand in the great global
game.

De Gaulle no doubt defined his permanent goals on the basis of his
understanding of history and geography. But he was a supreme oppor-
tunist in his pursuit of them, following through on policies which gave
promise of success, muting or dropping those which failed, devising new
ones as world circumstances and the exigencies of France's own position
required. This flexibility of means was most evident and most important
in his interrelated dealings with the United States, the Federal Republic,
and the Soviet Union in two distinct phases: the first in an orthodox cold
war framework; the second, from 1964 on, in a bolder movement toward overcoming the consequences of the cold war in Europe. In both
phases he challenged the postwar European system. Had he succeeded
in his first effort the balance of power within the Euratlantic subsystem
would have been changed, to France's advantage. Had his second
effort been successful the fundamental structure of the bipolar system
would have been dismantled, or put on the road to being so.

Throughout most if not all of de Gaulle's rule France's relations with
the United States were more important to him than those with any other
country because the status recognition which he craved for France could
only be accorded by the United States as the greatest power in the
world—a fact he never doubted—and the most important participant in
the web of military, political, and economic relationships in which
France, however independent he proclaimed it to be, had no choice but
to participate. He tried at first to win recognition of France's status by
means of the 1958 proposal for a tripartite directorate to manage the
cold war globally—an arrangement, it should be noted, which would
have been not within but above the Atlantic alliance and other regional
groupings in which the three powers participated.

When the Americans refused this direct proposal, de Gaulle then set
about coercing them into accepting his demand, by progressively di-
minishing France's cooperation in and outside the alliance and by trying
to organize a French-led West European bloc which would magnify its
voice in alliance councils. If the United States would not deal with France
willingly on the basis de Gaulle desired, he would so arrange things as to
force it to do so if it wished to implement its own highest priority
European policies.

De Gaulle no doubt really feared the encroachment of American control on French independence through the alliance, and in other ways too. He was not the only Frenchman to do so. But he believed also that NATO, as the main instrument of U.S. hegemony in Western Europe, was a hostage which he could threaten to bring the Americans to grant to France what they had denied. The substance of integration no doubt irked him, yet he chose to take eight years, including four after the end of the Algerian war, to get to the point of terminating it as regards France. During those years he reduced French cooperation with the alliance step by step, in a kind of Chinese water torture aimed to induce the United States to renegotiate France's place in the structure.

We cannot be quite certain whether or not France might have been kept in the NATO military structure on terms compatible with its effectiveness because the American government would not negotiate with de Gaulle. It seemed to assume that his initial demands were also his last word—not necessarily the case with him or with any party to a negotiation—and that his talk of independence was to be taken literally. Indeed, it seemed to want this to be the case to avoid even the thought of negotiating with this challenger of its leadership and wrecker of its plans (in Indochina as well as in Europe!). It was easier to believe that de Gaulle really had the means as well as the ambitions of a Napoleon (just as some could take Brandt for Bismarck or Ho for Hitler) and had to be resisted accordingly than to examine the specific relation of forces, which he understood quite well. As so often, analogy paralyzed analysis.

Those allies dealing with de Gaulle's France had better reason to weigh its means of action—or lack of them—than to become obsessed with its intentions. They might have been able to risk negotiations with him if they had appraised him realistically as the leader of an important ally which, however, lacked the means to blow down the firm and imposing Euratlantic edifice. Since they would not negotiate, de Gaulle predictably disintegrated France from NATO's military system, but only when it became clear that neither persuasion nor coercion would lead the United States to give France the status he wanted. At the same moment, however, international circumstances seemed to open up an even more dazzling prospect for French policy to dangle before the Germans and others: reunification of Europe from the Atlantic to the Urals by means of the dismantling of the two-bloc system and the ending of superpower hegemony. If France could not obtain a satisfactory role within the system, it might hope to achieve an even greater one by disrupting it.

After the Cuban missile crisis de Gaulle was convinced that the changes of a Soviet attack on Western Europe were next to negligible, because of changes in the Soviet system, Soviet preoccupation with the Chinese problem (which he recognized early), and Soviet respect for American power. He knew that whatever he did the United States could not withdraw its protection from France while continuing to give it to Germany and other neighboring states, for France had no frontier with the Soviet bloc and no cause for bilateral conflict with the East. If he withdrew France from NATO integration in 1966 but emphasized continued loyalty to the Atlantic Treaty and to the alliance, it was because he wanted leverage, not isolation. France therefore continued to participate in the North Atlantic Council and in certain other alliance activities and programs and to maintain its forces in Germany. His purpose was to lead the other allies, not cut France off from them; to reduce American power but not eliminate its still essential presence in the European balance of power; to induce the Soviet Union to negotiation by opening the prospect of reducing U.S. power in Europe, but not dismantling the Euratlantic system without getting the Russians to make reciprocal moves in the East.

Thus adequately covered against a negligible danger, de Gaulle began to argue that all the West Europeans, not only France, no longer had to pay the price of political and economic dependence on the United States to maintain a kind of protection which the Americans, in their own interest, could not withdraw, and which, in any case, was both less needed and less dependable than before. Insofar as there was a residual danger of Soviet attack and a legitimate doubt about the efficacy of the American guarantee, the French *force de dissuasion* would be there, in European hands, allegedly able to trigger nuclear war and by this potential to deter the USSR from taking the chance.

The core element of this new French policy, as of de Gaulle's policy at all times, was the Federal Republic. If France could speak for the FRG (and the other four) as well as for itself, its voice would have to be listened to. De Gaulle therefore tried at all times and by all means to win West Germany as France's main partner in a Western European bloc which should eventually be able to deal as an equal with the United States and the Soviet Union. During the tense period of the Berlin crises (1958–60 and 1961–62) and up to the end of the Adenauer era, de Gaulle played on German fears that the United States might sell out their interests in a "new Yalta" whereby Europe and Germany would remain permanently divided and under the control of the two super-powers. These arguments had some appeal to Adenauer, and in the dawn of détente following the Cuban crisis he and de Gaulle were the last of the cold warriors. Yet de Gaulle failed to establish a Franco-German nucleus to counter U.S. policy. The Franco-German treaty of

January 1963 seemed for a moment to represent the consummation of his hopes. But Adenauer could not line up his country in what seemed in the circumstances (after de Gaulle's veto of British entry into the EEC), a challenge to the American-led system. With an American blessing, the German parliament sterilized the treaty by adding to it a preamble reaffirming Atlantic orthodoxy. A few months later Adenauer left office.

De Gaulle reversed his line almost at once and began to suggest that Germany's hope for reunification lay in détente between the two halves of Europe, a détente to which Bonn could contribute by loosening its ties with Washington. Taking France out of NATO integration as his contribution to this process, he held out reunification as bait to the Germans and as an alternative to their intimate ties to Washington. He believed the tide of German politics was beginning to flow in this new direction and that Franco-German relations could flow with it.

It should be clear from this discussion that de Gaulle's policies toward the Soviet Union were to a considerable extent arrived at, whether wishfully or cynically, as a by-product of other calculations. His initial cold war orthodoxy served his purposes with respect to the United States and the Federal Republic. So did his shift after 1963 from a rigid to a more open approach towards the Soviet Union, obviously with the hope of using the Soviet Union as a lever to help him develop the French-led European bloc which he had not been able to establish. In this phase he argued that Soviet policy was changing and that there was a possibility of what he called détente, entente, and cooperation in Europe—provided that the European countries, and especially the Federal Republic, followed France's lead in emancipating themselves from dependence on the United States, the sine qua non of a parallel loosening of the Eastern bloc. The USSR might eventually agree to a settlement on a basis other than the status quo of a divided Europe—and divided Germany—but only if the Western European states played their own part in the process of dissolving the two blocs rather than rigidly—and hopelessly—waiting for the day when the USSR would give up its satellites to an American-dominated Western bloc or, worse, when the two superpowers would ratify their joint condominium over Europe at Europe's expense.

By visiting the Soviet Union in 1966, soon after taking France out of NATO integration, de Gaulle succeeded in scoring a considerable public relations coup. In this context his Atlantic policy did not appear as the mere tearing down of established institutions but as part of a constructive effort to bring about a settlement of frozen postwar European problems. De Gaulle's long-range vision for Europe was not made very explicit, however. It seemed to imply a withering away of both the

Eastern and Western blocs in some reciprocal way and the reunion of the continent, obviously in the loosest manner, from the Atlantic to the Urals. What de Gaulle had in mind was not a quick settlement but a long-term process which in itself would benefit France. He believed that the Soviet Union would inevitably become more preoccupied with its relations with China and, therefore, more concerned to settle trouble-some European questions in its rear. Further, the status quo, including Soviet control of Eastern Europe, was not a viable long-term system and eventually the Russians would realize this. In the meantime, he himself tried to nudge the Germans and others in Western Europe towards realizing what they too must do to promote a European settlement—namely, assert their own political identity and come out from behind the shadow of the United States.

For all his ambiguity on the subject, it does not seem that de Gaulle expected to exclude the United States from a European settlement, or that American or Russian influence would disappear from Europe after-ward. But he wanted to encourage the Europeans placed between the two colossi to take initiatives in the matter themselves, to talk to Moscow bilaterally about it, and to come to feel that as Europeans they should not and need not rely on U.S. diplomacy to take advantage of the new opportunities opening up in Europe. De Gaulle was thus involved in a long-range campaign of European consciousness-raising.

Whether France would have benefitted from a drift of events in the direction he desired is an open question. As an opponent of the Euro-pean status quo, which he liked to suggest was established at Yalta, de Gaulle could not fail to see that his own analysis and policy pointed forward to the eventual reunification of Germany as a natural event. He certainly had no reason to wish that the West Germans would miss this implication of his views. Support for reunification by means of gradual détente was obviously useful to him in his relations with the Germans, and he tried to suggest to them that their Atlantic ties stood in the way of progress toward their great national aspiration. Of course, de Gaulle also believed that the Germans would have to sacrifice more to reunification than their dependence on Washington. Among other things, they would have to accept the Oder-Neisse frontier (he had said so publicly as early as 1959) and continued non-nuclear status. Probably he thought that a united Germany would be armed, but within a carefully prescribed secu-rity framework which would make the arrangement acceptable to its neighbors, West and East.

But German-Soviet bilateral talks, which he favored, and eventual German reunification, might have been less beneficial for France's leadership than de Gaulle believed. Indeed, he may have been risking its security in pursuit of an ephemeral show of leadership by encouraging such West German hopes. No doubt he expected that a united Germany, if that ever came about, could be managed by the cooperative effort of all its neighbors, East and West, and that in this process France would have a pivotal role both as Germany's friend and ally and as its number one warder. But this was a bold policy, and the other West European governments, less ambitious than de Gaulle and therefore less willing to take risks, did not accept it. No doubt they saw his attempt to reduce American influence in Europe as likely to lead not only to a diminution of their security but to the possibility of releasing the Germans, united or not, from the constraints placed on them since the war. Of course de Gaulle might have done without the support of the smaller European countries if he could have won the West Germans and the Russians to his ideas. But he could not, and in the attempt he completed the diplomatic isolation of France in Western Europe which his NATO and European community policies had begun.

De Gaulle was right that German opinion was moving toward a more flexible approach with respect to Eastern Europe, but the shift proved not to be of much use to France nor to de Gaulle's European leadership aspirations. But to give up hope of winning over the Germans would have meant, for de Gaulle, giving up hope of organizing a Western European bloc which could deal as a diplomatic equal with the United States and the USSR. To give up *that* hope would have been equivalent to having to admit, which was the case, that France—however independent it might be—was also diplomatically isolated. He thus persevered in his effort to persuade the Russians, Poles, and others to adopt a more conciliatory attitude toward the Federal Republic, and to persuade the West Germans to follow his own example vis-à-vis the East.

But the Germans did not do so in his time, and even before he left office in April 1969 his basic goals had been frustrated by the Warsaw Pact invasion of Czechoslovakia. This, ironically, turned out to be a spur to a new kind of German Eastern policy—one which, as I discussed in the last chapter, accepted and ratified the postwar status quo in the hope of ameliorating and in the long run modifying it. But this was the antithesis of what de Gaulle had sought. His dream of a gradual loosening of both the Western and Eastern blocs was shattered by the demonstration of Soviet determination to maintain Russian control over Eastern Europe. The détente that was to be built in light of that fact was not de Gaulle's détente.

Compared to the grand policy of relations with the United States, the Federal Republic, and the Soviet Union, de Gaulle's dealings with the European community were second level, exploitative, and defensive.

Ironically, the results of his actions toward it have been more lasting than those on the plane of his higher interest. As noted in the preceding section, his actions in some ways permitted the community to take shape and permitted France to take its full part more readily than might have happened if he had not returned to power in 1958. In other ways, of course, his influence was negative.

The community was most interesting to de Gaulle as an aspect of his attempt to establish a special relationship with the FRG, which set great value on the community, and as a possible vehicle for forming a French-led political bloc based on the Franco-German entente. Hence, he readily accepted the Rome treaties when he returned to power despite his earlier ideological opposition. His veto of British membership in January 1963 is perhaps best understood in terms of this policy, for France could reasonably expect (at that time) to be the most powerful member of a Europe of Six but not of one that included another major power, Great Britain (even if the latter had not, as de Gaulle claimed, proved that it would be an American "Trojan Horse" by renewing its special nuclear relationship with the United States a month before at Nassau).

During this period the community rapidly took form according to the treaty, and ahead of the prescribed timetable as far as economic integration was concerned. But de Gaulle's hope also to establish a confederal political community of the six came to nothing, not so much because his proposal for structured political consultations was so repellent in itself (the members have since moved in that direction) but for two other reasons: because the other five strongly resented his brutal rejection of integration even in principle, and because they saw in his plan a desire to establish a European grouping under French leadership which would distance itself from the United States. De Gaulle never brought any of them to accept the latter, notwithstanding his often ingenious use of every available strategic, political, and economic issue—of which there were many—to try to arouse in them a sense of their separateness from the United States. His failure after so many attempts cannot be attributed only to their resentment of the visible contempt he showed toward them. Rather, it provided a proof of how small that separateness was, in their perceptions and in fact, even in the face of serious policy differences between the United States and some of the European allies on strategic, economic, and other problems.

Once de Gaulle's hopes to use the community for his own political ends faded, his limited positive interest in it also declined. What remained was his fear of the implications of integration. Not only did he refuse to go along with any of the steps proposed to strengthen political integration in the community (though he accepted speedups in its time-table for economic union), but in 1965 he created a major crisis when he came to believe that the commission and the other five members were trying to force France to accept greater central powers for the Brussels authorities as the price for establishing the common agricultural policy (CAP) which had already been agreed to in principle. The French attack seemed so virulent that many, reading the general's statements and those of his ministers, concluded that the continued survival of the community's institutions in their integrated form was no longer compatible with French membership.

De Gaulle was probably bargaining for the best terms he could get. In the end the institutions did survive, the details of the CAP were worked out, and de Gaulle not only stopped the proposed enlargement of the commission's prerogatives but also blocked implementation of the treaty clauses providing for less than unanimous decisions by the council of ministers. This outcome was paradoxical. Considering that the community existed only on paper when de Gaulle took office in 1958 and was a flourishing economic union when he departed the scene, his legacy to France in this respect was one of the more ironical facets of a career filled with ironies. But, as previously discussed, he clearly bears some—though not all—of the responsibility for weakening the European spirit and preventing further institutional evolution thereafter. By doing that, he perhaps blocked the growth of what would have been a more serious challenge than the one he himself mounted to the structure of the Euratlantic subsystem and the U.S. leadership of it which he so much deplored.

De Gaulle's largely successful effort to maintain close ties with the French colonies to which, willingly or unwillingly, he gave independence, is an interesting chapter of his foreign policy but of significance here only to the extent that it was meant, like his European policy, to magnify France's voice and make its claims to world power status more valid. Certainly the ties which he maintained with ex-French Africa and the deference many of its leaders paid him enhanced his image as a global statesman. Even more important were the way he managed to make the loss of Algeria in 1962 seem a success of French statecraft and, building on that, the use to which he then put France's relationship with the new country. For it showed that the French government could maintain close ties not only with conservative African regimes but also with radical ones, such as that in Algeria.

This, in turn, highlighted a wider French policy of trying to take the lead of, or at least to become an inspirational symbol for, those third world countries that were trying to disassociate themselves from what de

Gaulle called "the two hegemonies." In his speeches and in his extensive travels, de Gaulle called on the countries of Asia, Africa, and Latin America to assert their independence from the two superpowers, to do in their parts of the word what he was doing in Europe.

This third world aspect of de Gaulle's policy became most marked in 1964, following on and to some extent resulting from the setback to his European hopes the preceding year. De Gaulle's advocacy of the neutralization of Indochina, which the American government of the mid-1960s found fully as devilish as his blocking of its dream of European unity, was a special case of a general policy of encouraging the subtraction of the third world from cold war competition—the extension to the world of what he was advocating in Europe at that time—and the drying up of the cold war for lack of territory in which the superpowers would be permitted to compete. These policies won him the praise of Sukarno, Sihanouk, Nasser, and Nkrumah but little else. French recognition of Communist China in January 1964 also created a stir at the time. But, while it was a blow directed at that Moscow-Washington axis symbolized by the 1963 test ban treaty that de Gaulle deplored, this gesture also did little to strengthen France's global leverage.

De Gaulle's intellectual agility and his well-cultivated capacity to shock and amaze concealed the fact for many years that most of his initiatives had no follow-up. He failed to establish a firm partnership with Germany, or secure the leadership of a coherent European bloc, or take even a first meaningful step toward negotiating the end of the cold war division of Europe and the superpower hegemony over its two halves. The determination of the superpowers to maintain the status quo in Europe, and the acceptance or acquiescence of the European countries (satisfied, resigned, or coerced, as the case was) in the international structure in which they lived—the theme of this book—were too much for de Gaulle's farreaching and diverse attempts to change things. This was clear from 1963 on, however well de Gaulle's theater convinced many—to their horror or delight—of the contrary.

The six-day Middle East war in June 1967 probably showed de Gaulle himself, if not others, that the forces arrayed against his dreams were overwhelming. The extreme bitterness he displayed afterward toward both Israel and the United States reflected deeper feelings than chagrin that the former had launched a preemptive war against his advice and, what was worse, had scored a great triumph. What was lost was his dream of reducing the dependence of the Middle Eastern states on the superpowers. War reaffirmed the dependence of Israel on the Americans and of the Arabs on the Russians—that is, it polarized the Middle

East. Worse, it brought the United States and the Soviet Union into direct collaboration to end the conflict and prevent its spread.

The Glassboro meeting of President Johnson and Prime Minister Kosygin in July, hailed by most as a step toward peace and détente, was a black day for de Gaulle. The superpowers, having confirmed the status quo in the Middle East, now seemed likely to do so in Europe at a "new Yalta," thus checkmating his policy of détente, entente, and cooperation from the Atlantic to the Urals. His problem was admirably summarized by *The Economist*:

> But if Russia and America are not going to retire from the world, they will have to do the opposite. They will have to make sure they have a real grip on things. This means, at the very least, agreeing that there are certain parts of the world which are too important to both of them to be allowed to fall wholly under the control of either, *or of anybody else*. It means a pretty precise definition of their essential spheres of influence in these areas, and an agreement to make these spheres stick. *It has already been done in Europe*. It needs to be done in south-east Asia and the Middle East too. . . . What it amounts to is the beginning of a loose, informal and indirect *condominium* over certain specified regions. Put it another way: it amounts to the beginning of a rudimentary form of international government.[7]

It would be difficult to find a more precise description of de Gaulle's abiding nightmare than this. It is not fanciful to speculate that his politically pointless behavior in Quebec a month later can be traced to the sense of impotence and defeat which the events of that summer laid on him.

De Gaulle's failure became clear to all in 1968 with the domestic upheaval in May, which shook the French economy and revealed the internal weaknesses of his rule, and the Warsaw Pact invasion of Czechoslovakia in August, which showed again to those like him who may have doubted that the Soviet Union's permissiveness toward change in Eastern Europe was much too limited to sustain the kind of hopes he had tried to nourish. His resignation from office in April 1969 was, from the point of view of foreign policy, an anticlimax.

Under de Gaulle's successors as under his predecessors, France was still a special case from the viewpoint of Atlantic orthodoxy. Georges Pompidou continued to keep France in the global game but he also

7. *The Economist* 224 (July 15, 1967), 188. Emphasis added.

moved to get rid of some of the liabilities de Gaulle had hung on French policy. He took advantage of the changed approach of the Nixon-Kissinger policy toward Europe to carry out a certain rapprochement with the United States. He also dropped the French veto on Britain's accession to the European community, not so much, probably, because he feared the economic power of the Federal Republic and wanted the United Kingdon to help provide balance in the community (on the contrary, France in those years hoped to catch up with the FRG) as because he understood that French leadership policy in Europe could not go anywhere unless France's alienation of the five, centered specifically though not exclusively on the veto, was ended. He even took up, in his own way, a policy of promoting European decisionmaking in common, though short of integration, and abandoned the theological debate between federalism and confederalism which de Gaulle had relished to his cost. It was in this phase that the community tried to launch a monetary and economic union for which the conditions, internal and external, did not exist.

The true Gaullist spirit had a last upsurge in the final months of Pompidou's rule when his foreign minister, Michel Jobert, responded to the American government's attempt to define a lasting relationship with the Europeans on American terms (the year of Europe) with a biting defense of Europe's, and France's, autonomy. But Jobert persuaded no one, and the energy crisis, which he tried to exploit in the Gaullist manner, imposed a de facto cooperation between the two sides of the Atlantic to which France could offer no alternative that the other Europeans found realistic.

The Giscard regime that followed Pompidou's has seen a further fading of the spirit of French particularism in foreign policy. The French have continued to cultivate as close ties as possible with third world countries and have led the community toward a more pro-Arab policy—no difficult thing in light of OPEC's power. But economic problems and the diminution of prospects for an active détente policy have left France little latitude or opportunity for trying to organize and lead Europe or differentiate it from the United States. French relations with the latter, therefore, have improved considerably. France under Giscard has not been a model ally for the United States, any more than it ever was or is likely to be. But its policy has not been designed to pose a significant challenge to the Euratlantic system, nor has it done so.

CHAPTER 11

Toward the Future

The European state system developed by the cold war and completed by the arming of Germany in 1955 remains intact today. It will continue to be challenged by developments in the years to come, as it has been in the past. Many of these challenges will be like earlier ones: tension between the two blocs; relaxation of tension between them; the chronic strains inherent in the Soviet Union's coercion of the Eastern subsystem; the many divisions among the members of the Western subsystem; the possibility of greater unity in Western Europe. A new challenge, not yet in focus, is the prospect that economic difficulties and political realignments within the advanced countries may call into question their internal stability and the relations between them. And beyond all the challenges we have known or can imagine are others yet undreamed of.

These challenges of the future will have to contend against the hard factors which have maintained the structural stability of the European state system against the many serious challenges of the last quarter-century:

—The Soviet Union is likely to maintain its strategic and political dominance over Eastern Europe. The peoples and even the governments of Eastern Europe, each in its way, would welcome a loosening of the ties that bind them to the Soviet Union. But they must recognize after the experiences of 1953, 1956, and 1968 that their scope for action is limited. There will be constant and sometimes dangerous tension in Eastern Europe, occasional outbursts against the system of Soviet control and adaptive change within it which may make life more tolerable for the people, but probably no more structural change in the essential power relations than there has been hitherto.

—The overwhelming power presence of the Soviet Union in Eastern and Central Europe will continue to be seen by most Western Europeans as a threat to their security. For them, the liberalization or tightening up of Soviet society, the movement of Soviet policy to and from tension and détente, are secondary. What has mattered to them, and has not changed, and is most unlikely to change, is Soviet power and proximity.

—Unless Western Europe bends its energies to trying to balance Soviet power, which is most improbable and perhaps impossible to achieve, the countries of Western Europe are likely to continue to want to maintain a visible and structured alliance with the United States—in fact, the Atlantic alliance we have—to provide them the security which the *European* balance of power will no more be able to provide by itself than it has since 1945. The United States, for its part, will almost certainly continue to play its established role in the Euratlantic subsystem.

—The allies will continue as before to be divided by many differences of interest and policy, in and out of Europe. But the ties of alliance will be reinforced by common interests of other kinds, not least by the understanding of the member states that they have no real alternative to maintaining an effective and cooperative economic system among them.

—The solution to the German problem which has been brought about by Soviet policy in Eastern Europe and by the Western European and American response to that is by now, and will probably remain, generally acceptable or at least tolerable to most Europeans, East and West, and even to the West Germans, who continue to understand the power facts of life in Europe and to place the Federal Republic's security ahead of an impossible isolationism or an unpromising and dangerous pursuit of reunification.

These premises of the European system are probabilities for the future, not certainties. They may be eroded or bypassed by new challenges. But they are weighty elements of the situation. The experience of the last decades suggests that these factors of stability are more deeply rooted and better understood in Europe than has been commonly thought. The Europeans themselves seem to have acted over the years as if they understood the analysis presented here—which, after all, is drawn from their own historical experience. For these reasons, and assuming also the continued commitment of the superpowers to the system they have built, the factors of stability will not be lightly swept away by new or renewed impulses for structural change. The state system which up to now has so well reflected the true balance of power in the Europe that has emerged from the crises of the twentieth century has a strong lease on the future.

Selected Bibliography

Alperovitz, Gar. *Atomic Diplomacy: Hiroshima and Potsdam*. New York; Vintage Books, 1965.

Backer, John H. *Priming the German Economy: American Occupational Policies 1945–1948*. Durham, N.C.: Duke University Press, 1971.

Bergsten, C. Fred. *The Dilemmas of the Dollar*. New York: New York University Press, 1975.

Brown, Seyom. *The Faces of Power*. New York: Columbia University Press, 1968.

Brzezinski, Zbigniew. *Alternative to Partition*. New York: McGraw-Hill, 1965.

Buchan, Alastair. *The End of the Postwar Era*. New York: E. P. Dutton, 1974.

Calleo, David. *Europe's Future: The Grand Alternatives*. New York: Horizon Press, 1965.

―――. *The Atlantic Fantasy: The U.S., NATO, and Europe*. Baltimore: The Johns Hopkins Press, 1970.

Calleo, David P., and Rowland, Benjamin M. *America and the World Political Economy*. Bloomington: Indiana University Press, 1973.

Chace, James, and Ravenal, Earl C., eds. *Atlantis Lost: U.S.-European Relations After the Cold War*. New York: New York University Press, 1976.

Clemens, Diane Shaver. *Yalta*. New York: Oxford University Press, 1970.

Cleveland, Harlan. *NATO: The Transatlantic Bargain*. New York: Harper and Row, 1970.

Cleveland, Harold van B. *The Atlantic Idea and Its European Rivals*. New York: McGraw-Hill, 1966.

Cooper, Richard N. *The Economics of Interdependence: Economic Policy in the Atlantic Community*. New York: Mc-Graw Hill, 1968.

Davis, Lynn Etheridge. *The Cold War Begins: Soviet-American Conflict Over Eastern Europe*. Princeton, N.J.: Princeton University Press, 1974.

Diebold, William, Jr. *The United States and the Industrial World*. New York: Praeger, 1972.

Feis, Herbert. *From Trust to Terror—The Onset of the Cold War, 1945–1950*. New York: Norton, 1970.

Gaddis, John Lewis. *The United States and the Origins of the Cold War, 1941–1947*. New York: Columbia University Press, 1972.

Gardiner, Lloyd C. *Economic Aspects of New Deal Diplomacy*. Madison: University of Wisconsin Press, 1964.

———. *Architects of Illusion*. Chicago: Quadrangle Books, 1970.

Gardner, Richard N. *Sterling-Dollar Diplomacy*. New York: McGraw-Hill, 1969.

Gerbet, Pierre. *La genèse du plan Schuman*. Lausanne: Université de Lausanne, 1962.

Gimbel, John. *The American Occupation of Germany*. Stanford, Calif.: Stanford University Press, 1968.

———. *The Origins of the Marshall Plan*. Stanford, Calif.: Stanford University Press, 1976.

Graml, Hermann, et al. *The German Resistance to Hitler*. London: B. T. Batsford Ltd., 1970.

Graubard, Stephen R., ed. *A New Europe?* Boston: Houghton Mifflin, 1964.

Griffith, William E., ed. *The Soviet Empire: Expansion and Détente*. Lexington, Mass.: Lexington Books, 1977.

Halle, Louis J. *The Cold War as History*. New York: Harper & Row, 1967.

Hanrieder, Wolfram F. *West German Foreign Policy, 1949–1963*. Stanford, Calif.: Stanford University Press, 1967.

Herring, George C., Jr. *Aid to Russia, 1941–1946*. New York: Columbia University Press, 1973.

Herz, Martin F. *Beginnings of the Cold War*. Bloomington: Indiana University Press, 1966.

Holborn, Hajo. *The Political Collapse of Europe*. New York: Knopf, 1951.

———. *A History of Modern Germany, 1840–1945*. New York: Knopf, 1969.

———. *Germany and Europe*. Garden City, N.Y.: Doubleday, 1970.

Jones, Joseph M. *The Fifteen Weeks*. New York: Viking, 1955.

Kelleher, Catherine McArdle. *Germany & the Politics of Nuclear Weapons*. New York: Columbia University Press, 1975.

Kennan, George F. *Russia, the Atom, and the West*. New York: Harper, 1958.

———. *Russia and the West Under Lenin and Stalin*. Cambridge, Mass.: Harvard University Press, 1960.

Kissinger, Henry A. *The Troubled Partnership*. New York: McGraw-Hill, 1965.

Kolko, Gabriel. *The Politics of War: The World and United States Foreign Policy, 1943–1945*. New York: Random House, 1968.

———. *The Roots of American Foreign Policy*. Boston: Beacon Press, 1969.

Kolodjiez, Edward A. *French International Policy Under de Gaulle and*

Pompidou: The Politics of Grandeur. Ithaca, N.Y.: Cornell University Press, 1974.

Kuklick, Bruce. *American Policy and the Division of Germany.* Ithaca, N.Y.: Cornell University Press, 1972.

La Feber, Walter. *America, Russia, and the Cold War, 1945–1971.* 2d ed. New York: Wiley, 1972.

Landes, David S., ed. *Western Europe: The Trials of Partnership.* Lexington, Mass.: Lexington Books, 1977.

Levin, N. Gordon, Jr. *Woodrow Wilson and World Politics.* New York: Oxford University Press, 1968.

Lieberman, Joseph L. *The Scorpion and the Tarantula.* Boston: Houghton Mifflin, 1970.

Lippmann, Walter. *The Cold War.* New York: Harper, 1947.

McGeehan, Robert. *The German Rearmament Question.* Urbana: University of Illinois Press, 1971.

Maddox, Robert James. *The New Left and the Origins of the Cold War.* Princeton, N.J.: Princeton University Press, 1973.

Maier, Charles S. "Revisionism and the Interpretation of Cold War Origins," *Perspectives in American History* 4 (1970): 313–47.

May, Ernest R. *"Lessons" of the Past: The Use & Misuse of History in American Foreign Policy.* New York: Oxford University Press, 1973.

Mayer, Arno J. *Political Origins of the New Diplomacy, 1917–1918.* New Haven: Yale University Press, 1959.

——— . *Politics and Diplomacy of Peacemaking.* New York: Knopf, 1967.

Merkl, Peter H. *German Foreign Policies, West and East.* Santa Barbara, Calif. and Oxford, England: Clio Press (American Bibliographical Center) 1974.

Miller, Lynn H., and Preussen, Ronald, eds. *Reflections on the Cold War.* Philadelphia: Temple University Press, 1974.

Neustadt, Richard E. *Alliance Politics.* New York: Columbia University Press, 1970.

Newhouse, John. *De Gaulle and the Anglo-Saxons.* New York: Viking, 1970.

Notter, Harley A. *Postwar Foreign Policy Preparation, 1939–1945.* Washington: Department of State, 1949.

O'Connor, Raymond G. *Diplomacy for Victory: FDR and Unconditional Surrender.* New York: Norton, 1971.

Paterson, Thomas G., ed. *Cold War Critics.* Chicago: Quadrangle Books, 1971.

——— . *Soviet-American Confrontation.* Baltimore and London: The Johns Hopkins University Press, 1973.

Penrose, E. F. *Economic Planning for the Peace.* Princeton, N.J.: Princeton University Press, 1953.

Pfaltzgraff, Robert L., Jr. *The Atlantic Community: A Complex Imbalance.* New York: Van Nostrand Reinhold, 1969.

Pierre, Andrew J. *Nuclear Politics: The British Experience with an Independent Strategic Force, 1939–1970.* London: Oxford University Press, 1972.

Planck, Charles R. *The Changing Status of German Reunification in Western Diplomacy, 1955–1966.* Baltimore: The Johns Hopkins Press, 1967.

Post, Gaines, Jr. *The Civil-Military Fabric of Weimar Foreign Policy.* Princeton, N.J.: Princeton University Press, 1973.

Richardson, James L. *Germany and the Atlantic Alliance.* Cambridge, Mass.: Harvard University Press, 1966.

Rose, Lisle A. *After Yalta.* New York: Charles Scribner's Sons, 1973.

———. *Dubious Victory: The United States and the End of World War II.* Kent, Ohio: The Kent State University Press, 1973.

Rosecrance, Richard, ed. *America as an Ordinary Country.* Ithaca, N.Y.: Cornell University Press, 1976.

Seabury, Paul. *The Rise and Decline of the Cold War.* New York: Basic Books, 1967.

Sherwin, Martin J. *A World Destroyed: The Atomic Bomb and the Grand Alliance.* New York: Knopf, 1975.

Shonfield, Andrew, ed. *International Economic Relations of the Western World, 1959–1971.* 2 vols. New York: Oxford University Press, 1976.

Shulman, Marshall D. *Beyond the Cold War.* New Haven: Yale University Press, 1966.

Siracusa, Joseph M. *New Left Diplomatic Histories & Historians: The American Revisionists.* Port Washington, N.Y.: National University Publications, Kennekat Press, 1973.

Solomon, Robert. *The International Monetary System, 1945–1976.* New York: Harper & Row, 1977.

Steel, Ronald. *The End of Alliance: America and the Future of Europe.* New York: Viking, 1964.

Stillman, Edmund, and Pfaff, William. *The New Politics: America and the End of the Postwar World.* New York: Coward McCann, 1961.

Taylor, A. J. P. *The Struggle For Mastery in Europe, 1848–1918.* London: Oxford University Press, 1954.

Ulam, Adam B. *Expansion and Coexistence: The History of Soviet Foreign Policy, 1917–1967.* New York: Praeger, 1968.

Welch, William. *American Images of Soviet Foreign Policy.* New Haven and London: Yale University Press, 1970.

Wilcox, Francis O., and Haviland, H. Field, Jr., eds. *The Atlantic Community*. New York: Praeger, 1963.

Willis, F. Roy. *France, Germany, and the New Europe, 1945–1967*. Stanford, Calif.: Stanford University Press, 1968.

Wolfe, Thomas W. *Soviet Power and Europe, 1945–70*. Baltimore and London: The Johns Hopkins Press, 1970.

Yergin, Daniel. *Shattered Peace: The Origins of the Cold War and the National Security State*. Boston: Houghton Mifflin, 1977.

Index

Acheson, Dean, 122, 133
Adenauer, Konrad: Franco-German cooperation and, 183, 223, 234–35; German rearmament and, 160–61
Africa, colonial rivalries in, 10, 14
Allied Control Council for Germany, 55, 56
Alsace-Lorraine, Franco-German rivalry over, 21, 27
Asia, colonial partition of, 14
Atlantic Charter (1941), 82, 90, 99, 100
Atomic energy. See Nuclear weapons
Austria-Hungary: attack of, on Serbia, 16, 17; dissolution of, 31; industrial growth of, 13; military development of, 11; population growth in, 12; in World War I, 20, 21
Austro-German Alliance (1879), 15

Badoglio, Marshal Pietro, 46, 47
Balkan states: Allies' power struggle in, 49–52; Balkan wars (1912–13), 16; German seizure of, 43; Soviet control of, 48–49, 68
Baruch, Bernard, 122–23
Battle of the Bulge, 54, 55
Belgium, German violation of neutrality of, 17, 18
Benes, Eduard, 50, 120–21
Berlin: 1958–60 and 1961–62 crises of, 175–76, 182; Soviet blockade of, 153–54
Bethmann-Hollweg, Theobald von, 15, 21n
Bismarck, Otto von, 14
Boer War, British foreign policy and, 15
Bohemia, post-World War I position of, 31
Bolshevism: Poland as defense against, 24–25; in Russia, 65, 66, 67; as threat to European governments, 22–23, 24, 25; United States troops against, 60; Wilsonianism and, 62
Bowman, Isaiah, on Russian interests, 87
Brandt, Willy, 185
Brest-Litovsk, Treaty of (1918), 20, 21, 31; effect on Soviet policy, 64, 65
Bretton Woods Conference, international

financial system of, 81, 82–83, 197, 199, 200–07
Brezhnev, Leonid, 170
Bruning, Heinrich, 36n
Brussels, Treaty of (1948), 138
Bulgaria: Soviet satellization of, 48–50, 70, 119; Truman administration policy on, 98
Bullitt, William, 53
Byrnes, James, 98, 124, 150, 152, 155

Casablanca Meeting (1943), 44, 45, 47
Charles V, threat of, to European state system, 7
Charles VIII, beginning of state system and, 2
China, Soviet conflict with, 170, 176
Churchill, Winston: at Casablanca Meeting, 45; iron curtain speech, 123; Mediterranean strategy of, 50, 51–53; Soviet territorial claims and, 49–50, 56, 94, 95–96, 99
Clemenceau, Georges, 25, 26
Cold war: Berlin blockade and, 153–54; George Kennan's influence on, 126–28; modern state system and, 130–31, 137, 140–41, 165; Poland and, 92, 95, 97, 106, 109–11, 118; postwar Germany and, 147–49, 165; Truman administration and, 97, 101, 103, 111–14, 122–26; United States economic policies and, 103–06, 107; Walter Lippmann's view of, 128–30; World War II strategies and, 43–44, 53
Colonialism: in Africa, 10, 14; in Asia, 14; British, 10; French, 231, 239–40; German, 14–15, 16; in Middle East, 10
Committee for the Challenges of Modern Society, 215n
Common Market. See European Economic Community
Communism, 36, 73, 94; United States opinion of, 111–12
Communist Information Bureau (Cominform), 121, 135–37